Mental Health in a Multi-ethnic Society

As services in the community continue to replace institution-based care there is an increasing need for professionals from medical, social work, clinical psychology, nursing and other backgrounds to address the diverse needs of a multi-ethnic society using a common frame of reference. Those who provide mental health services must now face up to challenges from service users and strive for a closer, more effective working relationship with voluntary organisations. *Mental Health in a Multi-ethnic Society: A Multi-disciplinary Handbook* addresses all these issues. It offers an approach to the meaning of mental health and suggests constructive and imaginative ways of providing care for people with mental health problems.

Contributions from a multi-ethnic team of professionals are organised in three parts: 'Current setting' describes the background to contemporary mental health services, the legal framework and the role of the voluntary sector, and examines the experience of black people. 'Confronting issues' considers practical problems in delivering services to a multi-ethnic society and offers some innovative approaches. The final part, 'Seeking change', draws together the various issues in order to indicate a way forward, with suggestions for change on both a practical and theoretical level.

Intended primarily as a handbook for practitioners working in the mental health field, it is also suitable for multi-disciplinary trainings, basic trainings and in-service postgraduate trainings in a variety of professions including social work, psychology, psychiatry and nursing.

Suman Fernando is a Senior Lecturer in Mental Health at the Tizard Centre, University of Kent at Canterbury, and Honorary Consultant Psychiatrist at Enfield Community Care Trust, Middlesex.

Mental Health in a Multi-ethnic Society

A Multi-disciplinary Handbook

Edited by Suman Fernando

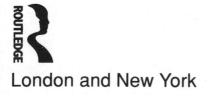

London and New York

First published 1995
by Routledge
11 New Fetter Lane, London EC4P 4EE

Simultaneously published in the USA and Canada
by Routledge
29 West 35th Street, New York, NY 10001

Reprinted 1996

Routledge is an International Thomson Publishing company   I(T)P

Typeset in Times by
Ponting–Green Publishing Services, Chesham, Bucks
Printed and bound in Great Britain by
TJ Press (Padstow) Ltd, Padstow, Cornwall

British Library Cataloguing in Publication Data
A catalogue record for this book is available from the
British Library

Library of Congress Cataloguing in Publication Data
A catalogue record for this book is available from the Library
of Congress

ISBN   0–415–10536–6 (hbk)
ISBN   0–415–10537–4 (pbk)

To all those who meet racism or cultural intolerance in the field of mental health.

Contents

Illustrations

Contributors

Tanzeem Ahmed. Tanzeem is a psychologist with a background in 'child guidance' and research into cognitive development of children. Currently, Tanzeem is the Director of Confederation of Indian Organisations and she has managed three research projects in the field of community mental health focusing on individual experiences and voluntary organisations.

William Bingley. A lawyer by training, William was Legal Director of the National Association for Mental Health (MIND) for six years in the 1980s before becoming the Executive Secretary of the working group that prepared the Mental Health Act Code of Practice. In 1990, he was appointed the first Chief Executive of the Mental Health Act Commission, a position which he still holds.

Deryck Browne. Deryck is Policy Development Officer with the National Association for the Care and Resettlement of Offenders (NACRO). With a background of African-American studies and forensic behavioural science, Deryck has researched the psychiatric remand process as it affects black defendants and, more recently, the impact of race on civil detention ('sectioning') under the Mental Health Act 1983.

Suman Fernando. A consultant psychiatrist and former Mental Health Act Commissioner, Suman is involved in consultancy, training and research in the mental health field. He is Chair of the Board of Directors of Nafsiyat (Inter-cultural Therapy Centre) and a member of the Council of Management of MIND. Suman has written two books, *Race and Culture in Psychiatry* (Routledge, 1988) and *Mental Health, Race and Culture* (Macmillan/MIND, 1991).

Peter Ferns. Peter is a qualified social worker with experience of services for people with learning difficulties and of mental health services. He has a wide experience of consultancy in both the statutory and voluntary sectors, specialising in community care and issues involving race. Peter has been involved in the training of professionals in the mental health field for many years.

Sue Holland. Sue has pioneered 'social action psychotherapy' services in working-class multi-racial London neighbourhoods for 20 years. Currently, she is a consultant clinical psychologist with South Buckinghamshire NHS Trust, working specifically with Black and Asian minorities. Recently, Sue was given the newly established Award for Challenging Inequality of Opportunity by the British Psychological Society (BPS).

Inga-Britt Krause. Britt is a family therapist at the Marlborough Family Service in London, and a tutor on the Diploma Course in Inter-cultural Therapy at University College. With Ann Miller, she is involved in the Asian Families Community Project based at the Marlborough. Britt is an anthropologist who has worked in a Hindu community in the Himalayas and with Punjabis settled in Britain.

Vivien Lindow. Vivien is an independent consultant, researcher and writer in the field of user involvement in mental health services. She is an active member of the psychiatric system survivor movement, including 'Survivors Speak Out', and is involved in the training of professionals working in the mental health field. Vivien is an elected member of the Council of Management of MIND.

Mita Madden. Following extensive experience in social work, Mita has been involved in training in the mental health field for many years, with a special interest in anti-racist/discriminatory practice and in user/carer empowerment issues. Currently, she is Training Officer, Social Services Department, London Borough of Harrow.

Ann C. Miller. Ann, a family therapist, is Principal Clinical Psychologist at the Marlborough Family Service. With Britt Krause, she is involved in the Asian Families Community Project based at the Marlborough. She is director of the joint Malborough/University College London Diploma in Family Therapy which has developed teaching in relation to racism and culture. Ann also teaches at the Institute of Family Therapy in London.

Parimala Moodley. In the 1980s Parimala set up a unique service in Camberwell – the Maudsley Outreach Service Team (MOST), for outreach work with (mainly) black clients with mental health problems living in the community. She is now a consultant psychiatrist in South London and also Chair of the Transcultural Psychiatry Society (UK) and the Transcultural Interest Group within the Royal College of Psychiatrists.

Mina Sassoon. Mina has extensive experience of working with user groups and ethnic minority communities while working in the voluntary sector, including local MIND Associations and Good Practices in Mental Health (GPMH). Currently, she is Training Officer in Mental Health and Ethnicity for North West London NHS Trust.

Lennox Thomas. Lennox is the Clinical Director of Nafsiyat (Intercultural Therapy Centre) and joint Course Director of the Diploma in Intercultural Therapy at University College, London. With a background in psychiatric social work and probation before training in psychoanalytic psychotherapy, Lennox works as an individual and family therapist with an interest in the psychological development of the Black child.

Amanda Webb-Johnson. As a primary school teacher, Amanda had an interest in multicultural and anti-racist education and spent a year in India researching the education of children. Later, while working at the Confederation of Indian Organisations, Amanda carried out the research for the reports *A Cry for Change* (Confederation of Indian Organisations, 1991) and *Building on Strengths* (Confederation of Indian Organisations, 1993). Amanda is a trained counsellor and also works at Voluntary Services Overseas.

Acknowledgements

Although the views expressed in each chapter are those of the author(s) concerned, they have been influenced by many colleagues and friends in various organisations and settings, in particular the Transcultural Psychiatry Society (UK); Survivors Speak Out; Nafsiyat (Intercultural Therapy Centre); MIND; the Marlborough Family Service; Good Practices in Mental Health; Clinical Psychology, Race and Culture Special Interest Group of the British Psychological Society and the confederation of Indian Organisations. In addition, the editor acknowledges the encouragement and help of numerous people in the field of mental health.

The extract from the video 'From anger to action' is published with the permission of Mental Health Media. The extract from 'Still I rise' in *And Still I Rise* by Maya Angelou copyright © 1978 by Maya Angelou is reprinted by kind permission of the publishers, Virago Press and Random House, New York. The extract from 'Untitled' in *Survivors' Poetry: From dark to light* is reprinted by kind permission of Premila Trivedi.

Introduction

Suman Fernando

The change in emphasis from institution-based psychiatry to mental health care based in the community is affecting services across Europe and North America, and involves a change in ways of thinking about health and illness. Essentially it means a shift from 'symptoms-thinking' to 'needs-thinking', from looking for illness to promoting health. This transformation is foreshadowed in changes in the language used in many circles and attempts to look anew at the ideologies and concepts that inform the development of services as indicated in recent policy documents (MIND, 1993a, 1993b) and papers (Cobb, 1993; Wood, 1993; Darton *et al.*, 1994) issued by the National Association for Mental Health (MIND). The term 'mental health problem' has replaced, to some extent, 'mental illness'; people formerly called 'patients' are increasingly referred to as 'service users'; and rather than (psychiatric) treatments, 'interventions' are planned – with the totality being subsumed within the concept of promoting 'mental health care', not the eradication of 'mental illness'. There is much more talk about services based on needs-assessment (rather than diagnosis), and multi-disciplinary community teams are being seen as the basis of mental health services, with the (medical) general practitioner and hospital-based psychiatrist being one of a team and not necessarily its leader. The government's White Paper *Caring for People* (DHSS, 1993) sees the assessment of need as a 'cornerstone of community care'. In the midst of all this, one hears and reads about the need to address the diversity of need in a multicultural society, and about the inequities caused by racism.

Although community care is envisaged as the foundation, there is little doubt that hospital care is to continue as an important part of the total mental health service. However, the exact balance between hospital care and community care within a mental health service is extremely uncertain, and is likely to depend on many legal, social and political factors. First, as the law stands at present, compulsory treatment (under provisions of the Mental Health Act 1983) cannot be given unless a person is an in-patient of a hospital. Second, the extent to which community services are likely to be able to provide sufficient care – within the resource limits set by the availability of funding, voluntary commitment, etc. – to enable community care to cater for people with all types of mental health problems, including those who have developed dependency because of institutionalisation (the 'long stay') as well as those being identified (by psychiatry) as 'the new long stay', is not clear. Third, and most importantly, the intolerance of deviancy by society at large may compel mental health services (politically or through force of circumstances) to continue, at least to some extent, its traditional function of 'putting away' people unwanted by society.

This is a book for professionals working in the mental health field and for those who are training to do so. It is not geared to any particular professional group. Indeed the book was conceived as a common text for all professional groups working (or training to work) in the statutory services – that is, those services under the direction of Social Service Departments and Hospital Trusts operating under the National Health Service. The editor and several of the authors who have contributed to this text have experienced recent changes in management structures within Health and Social Services as a result of changes in the organisation of responsibilities between Health and Local Authority enunciated in the Community Care Act 1990 – changes which clearly influence the framework in which professionals work. However, we feel that on the whole, professional workers at the grass roots, although influenced by changes in management structures, to a great extent carry on regardless. Therefore, this book does not seek to evaluate or discuss the changes resulting from new structures in Social Services and the National Health Service, except in referring to their impact on professional practices when necessary – especially in the last chapter, when the future prospects for mental health services are considered.

Many of the 'mission statements' of Hospital Trusts, and policies enunciated by Social Service Departments reflect the change in orientation of mental health services from being predominantly hospital-based to being mainly based in the community. The aims of the services are usually articulated in terms of meeting mental health needs. However, relatively little attention has been given to a crucial issue, namely the training of professionals who are supposed to run such mental health services. Nor has there been much consideration of theoretical issues that would inform such training. At present, multi-disciplinary work is often disjointed because of wide divisions between the ideologies of different professional groups and the lack of adequate training schemes to bring professionals together. There is little agreement about fundamental issues such as working concepts of 'mental health' or 'needs', between, on the one hand, the (hospital-based or ex-hospital-based) psychiatric personnel – mainly psychiatrists – and, on the other, socio-culturally inclined mental health workers – including many trans-cultural psychiatrists. A recent publication by the former group *Measuring Mental Health Needs* (Thornicroft *et al.*, 1992) sees 'needs' in terms of illness models requiring treatment. But as community care replaces institutional models of practice, cross-disciplinary training must emerge. A common frame of reference, at least on basic issues, must evolve – or be manufactured – and for this to happen a common text is essential. Unfortunately there is (at present) no publication that could be described as a comprehensive text or handbook suitable for all disciplines working in mental health services. The aim of this book is to redress this deficiency while focusing on the multicultural nature of society that the services are supposed to benefit.

The culture of training in all the professions involved in mental health care has been, up to now, one based primarily on considering mental health problems in terms of 'illness'. Therefore, however much we try to modify our 'illness-based' attitude to the meaning of 'health' or move away from it, the natural – almost the *normal* – tendency in all professional work is to think of health as the converse of illness. Moreover, whenever there is pressure on a professional to explain some serious problem or to account for some seemingly unreasonable behaviour on the part of a fellow being, the tendency is to fall back on some sort of variation of the illness model. Thus, when there is publicity about some mishap affecting someone who has the 'mental illness' label, the main discussion centres on the extent of 'illness' – as if 'illness' is something that can be clearly defined. A recent example is that of the tragedy involving Christopher Clunis, resulting in recommendations that concentrate on ways of 'treating' the 'illness' early (Ritchie *et al.*, 1994), with no reference to service provision based on 'needs assessment' but a deference to the traditional 'treatment of illness' approach. In many of these situations, there is also often a tendency to make assumptions without too much thought – assumptions that are often no more than a reflection of popular (and inaccurate) stereotyping.

In recent years, both psychiatry and clinical psychology have been subject to criticism that has attracted much attention. The concepts of illness and therapy have been attacked from within the professions themselves – for example, in *The Manufacture of Madness* by Thomas Szasz (1969), *Against Therapy* by Jeffrey Masson (1988) and *Toxic Psychiatry* by Peter Breggin (1991). However, this criticism has had very little impact on day-to-day hospital-based services or on many of the changes that have taken place in the move from institutional to community care. MIND's policy documents lack the rhetoric of Szasz, Masson and Breggin but express the dissatisfaction heard on the ground and voiced increasingly strongly by service users. Basically, the pressure is for the disciplines that provide mental health services to become sensitive to social issues, such as sexism and racism, to user involvement and to the real needs of people in trouble. Some professionals have taken up these calls (e.g. Howitt, 1991; Fernando, 1991), but the extent to which they have affected the training of professionals has been negligible.

A major problem in the training of professionals for mental health work has been the lack of an overall approach that encompasses, as a totality, the various facets of a modern Western society – relating these to concepts of mental health and interventions designed to maintain such 'health'. Such an approach needs to be informed by clear analyses of social realities (of society), the traditions, and indeed history, of the professional groups involved, the place of voluntary organisations and finally (and perhaps most importantly), the perceptions and views of the users of the services. This book is an attempt to redress this imbalance.

Nothing in the field of mental health can possibly be explored in a social vacuum – not problems, 'illness', health, interventions, legal issues nor indeed anything else that has a bearing on mental health care. And one of the significant social issues of our time is racism, so that it is inevitable that racism is a part of the scene in most, if not all, of the chapters in this book. Unfortunately considerable confusion exists between what is 'racial' and what is 'cultural', and this has played a not insignificant part in allowing 'cultural racism' (also called the 'new racism') to replace 'biological racism' (Barker, 1981; Gilroy, 1987; Husband, 1994). The concept of 'ethnicity' appears to get over this problem – but does it? In fact, the terms race,

culture and ethnicity (and their derivatives) are often used rather
loosely, almost interchangeably. The usual meanings and uses of
these terms have been discussed fully elsewhere (e.g. Fernando, 1991)
and will be summarised here.

The word 'culture' denotes a way of life (family life, patterns of
behaviour and belief, language, etc.), but it is important to note that
cultures are not static, especially in a community where there are
people from several cultures living side by side. Reference to race
does not necessarily imply support for the thesis that people are
inherently 'different' because of certain inherited characteristics that
are related to skin colour, but it does imply that people are treated
differently because of skin colour – that the concept of race is a social
reality. The term 'ethnic' generally refers to a sense of belonging
based on both culture and race and is used sometimes when the term
'culture' or 'race' is inappropriate or undesirable for various reasons.
Although there is no consistent way in which the term 'black' is used
to describe people, it may be used in what is called a 'political sense'
– to refer to people identified not just by the colour of their skin but
more generally as those who trace their ancestry to populations that
were and/or are subjugated and exploited, etc. by people who are
known as 'white people'.

The title of this book refers to a 'multi-ethnic' society, a term
which encompasses both the racial and cultural identities of the
people who constitute British society. However, sometimes this
society is referred to as 'multicultural' or 'multiracial' if either
'culture' or 'race' is being emphasised – in keeping with the
discussion in the previous paragraph (the hyphen being dropped to
indicate the unity implied in the words). Similarly, other words
referring to race, culture and ethnicity are used as appropriate to the
context. Each author has tried to steer a way through somewhat
variable understandings of the concepts of race, culture and ethnicity. Since they are from diverse professional backgrounds in both
the voluntary and statutory sectors, their approaches to questions of
race and culture vary and their perceptions of the meaning of mental
health are not always identical. As a result, some authors use the
capital 'B' or 'W' in designating people's race based on skin colour,
while others do not do so; some authors refer to 'patients', others to
'clients' and still others to 'service users'. The editor has not
attempted to introduce uniformity of terminology across chapters but
the meanings of terms and use of words are usually consistent within
each chapter. The diversity of views, styles and fashions points to

the fact that there are no easy answers to many questions in the field of mental health – nor to issues concerning race and culture. Ultimately, professionals need to think for themselves and that is essentially what training is all about.

The first part of the book deals with the context in which mental health services operate – its 'Current setting'. The second part, 'Confronting issues', addresses racial and cultural issues that arise in delivering these services in a multi-ethnic society. Finally in the third part, 'Seeking change', the various issues are brought together in order to indicate a way forward – not so much a 'blueprint' for the future as suggestions for change, starting from where we are now. All the chapters are informed by an awareness of the cultural diversity of British society, the realities of racism and the importance of social issues both in general and within the professions that control the mental health scene.

The training of mental health workers, and indeed the practice of professionals in the mental health field, must first and foremost address the question: 'What is mental health?'. Even more pertinently, it must address the issue of what mental health means in a multi-ethnic setting in terms of the practical politics of service provision. Although the definition of mental health must be built on an appreciation of contemporary social realities (with respect to questions of illness and health, issues of race and culture, etc.), it is not just a theoretical, academic definition of 'mental health' that is required, but an evaluation of what mental health actually means as a practical proposition.

Chapter 1 examines Western thinking about mental health and illness in a historical context, considers the concept of multiculturalism in the presence of racism and finally analyses the meaning of mental health in the light of discriminatory diagnostic practices. In Chapter 2, the question of 'therapy' is faced. After a general discussion of its meaning across cultures seen in a historical context, the chapter explores the seemingly mystical element in what goes for therapy and the dimensions of power in the interaction between professionals and service users.

Mental health services, like all other services, are provided within a legal framework. Chapter 3 analyses the main laws which constitute this legal framework, referring also to guidelines on practice issued by the Department of Health and to ways in which mental health legislation could change in the future. Chapter 4 examines in some depth – based on research carried out by the author – the experience of black people in their confrontation with the hard end of psychiatry – the 'sectioning' process – raising issues about the role of psychiatry in a racist society or, as some would contend, the racist role of psychiatry in society. A major question in the context of a multi-ethnic society is whether mainstream organisations can deliver appropriate services to members of black and minority ethnic communities, or whether the problems and needs of these communities can best be served by organisations representing these communities. In discussing the findings of their research in the Asian voluntary sector, the authors of Chapter 5 illustrate the difficulties encountered by voluntary groups and examine the future for the black voluntary sector in the light of the changes taking place in the resourcing of minority ethnic community groups.

The attempts to explore, or better still confront, problems faced by ethnic minorities in accessing and acquiring the sort of services best suited to their needs in a milieu where racism is minimised and cultural sensitivity maximised, are few and far between. Part 2 of this book attempts to provide some feel for what is happening in this area however. The viewpoints of service users from national user movements are sometimes canvassed in setting up services, but it is rare for these to play a significant role in the final analysis – and black users seem to be marginalised in the user movement itself. The reasons for these problems are explored in Chapter 6 by considering issues such as questions of power in the mental health system, especially in relation to racial and cultural matters. Then in Chapter 7, the place of race equality training for professionals in the field of mental health is discussed and the training courses described.

In Chapter 8, a black psychiatrist with first-hand experience of the psychiatric 'coal-face' considers the shortcomings in the present psychiatric system, and describes a service that has been successful in 'reaching out' to black people in the Camberwell district of South London – the Maudsley Outreach Support and Treatment Team (MOST). In Chapter 9, the founder of another project, the White City Project in West London – set up to provide help for depressed women caught up in a vicious spiral of social suffering (so common for people from black and minority ethnic communities) – describes that project and considers the theory behind the model of intervention used in the project.

In Chapter 10 two workers from the Marlborough Family Service in North London discuss the cultural dimension in the practice and theory of family therapy, and describe their ways of building a culturally sensitive (family) service that confronts the realities of racism. Following this, in Chapter 11, the director of Nafsiyat, a psychotherapy centre in North London that was established for the specific purpose of applying (if that is the correct word!) psycho-analytic psychotherapy across cultures, presents insights derived from his experience at this centre and considers theoretical and practical issues that have concerned the staff working there.

The third part of the book consists of one chapter (Chapter 12) written by the editor. Using the information, knowledge, insights and speculations contained in the eleven previous chapters as a jumping-off ground, this chapter seeks ways of moving forward in the field of mental health care. The principle of a community-based service is accepted and its meaning explored. An alternative to the medical diagnostic approach to psychiatric assessment is suggested, and the concept of therapy redefined. Changes in the meaning of culture and race are addressed, and some of the problems that may arise in assessing need and establishing change are considered. The agenda of this final chapter is set by the theme and ethos of the book – that *community care is about communities and mental health about people*, with individuals, families or societies seen in a context of social realities. The task of professionals in a multi-ethnic society is to provide services within and of communities, using hospitals sparingly, and addressing the needs of all ethnic groups. And that means recognising and taking account of cultural differences among the people in the area covered by the service and confronting the diverse ways in which racism is interwoven into society.

Part I

Current setting

Mental health is something we all aspire to and the provision of services for people with mental health problems is undoubtedly an obligation of society. As a result of various political, ideological and indeed economic forces within society, community care is emerging as a way of providing such services. Its implementation on a large scale in Europe and North America did not begin until the mid-1980s and is still in progress. The first part of this book considers the major elements in the *context* in which these changes are developing: the ideologies that inform the professional disciplines that dominate statutory services, the legal framework in which it has to operate, the experience of those disadvantaged in society and the role of the voluntary sector – all these determine the nature of what goes for mental health care in a modern society. This first part of the book attempts to tell it how it is, without considering in any detail possible ways of confronting the serious issues stated and implied.

Chapter 1

Social realities and mental health

Suman Fernando

Concepts of both race and culture are included in the term 'ethnic', and so a multi-ethnic society is both multicultural and multiracial. In attempting to explore the meaning of mental health in a multi-cultural setting, first, we need to see where we come from in terms of the culture of professional training – that is, to examine the origins of psychiatry and psychology, which, after all, have dominated and fashioned Western thinking about mental health and mental illness. Second, we need to appraise what we mean by saying that a society is multicultural, not forgetting how racism complicates the picture. Is it in fact realistic and appropriate to see different groups of people as 'having' different cultures and then seeing these cultures as, in some way, interacting with each other? Or is it preferable – more useful, more correct – to see all individual persons, or families, as culturally mixed, hybrid perhaps, with gradations of differences so that the margins between one culture and another are arbitrary – a matter of judgement affected by the model employed by the person making the judgement? Third, we need to determine the meaning of mental health in relation to culture in a context of racism, attempting to differentiate what is 'cultural' from what is 'racial'.

Since there is a likelihood of losing the overall meaning of mental health by breaking down important holistic issues into individual parts, this chapter will attempt to examine these questions by addressing them all together – as a whole, rather than by considering each in turn. The discussion will be informed by various types of data: first, historical information, because it illustrates the Western thinking which largely determines the traditions of the professions involved in mental health care; second, social, psychological and biological facts in relation to race and culture, since they affect very closely the lives of people who may suffer from mental health problems; and finally the conventions and practices of professionals and users of services.

This chapter will present a resumé of Western thinking about mental health and illness from a historical perspective, considering it in as wide a context as possible but geared to practicalities of service provision. Then it will outline some of the changes that have occurred in the recent past, culminating in the current shift from institutional to community care, and focusing on the British scene to note how racism and cultural issues have become evident in the course of these changes. Finally, general matters concerning race, racism and culture will be discussed, exemplified by current issues in the mental health scene.

PSYCHIATRIC THINKING IN THE CONTEXT OF CULTURE AND RACE

In the sixteenth century Descartes established the 'Cartesian' concept (Gold, 1985) of a strict division between mind and body (*psyche* and *soma*) which became a hallmark of Western thinking about human beings generally. It is on this theoretical basis that interest in matters to do with 'mind' developed. Later, as madness was seen as a medical problem, 'illness of the mind' became the basic model for understanding people regarded by society as 'mad'. 'Pathologies' of emotion, intellect, beliefs, feelings, thinking, etc. were identified and elaborated. Various theoretical concepts about illness of the mind were developed. Clearly, the models of 'mental illness' (and its subdivisions) that were built up over the years embodied a Western world view – the 'culture of psychiatry' (Fernando, 1988) – the main features of which are represented in Figure 1.1. Although this 'medical' approach (the illness-approach to problems) has paid off in the study of the body, it is still an open question as to whether it is appropriate to a study of the mind.

European studies of 'illness of the mind' initially drew mainly on Greek Hippocratic traditions (Simon, 1978) but later developed new theories. Thus many variations of the basic illness model exist in psychiatric circles as 'models of madness' (Siegler and Osmond, 1974): in psychodynamic terms (based on the writings of Freud), madness is explained as being derived from disorders in development – with pathology located in childhood; in neurological terms as brain disease; the inherited nature of illness sees madness as the end result of (inherited) deficiency or malfunctioning of the brain;

Mind–Body dichotomy

Mechanistic view of life

Materialistic concept of mind

Segmental approach to the individual

Illness = biomedical change

Natural cause of illness

Figure 1.1 Culture of psychiatry

the family interaction model holds that the whole family, rather than the individual, is 'ill'; and, in an extension of this model developed by Laing (1967), illness may be seen as a positive experience. Finally, 'eclectic' practitioners, drawing from a variety of models, evaluate illness in terms of many biological, psychological and social (causative) factors in what is sometimes called the 'bio-psychosocial model' (Holloway, 1994) – the exact constellation of factors that are relevant depending on the particular instance.

Western psychiatric research has focused on possible biological explanations of madness (usually represented by the diagnosis of 'schizophrenia') in terms of a mixture of genetic factors, altered brain dopamine systems, and structural abnormalities in the brain. None of these lines of research have produced definitive answers. One reviewer of the topic (Barnes, 1987) concludes: 'For every point about the biology of schizophrenia there is a counterpoint. Theories about the origin and disease process of schizophrenia are often built on a multitude of empirical observations and a paucity of hard facts' (p. 433). A more recent extensive review of the neurochemistry and neuroendocrinology of schizophrenia (Lieberman and Koreen, 1993) found a 'fragmentary body of data which provides neither consistent nor conclusive evidence for any specific etiologic theory'. In a recent book on schizophrenia, Jenner *et al.*, in a chapter reviewing neuro-biological research into the topic, conclude:

> In our opinion, what all these studies appear to indicate is that the finding of (more or less conspicuous) neurobiochemical, psy-chophysiological, psychoendocrinological, or neurophysiological

anomalies (when we proceed to study the working of the human brain) does not necessarily imply the existence of any sort of disease process (which could therefore be the only one capable of producing the anomalies).

(1993: 106)

All the models of madness currently used in psychiatric practice, especially the eclectic one that requires a sort of all-round specialist to evaluate the aetiological factors concerned, leave psychiatrists – rather than any other type of professional (not to speak of carer or service user) – with the power of making the final judgement about illness, its cause (if 'present') and treatment required. Thus the issue of power is inextricably involved in questions about the perceived nature of madness, the existence (or myth) of mental illness, and the basis for evaluating human problems that seem to encompass emotions and behaviour: an eminent professor of psychiatry states:

For psychiatrists it is particularly important to understand which conflicts we are encharged by power to dominate and regulate – small rational conflicts and those which are determined by nascent states. This is the object of psychiatric biochemistry, genetics and biostatistics.

(Jenner *et al.*, 1993: 136)

In Western culture today, the theme of 'illness' is consistently used in evaluating certain human problems. These are problems where individuals (1) present with distress, (2) are presented as disturbing other people, that is, causing distress, or (3) are designated as behaving in ways that society sees as deviant *and* irrational. The basic contention that influences theorising in these instances is that of a personal disturbance seen as a problem in the 'mind' associated with a biological change which is then conceived of as a mental disorder or 'mental illness' (see Figure 1.2). In other words, the process of psychiatry is to evaluate certain types of human problem in terms of illness by identifying a 'change' (from a hypothesised norm), giving it a name ('diagnosis'), evaluating the causation ('aetiology'), and finally making a judgement on interventions ('treatment') that are likely to counteract or alleviate the 'condition'.

In modern Western psychiatry, the aetiology of an illness is seen in terms of factors internal to the individual person (usually bio-chemical, genetic or physiological) or external to him/her (rela-tionships, stresses, etc.). In the extreme biological (or 'medical')

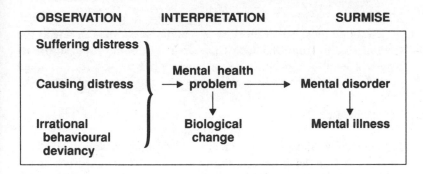

Figure 1.2 The psychiatric process

approach that characterises most hospital-based British psychiatrists, the extraneous factors are given little importance, being seen as 'merely' precipitants, and there is a tendency to assume that one particular, usually internal, factor such as a biochemical change or infection may be all important. Thus an illness may be called 'alcoholic psychosis' – implying that alcohol consumption is the only important factor involved – or a 'toxic psychosis' may be diagnosed when someone becomes confused while in the throes of an infective condition, such as pneumonia. But more importantly, assumptions are made about the likelihood, even certainty, of a single biochemical cause of an 'illness', such as 'schizophrenia', although it is associated with several factors. In the multi-factorial approach of eclectic thinking that is often found in well-established multi-disciplinary teams, external factors may be given as much, or even more, importance as internal factors and one causative factor is seldom looked for. But even here there is an assumption of a basic biological substratum underlying a change within the individual whenever an 'illness' is diagnosed. In the movement within traditional psychiatry (perhaps) erroneously termed social psychiatry, social factors are accepted as important but only as *precipitants*, rather than causes of illness (see p. 20).

Although wedded to an illness model of evaluating problems, psychiatry is not just a medical discipline; it is also a social institution. Together with its counterpart clinical psychology, psychiatry arose within a political and cultural context – serving purposes which were not merely academic or medical (see Chapter 2). From the very beginning, psychiatry was concerned with social control – and it still is. The type of control and the recipients of its actions are essentially determined by the socio-political context in which it operates. This aspect of psychiatry is codified in law as the Mental Health Act 1983 (see Chapter 3) but more importantly, its use of coercion and compulsion is accepted by society – indeed *expected* by society – and implemented inequitably (see Chapter 4).

Models of illness

Although psychiatry has its origins in the control and care of the 'insane', it then developed (in the West) as a way of analysing varied human problems in terms of illness. An equivalent way of thinking about human problems did not develop in other systems of medicine, such as the Ayurvedic system in India or African systems (discussed in detail by Fernando, 1991). Moreover, in non-Western cultures, the mind–body dichotomy does not dominate thinking about human life and its problems, and matters brought together (in Western culture) in psychiatry are seen in religious, spiritual, social, political, philosophical, psychological, ethical or medical terms (or varied mixtures of these). In other words, psychiatry, from a non-Western standpoint, may be seen as a mixture of all these brought together for social, ethnic, political and historic reasons. However, it is the Western (illness) model for evaluating human problems and controlling people that dominates the planning of systems of care for multiethnic societies in the West – and even more regrettably, that is copied by predominantly non-Western countries as a result of the imposition of Western ways of thinking.

During the past sixty years, the validity of the concept of mental illness as a purely medical matter has been seriously questioned by anthropologists (e.g. Benedict, 1935), sociologists (e.g. Scheff, 1966) and philosophers (e.g. Foucault, 1967). The essential critique has been that the labelling of people as 'mentally ill' deals with social deviancy – enabling society to 'put away' people who are unacceptable, if not an actual danger, to society – or else that such labelling invalidates feelings (e.g. angry feelings), beliefs, etc. that society wishes to suppress for political, social or other non-medical reasons. The social model goes on to explain the phenomenon of mental illness in terms of rule-breaking and labelling with subsequent role-playing. Psychiatrists have usually seen social theories to be alleging a conspiracy by psychiatrists and so they have reacted defensively. But more recently, doubts about the usefulness of the illness model are voiced within the profession of psychiatry itself (e.g. Jenner *et al.*, 1993) and certainly within other professions involved in mental health care (e.g. Bentall *et al.*, 1988; Bentall, 1990; Boyle, 1990). However, the illness model for defining mental health problems continues to thrive. Although information from various sources plays a part in defining illness, the way disease entities are constructed and named is socially determined at least in part. It is easy to see this in the case of (say) homosexuality, which was a disease until 1973 but not after that (Bayer, 1981), or drapetomania, the disease of black slaves characterised by the symptom of running away from captivity (Cartwright, 1851). But the case for considering diagnoses such as depression among Africans and cannabis psychosis in black people in Britain as socially constructed entities is equally valid (Fernando, 1991): depression was considered rare among Africans while they were thought to lack qualities such as 'a sense of responsibility' (Carothers, 1953), but became commoner after the advent of independent black African states when the perception of Africans changed (Prince, 1968). Cannabis psychosis – a diagnosis given almost exclusively to black people in Britain (McGovern and Cope, 1987) – is related to the stereotype of drug-intoxicated madness of black people (see Chapter 2). More recently it has become equally evident that racism, through stereotyping, plays a large part in the social construction of schizophrenia itself – the diagnosis that forms the bread and butter of everyday psychiatry. (Racism in the social construction of schizophrenia is discussed in Fernando, 1988, 1991.)

In short, the dominant theme in Western culture, implemented through psychiatry and psychology, is that problems to do with thinking, emotional reaction, feelings, fears, anxieties, depressions, etc. are conceptualised in terms of illness. Even family problems and social behaviour (as in 'psychopathy') and hatred and jealousy (as in 'pathological jealousy') are sometimes fitted into the illness model. And racist perceptions of black, brown, red and yellow people (so-called) have worked their way into this psychiatric system at all levels (see Chapter 2). Clearly, this Western way of conceptualising mental health problems is alien to Asian and African cultural world views and, perhaps if we think about it, alien to what many people feel even in Western countries. For example, speaking very generally, in Eastern thinking integration, balance and harmony, both within oneself and within the family or community, are important aspects of what may be considered mental health, while in

EASTERN	WESTERN
Integration and harmony	**Self-sufficiency**
Between person and environment **Between families** **Within societies** **In relation to spiritual values**	
Social integration	**Personal autonomy**
Balanced functioning	**Efficiency**
Protection and caring	**Self-esteem**

Figure 1.3 Ideals of mental health

the West, self-sufficiency, efficiency and individual autonomy seem to be important (see Figure 1.3).

The influence of racism complicating cross-cultural comparisons may be appreciated if the reader examines his/her initial reactions (i.e. without much thought) to Figure 1.3. Anyone trained in Western schools of thought will naturally see ideals of self-sufficiency, personal autonomy, efficiency and self-esteem as the correct basis for discussions about mental health. In other words, the ideals of mental health implicit in the thinking that underlies training would naturally adhere to the values which are derived from Western culture, because cultures are seen hierarchically on the basis of racist assumptions about where they 'come' from. Racism affects our perceptions of culture and these assumptions are incorporated into the training of professionals.

RECENT HISTORY OF SERVICE PROVISION

The start of the modern era of mental health care in Europe began in the 1950s and 1960s when there was a rapid decrease in the mental hospital populations in most European countries. This change may well have been a result of changes in attitude in Western Europe after the defeat of fascism, reflected in the development of the Welfare State in the UK, decolonisation in Asia and Africa, and a humanitarian approach to people generally. The part played by the advent of psychotropic medication in the mid-1950s is a matter of debate; in some Scandinavian countries the emptying of mental hospitals had actually started before these drugs were available, and there the change was attributed mainly to a change in staff attitudes. Whatever the underlying reasons for the changes, by the early 1960s there was an air of optimism that psychiatry was in the throes of a revolution. In 1961 the then Minister of Health for England announced a policy to close all mental hospitals within ten years, and two years later the 'community care blue book' was issued by the Department of Health and Social Services (DHSS).

In the 1950s and 1960s too some mental hospitals developed the 'therapeutic community' movement led by institutions such as Claybury Hospital in North East London (Shoenberg, 1972), and later Mapperley in Nottingham and Dingleton in Scotland – an approach referred to by Maxwell Jones (1968) as 'social psychiatry in hospital'. The movement established important ways of working with large groups of people and influencing behaviour by manipulation of the milieu in which people live. Special 'therapeutic communities' were established as treatment settings – for example, one for psychopaths at the Henderson Hospital in Surrey is still active. The search for 'alternatives to hospital' in the 1960s led to 'crisis intervention' – pioneered at Napsbury Hospital in St Albans by Scott (1960) – as a special type of 'social' therapy based on family work. Unfortunately the term 'crisis intervention' is now applied to many other forms of intervention, even sometimes to the compulsory removal of people from their families!

In the USA, Thomas Szasz (1962) in *Myth of Mental Illness*, challenged the traditional biological view of mental illness. Similar views in the UK led to the so-called anti-psychiatry movement of Laing and Esterson (Cooper, 1970). Although here, illness (particularly schizophrenia) was not denied as an individual reality, it was perceived as a way of coping within families – essentially families which used pathological forms of communication, such as 'double-bind' (Bateson *et al.*, 1956). A residential establishment, Kingsley Hall, was set up by this movement in East London in the late 1960s – described vividly in *Two Accounts of a Journey Through Madness* (Barnes and Berke, 1971). The Arbours movement, providing houses for people with mental health problems, is the modern counterpart of the original 'anti-psychiatry' movement.

However, the process of looking for alternatives to a hospital-based service within the overall NHS system continued unabated. The treatment of patients in small units in the community and the emphasis on community work from units attached to District General Hospitals (DGHs) grew fast in the 1970s. And everywhere, multi-disciplinary teams serving catchment areas or sectors of catchment areas became the standard aimed for. Finally in the 1980s, the shift to community care was given a new head of steam for (what one suspects to be) economic reasons – namely raising money by selling what had become very expensive land tied up in the mental hospitals. On the whole, over the years, the move to community care has been supported by most professionals, academics, carers and users, although many people have voiced reservations about the paucity of resources being allocated to fund the changes.

The first day hospital was the Marlborough Day Hospital in North London which Dr Joshua Bierer started in the 1950s, promoting a model of social psychiatry that perceived illness as a reaction to problems of living. By the mid-1960s, even very traditional hospitals, such as the Maudsley Hospital in Camberwell (South London), developed day hospitals; and day centres, hostels, group homes, etc. followed. This became the rehabilitation model of mental health care, written up as the so-called Camberwell Service Model (Wing and Haley, 1972). This type of quest for alternatives to the mental hospital was tested in Worcester (DHSS, 1970) and formulated as national policy in *Better Services for the Mentally Ill* (DHSS, 1975).

The rehabilitation model (Camberwell Service Model) is essentially a medical one, but its use is called 'social psychiatry' – a sort of application of the medical model of traditional institutional psychiatry in the community. People who develop mental illness, especially if they are diagnosed as 'schizophrenic', are seen as socially handicapped – so acute treatment in hospital is followed by rehabilitation, then by resettlement with long-term supports for supposedly stable residual handicaps. The revolving door is not avoided – the idea is rather to slow down the 'revolutions to a minimum by active rehabilitation and support (Watts and Bennett, 1983). This 'social psychiatry' emphasises social factors in aetiology and rehabilitation but sees illness as biological in nature (as described above). The community care model is something further on from the rehabilitation model. In this, resources reach out with services for people living in the community. Scull (1977) and others claim that a community approach of this sort allows people with mental health problems to be integrated with their neighbours within 'normal society', even where these ties have become strained or broken – the aim of therapy being to enable such people to establish social relationships. It is really a reversal of the ideas of 100 years ago – or even sixty years ago – which were essentially that society had actually caused mental health problems in the first place and 'mentally ill' people needed to be separated from society until they got over these problems, needing peace and quiet to do so. (Even so, doctors put in charge of these asylums took to introducing 'treatments' of various sorts, unwilling on the whole to be mere custodians.)

The official developments in the UK over the last twenty years have used the Camberwell Service Model of rehabilitation where in-patient services are combined with day hospital – to achieve continuity and easy movement between the two. Many psychiatric units in DGHs have been built on this model and generally it has been reported as successful – without any evidence to back this up. The failure to engage nearly half of those referred from acute care to chronic care (Beard *et al.*, 1974) has been identified as a major problem however. Observations in Camberwell itself indicate that most of the people who are classified as 'non-compliant' are from black and ethnic minorities (Moodley, personal communication, 1993), and another significant observation is that black and ethnic minorities are being diagnosed as 'schizophrenic' to a disproportionate extent in both hospital and community settings (Fernando, 1991). Further, black people are over-represented among those compulsorily removed from the community under mental health legislation (see Chapters 3 and 4).

A psychiatric system based on community mental health centres (*Riaggs*) is well developed in the Netherlands. The emphasis in the *Riaggs* is on counselling, with a team of workers attending to social and psychological needs aimed at preventing acute illness. The relatively easy access to *Riaggs* is combined with strict control on admissions to hospitals, and round the clock assessment teams in each city. Nevertheless, it seems that under-use of *Riaggs* by ethnic minorities (commonly called 'migrants' in many parts of Europe) is being noticed, coupled with possibly relatively high admission rates of these groups to mental hospitals. There is, however, apparent reluctance to see these as racial or even cultural issues.

The rehabilitation model does not address the question of alternatives to acute admission and so does not challenge the medical model of illness. Nor of course does it challenge discriminations based on racism, sexism or any other 'ism' causing inequities in society. It is reported that some places in the USA have moved away from the strict medical model; in the Madison Service in Wisconsin, handicaps are not considered an inherent aftermath of illness and the emphasis is on social care. There, a mixture of support and rehabilitation combined with 'crisis stabilisation', aims to eliminate the revolving door completely. Engagement is said to be high and drop-out low; it seems that financial pressures (coercion?) to comply may be used, but as yet the Service has not experienced any significant non-compliance. The Madison Service serves a population with a relatively low number of black people however, the main ethnic minority being Chinese (Radford 1993).

In noting all these changes one cannot ignore what might be termed the other side of the coin. First, there appears to be an increasing emphasis on forensic psychiatry and a rise of 'forensic patients' (paid for by public funds) in large private institutions, such as Kneesworth House Hospital and St Andrews Hospital, Northampton. Significantly, the approach to patients in these institutions is not dissimilar to that which used to prevail many years ago in the mental hospitals that are being closed. Second, it is the personal observation of the author – as a Mental Health Act Commissioner visiting hospitals in and around London – that locked wards, and even whole sections of hospitals, are being developed within general psychiatric units (often called mental health units). This may be a response to public pressure for psychiatric patients to be held in secure conditions and government policies such as the 'diversion from prison' scheme, whereby magistrates are encouraged to make strenuous efforts to 'divert' to hospitals potential prisoners who may be deemed 'mentally disordered'. (In the case of the 'diversion from prison scheme', an apparently humane policy is far from humane in its implementation.) These 'para-forensic' units are often referred to as 'intensive care wards', 'locked wards', or even 'rehabilitation wards' (!). Third, there is concern about the whole detention procedure (Browne, 1995 and Chapter 4), and the use of very high doses of medication, especially for black patients (Mental Health Act Commission, 1991, 1993). So, while community care encourages non-medical models of care, the concept of illness as an explanation of socially undesirable behaviour perceived as dangerous is being powerfully reinforced in the forensic and 'para-forensic' field, covering over social issues of poverty, homelessness and racism.

Another issue that applies on both sides of the Atlantic, and one that may have serious consequences, is the growing tendency in psychiatry to emphasise biochemical and genetic factors, rather than environmental and social ones, as causes of 'illness' and violence – for example, in the so-called 'violence initiatives' in the USA allegedly to identify and 'treat' children who are predicted as likely to become violent adults (Breggin and Breggin, 1993). In *The Language of the Genes*, Steve Jones (1993), a leading British geneticist, warns against the confusion between nature and nurture in the misuse of modern genetic knowledge for 'biologising of behaviour' and the 'geneticising of crime', pointing out the similarity of these tendencies to the eugenic ideology and the racist IQ movement of the earlier part of the twentieth century (Jones, 1993: 180). With rising poverty, racism and homelessness, there is a risk that social problems become medicalised and violence in society is attributed to heredity, culture and (by implication at least) race. The mental health services are likely to get drawn further into the morass of social control unless firm action is taken to prevent this happening.

RACISM, MULTICULTURALISM AND STEREOTYPES

The classification of human beings into 'races' based on visible physical characteristics, particularly skin colour, has a long history in Western Europe. According to Molnar (1983), Blumenbach decided that a skull recovered from the Caucasus Mountains closely fitted his image of the skulls of a particular 'race' of people and the term 'Caucasian' became a term applied to people from Europe, North Africa and the 'Middle East', later extended to all 'white-skinned' people. Race classification gradually centred around three main types – Negroid, Mongoloid and Caucasoid – black, yellow and white. As theories about racial differences were tested against scientific observations, particularly in genetics, the notion of genetic consistency of individual races was abandoned and race boundaries defined by colour were found to be arbitrary (Dobzhansky, 1971). The idea of a 'racial type', and 'race' itself, is no longer useful in human biology (Jones, 1981).

It should be noted in passing that, while the assumption of racial groups being biologically distinct from each other is not correct in scientific terms, race as a marker may be useful in a very limited way. For example, certain genetically transmitted conditions, such as Tay-Sachs disease, sickle cell trait or sickle cell disease, and cystic fibrosis may be suspected when there is evidence (from physical appearance) of East European Jewish, West African and

North European ancestry respectively (Molnar, 1983); so race may be used as an initial indicator to detect people who may be vulnerable to these conditions. But this use of 'race' in no way challenges the overall conclusion that scientifically, 'as a way of categorising people, race is based upon a delusion' (Banton and Harwood, 1975: 8).

Although race is a scientific myth, it persists as a social entity for historical, social and psychological reasons – in fact for all the reasons that result in racism. And skin colour remains the most popular basis for distinguishing one race from another. When a group of people are perceived as belonging to a racial group, the assumption is of a common ancestry. When a society is referred to as 'multi-racial', the implication is that it contains people whose ancestries vary; but more importantly, that these ancestries are related to their heritage, their biological make-up – their 'blood'.

Racism is not a uniform entity but one that varies from place to place, often determined by historical events as much as by contemporary social situations; in fact, it is more correct to talk of racisms rather than racism (Hall, 1978). And as Gilroy (1993) states:

a perspective that emphasises a need to deal with racisms rather than a single ahistorical racism also implicitly attacks the fashionable over-identification of race and ethnicity with tradition, allowing instead the opportunity to develop a view of contemporary racisms as responses to the flux of modernity itself.

(1993: 22)

Clearly, racism is not a new phenomenon in Britain or anywhere else. However its relationship to considerations of culture and mental health care requires a very special analysis. Groups of people identified in racial terms have been present in the UK for many years, especially in areas such as Liverpool and Bristol. However, it was the advent of black- and brown-skinned people in fairly large numbers in the 1950s that has given rise to a recognisable rise in racist antagonism, gradually mounting in the 1960s to reach a very high level in the 1990s, with no sign of abating. This has clearly affected mental health services very considerably, and racism is a major consideration for community-based services in a multicultural society.

Racism is fashioned by racial prejudice and underpinned by economic and social factors. When racism is implemented and practised through the institutions of society, it is called 'institutional racism'. Although race prejudice and racism are related concepts, they should be distinguished from each other. Race prejudice is basically a psychological state, a feeling or attitude of mind, felt and/ or expressed as 'an antipathy based upon a faulty and inflexible generalisation' (Allport, 1954: 9); at a deeper level it may be likened to a superstition (Fryer, 1984). Racism, however, is a doctrine or ideology – or dogma. Race prejudice and racism often go together, but unlike prejudice, racism is recognised by the behaviour of an individual and/or the way an institutional system works in practice – though (racially prejudiced) attitudes of mind that are recognisable and consciously held may be present also. And racism is associated with power – the power of one racial group over another. Wellman (1977) argues that an attitude such as prejudice must be seen within its 'structural context' – the distribution of power within the society, political constraints arising from external influences, rivalries between social classes, etc.. Once racial prejudice is embedded within the structures of society, individual prejudice is no longer the problem; it is racism that is the active principle. Racism is then essentially about 'institutionally generated inequality' based on concepts of racial difference; although it affects the behaviour of individuals, 'prejudiced people are not the only racists' (Wellman, 1977: 1).

Racism has been socially constructed over hundreds of years and its origins are lost in the history of Western culture (Banton and Harwood, 1975). It is carried in systems of education, advertising, propaganda, political manipulation, economic pressure, and the ordinary 'common sense' of the person-in-the-street. At a personal level, racism is a way of behaving (with or without an attitude of prejudice) that people learn and absorb through experiences in their upbringing and in everyday life events. It should not be seen as a deviancy from the norms of the culture but, on the contrary, as very much a part of it – perhaps central to it.

The background to British racism is somewhat different from that in other parts of the Western world. Although traditionally welcoming European refugees fleeing persecution, the British have never held a favourable attitude towards the immigrant who chooses to migrate to Britain. Moreover, immigrants to Britain from parts of the world that used to form the British Empire are viewed with the sort of racism that thrived in that empire, but without the imperial paternalism that existed there towards the 'native'. British racism today is seen in the derision implied in the term 'immigrant' – often used to describe all black people wherever they were born rather than to describe real immigrants from (say) Ireland – and the contempt implied when people are referred to as 'coloureds' or 'Pakis'. Racist practice in Britain today tends to include everyone denoted on the basis of skin colour as not being 'White' in one large group of 'Blacks', only slightly separated into Asians, African-Caribbeans, Cypriots, etc..

Stuart Hall *et al.* (1978) argue that British racism of the 1970s was fashioned by the socio-political crisis in post-war Britain. Various aspects of this crisis were articulated through 'race', identifying black populations as the enemy – this time the enemy within. Places where black people settled were identified as 'ghettos' and racial politics was articulated through debates about 'law and order', 'inner city deprivation' and 'mugging'. In the early 1980s, Barker identified a change in the articulation of racism in the British context, and noted that a belief in the inferiority of the out-group is no longer necessary for their exclusion (Barker, 1981). Husband (1994) describes how cultural difference is emphasised as a basis for separating one group from another, and the (alleged) *naturalness* of in-group preference and out-group hostility is legitimised by socio-biological notions of what culture means – represented by writings of Lorenz (1966, 1974) and Morris (1967, 1969) . Thus the very recognition of cultural difference – apparent *sensitivity to culture* – becomes the basis of racist doctrines and, worse still, racist action.

Paul Gilroy (1993) carries this argument further to encompass discussions about race and culture which are of significance to understandings necessary for mental health work. Gilroy reckons that British racism now 'frequently operates without any overt reference to "race" itself or the biological notions of difference which still give the term its common-sense meaning' (1993: 23). While the crisis in Britain involves uncertainty about (British) cultural identity, the definition of 'race' – presented as a matter of difference rather than hierarchy – has become an acceptable basis for describing people. In this context, 'culture', as an immutable, fixed property of social groups, has become confounded with 'race', and racism is articulated in cultural terms. Black people are seen as forever outside the British culture, 'locked in the bastard culture of their enslaved ancestors, unable to break out into the "mainstream" alternative' (p. 25) – or, to quote the title of one of Gilroy's earlier books (Gilroy, 1987) *There Ain't No Black in the Union Jack*.

Gilroy's contention that British racism is now marked by the importance given to 'culture rather than biology', means that by implicitly going along with a definition of race as culture, by emphasising 'cultures' of essentially 'racial' groups, and by failing to challenge the muddle between what is 'cultural' and what is 'racist', many anti-racists and others working in the mental health field may well be colluding in perpetuating British racism. Thus it is extremely important to grasp the significance of current analyses of British racism when considering mental health services in multi-ethnic Britain.

Background to racism in mental health services

Most cross-cultural studies in the first forty years of this century designated, perceived and reported non-Western cultures as 'primitive' cultures. Demerath (1942), reviewing a spate of such studies, observed that some of the non-Western societies that had been studied 'were not truly primitive, but on the contrary were either traditionally literate, or had been exposed to Euro-American culture' (1942: 705) – i.e. suggesting that not all non-Europeans were 'primitive' since some had languages of their own or had become civilised by contact with Europeans! An important review by Benedict and Jacks (1954) of studies on Maoris of New Zealand, indigenous Fijians, Hawaiians of the USA, and people of so-called 'Negro Africa', was entitled 'Mental illness in primitive societies' – a review which, according to Torrey (1973) was largely responsible for the acceptance of the universality of schizophrenia by mainstream psychiatry. The cross-cultural usefulness of the concept of schizophrenia is now seriously challenged (see Kleinman, 1988; Fernando, 1991).

Although not now stated overtly, the (racist) attribution of primitiveness to non-Europeans (i.e. peoples seen as originating in Africa, Asia and the Americas) and their cultures has persisted in the thinking of (Western) psychiatry, casting doubt on the objectivity of psychiatric studies on people seen as such. Freud saw similarities between 'the mental lives of savages and [European] neurotics' (1913: 1) in his *Totem and Taboo*; and Devereux (1939), an anthropologist, viewed non-Western healers (generally referred to as 'shamans') as neurotics or psychotics. Today, the universalist psychiatric doctrine, that Western psychiatric concepts, illness-models and treatment needs have a global relevance, subsumes within it a distinct racist judgement of cultures and peoples – often only partially concealed. It surfaces, for example, in the theory devised by Leff (1973), a psychiatrist at the (British) Institute of Psychiatry, which seeks to explain his 'observation' that people from industrially developed countries show a superior level of emotional differentiation when compared to those from 'developing' countries and black Americans. A similar way of thinking is shown by Bebbington (1978), also from the Institute of Psychiatry, in a review of depression: Bebbington uses the term 'primitive cultures' to mean non-Western cultures, and more significantly, argues for 'a provisional syndromal definition of depression as used by a consensus of Western psychiatrists against which cross-cultural anomalies can be tested' (1978: 303). In other words, the 'depression' of non-Western peoples is hailed as an 'anomaly' and the paper indicates that these so-called anomalies are found among black Americans, Africans, Asians and 'American Indians'. It is not necessarily the racial prejudices of individual research workers that is expressed in these theories and ideas, but the pervasive influence of a racist ideology within which they carry out their work.

Current practitioners tend to ignore the racist dimensions of their disciplines and therefore it is usual for no action to be taken to counteract the effects of racism in practice. Consequently, not only are racist traditions perpetuated, but racism in Western culture continues to permeate into the disciplines in their research, theory and practice. Although there is some concern in Britain about racism in psychiatry, this has not led to the adoption of any particular strategies to counteract it. In a recent book directed at British psychiatrists (Fernando, 1988), the author has suggested some possible strategies to detect and combat racism, and successive Biennial Reports of the Mental Health Act Commission (1987, 1989) have identified the needs of black and ethnic minorities as a priority, quoting the disadvantages that are being suffered by black people in Britain because of racism.

Multiculturalism and mental health

In the context of current British society, 'multiculturalism' means that British society has within it strands from various cultural traditions mixed up together. These stem from waves of immigration over many years though mostly since the 1939–45 war, the subsequent collapse of British rule overseas and the turmoil resulting from the long-term effects of colonialism and slavery. The main cultural elements in British society can be identified as Asian and African-Caribbean, with less strong influences from Greek-Cypriot, Turkish-Cypriot, Polish and Jewish cultures. Clearly one can speak of Asian groups, African-Caribbean groups, etc. and see them as 'cultural' groups, and some commonality of need may be related to 'culture' in this sense. But much more often, commonality of need is directly related to common experience in society often based on perceived 'race'. If racism had not determined such common experience, cultural need would be no more an issue for Asian or African-Caribbean people than it is for (say) Jewish or Polish people. Thus notions about culture are inevitably complicated by racism, especially racism in institutional processes, including the training currently given to professionals and many of the ways of working that are currently pursued.

The significance for mental health services of the way multi-culturalism is expressed in contemporary British society arises from several issues. First, there is the carry-over into professional per-ceptions of images carried in society of (say) subservience, aggressiveness, etc.. These images may be constructed politically (i.e. for political reasons) or merely arise through traditional ideas passed on 'culturally' (i.e. in popular common sense) and tend to fill gaps in professional knowledge about individuals that may be seen as unusual or 'exotic'. Second, cultural sensitivity in service pro-vision is often associated with a blindness to individual needs of persons and families. For example, service planners may make assumptions in service provision based on 'cultural need' (e.g. family stress from male domination of the household) taking preced-ence over individual need (e.g. for housing or child care). Both the 'image' problem and 'culturalisation of need' problem relate to the issue of stereotyping. Stereotypes are assumptions which may apply vaguely, inaccurately or not at all to a number of people, but which do not necessarily fit the situation of any one person. Allport differentiates a stereotype from a category:

> For example, the category 'negro' can be held in mind simply as a neutral, factual non-evaluative concept, pertaining merely to a racial stock. Stereotype enters when, and if, the initial category is freighted with 'pictures' and judgements of the negro as musical, lazy, superstitious, or what not . . . . They are sustained by selective perception and selective forgetting . . . they aid people

in simplifying their categories; they justify hostility; sometimes they serve as projection screens for our personal conflict. But there is an additional and exceedingly important reason for their existence. They are socially supported, continually revived and hammered in, by our media of mass communication – by novels, short stories, newspaper items, movies, stage, radio, and television.

(1954: 191–2)

The strength of stereotypes in a racist discourse, brilliantly enunciated in Frantz Fanon's *Black Skins, White Masks* (1952) and Edward Said's *Orientalism* (Said, 1978), derives from the fact that a stereotype is more than a misrepresentation; Homi Bhabha (1994) sees it as an arrested fixated form of representation similar to a fetish in the Freudian sense (i.e. reactivating deep-seated fantasies and anxieties). Certainly, political forces perpetuate their influence; in psychiatric practice, stereotypes are, to a large extent, the medium for political manipulation and the exercise of (racist) power. Many of the stereotypes of black people originate in the era of colonialism and slavery. And as Sartre (1948) said of Jews in the past and as Fanon highlights so clearly, black people often believe the stereotypes that others have of them – or, at least, behave as if they do, thereby helping to maintain their own oppression. The influence of stereotypes in psychiatric diagnosis, psychological testing and evaluation, and in social assessments, is often under-estimated even when recognised. (This is discussed further in Fernando, 1988, 1991).

MODELS OF MENTAL HEALTH

In traditional Western (usually medical) circles, mental health is generally conceptualised as something wider than, or perhaps somewhat different from, the absence of mental illness, but closely related to, if not identical with, 'normality'. However, the meaning of normality is a subject of much controversy (Offer and Sabshin, 1966) even within the limited ways that psychiatry usually sees it – in a narrow eurocentric perspective of white middle-class culture. The American psychiatrist Sabshin (1967), looking at it from a simplistic American perspective, describes four approaches to normality as used by psychiatrists in the USA. These are: normality meaning health as the absence of illness; normality as an ideal state of mind (something we all aspire to perhaps and few achieve); normality as the average level of functioning of individuals within the context of a total group (something that most of us have to settle for, perhaps); and normality as a process that is judged by the functioning of individuals over a period of time (as a sort of good or acceptable behaviour). Even such a simplified approach becomes extremely .complicated in the context of a multicultural society beset by racism, but it is a starting point for discussion of mental health.

Suppose mental health is something similar to normality. Is normality then – or, one might say, mental health – an ideal mental state of happiness, stability or soundness? Or is it an ability to keep a stable internal state of mind (of an individual) irrespective of environment – a sort of strength of mind – that is more or less the dictionary meaning in the seventh edition of *The Concise Oxford Dictionary* (Sykes, 1982)? Perhaps the nearest to a working hypothesis is the concept of mental health as a sort of stable internal state of mind whatever happens outside. For if we look any further, this too becomes very fuzzy and complex, for surely a mentally healthy person is not someone who does not react to circumstances and to people around her or him – a sort of automaton who does not get anxious or worried, never gets into crises, never gets depressed.

But if the concept of mental health is applied to communities or families rather than just individuals, the scene changes again, and talk of healthy attitudes, values and behaviour would lead on towards considering health as involving harmonious relationships all round, in body, mind and spirit. This approaches what sometimes seems to be available in older cultures. The indigenous Americans for example do not see themselves as whole people unless they are in constant communication with spirits; *nirvana* of the Buddhists and *samadhi* of the Hindus represent a loss of individuality in a holism that includes a force or consciousness outside the material self; and

the African is the possessor of a type of knowledge that teaches that reality consists in the relation not of men [and women] with things, but of *men* [and women] *with other men* [and women], *and of all men* [and women] *with spirits*.

(Lambo, 1969: 207, emphasis in original)

But here, in the materialistic Western society, we must be careful not to merely 'healthify' problems in the same way as we medicalise so much.

DISCRIMINATION, DIAGNOSIS AND 'TREATMENT'

The system of psychiatry and, therefore, most professionals in the mental health field, make no effort to allow for either ethnocentrism or racial bias in practice – nor do many professional know how to. Assessments usually fail to allow for ideologies about life, approaches to life's problems, beliefs and feelings that come from non-Western cultures, mainly because training (of professionals) is *of* Western culture. The causes of justified anger arising from racism in society are often not recognised because the black experience in society is not given credence, even if the existence of personal discrimination is recognised in a theoretical sort of way. The alienation felt by most black people is usually seen as *their* problem (and this often leads to 'treatment' aimed at suppressing their feelings) rather than a problem for society as a whole. And when the experiences and feelings of black people are recognised as significant, a disease or criminal model is used to conceptualise them because society (and possibly our own needs) promote this.

In such a context, stereotypical assumptions about black people play a big part in assessments that professionals make. In the case of the hard end of psychiatry (e.g. in the special hospitals), stereotyping of black violence (in media representations, etc.) leading to judgements about dangerousness is a tremendous problem for the profession and one that appears to be resulting in tragedies such as the deaths of three young black men in Broadmoor over the past few years (Prins *et al.*, 1993). Stereotypes also play their part in diagnosis. Psychiatric diagnoses carry their own special images which may connect up with other images derived from (say) common sense or tradition. Thus, alienness seems to be linked to schizophrenia (as a diagnosis) and to biological (or genetic) inferiority (as a human type). It is not difficult to see how race comes into both these concepts – alienness and biological inferiority. The result is a racial bias leading to an over-diagnosis of schizophrenia among black people who are seen (in common sense at least) as both 'alien' and 'inferior'.

When psychiatry is called upon to 'diagnose' dangerousness, common sense images of dangerous people seem to be the guide that is resorted to – often without much insight into the problems this raises. Indeed dangerousness and schizophrenia appear to be confused together in both lay minds and among many psychiatrists, general practitioners and social workers (Browne, 1995). And so racial bias gets compounded. The possibility of introducing a community treatment order is viewed with fear by many black people who already feel that they are being unnecessarily forced to have medication in high doses, but a recent report on a calamity in the community, popularly called the 'Clunis Report' (Ritchie *et al.*, 1994), endorses an increase in the social control of people 'diagnosed' as schizophrenic, without any reference to the exacerbation of 'indirect racial discrimination' (as described in the Race Relations Act (Home Office and Central Office of Information, 1977)) that this is likely to promote.

The problem of over-diagnosis of schizophrenia hinges on the nature of a psychiatric diagnosis and the nature of racial bias. Racial bias is concerned with racist perceptions and beliefs and racist practices incorporated into the diagnostic process; the question is not about accuracy of diagnosis and of 'mis-diagnosis', but what diagnosis means. To a trans-cultural or social psychiatrist, a diagnosis is a hypothesis – no more, no less. Sometimes it is useful – or rather it may be useful for a particular purpose – but often it is not so useful and sometimes it can be downright inappropriate or even damaging. So, in a psychiatric culture where there is racism and where racial bias is active, a correct diagnosis in the tradition of psychiatry and in line with the tools (of diagnosis) used, can still be a racist one and as such inappropriate. The fact is that with racism incorporated into the psychiatric system, a racist result is to be expected unless specific measures are taken to avoid it. This cannot happen until diagnosis is seen in a very different light or is dropped altogether to be replaced by a different system for the evaluation of mental health problems.

The Third Biennial Report of the Mental Health Act Commission (1989) reported an impression that high levels of medication were used for African-Caribbean patients in some hospitals. A recent study in Nottingham (Chen *et al.*, 1991) found that high peak doses of neuroleptic drugs were used mainly for African-Caribbean patients and also that these patients were more likely to be prescribed long-acting preparations given by injection. The question of psychotherapy is complex. The process that we call 'psychotherapy' is well known to be biased against working-class people and perhaps women (Masson, 1988), quite apart from being problematic for people from non-Western cultures. And issues of racism – and indeed sexism – in the therapeutic relationship are often not even recognised, quite apart from being addressed (Thomas, 1992).

Black/ethnic minorities more often:

Diagnosed as schizophrenic

Compulsorily detained under Mental Health Act

Admitted as 'offender patients'

Held by police under s. 136 of Mental Health Act

Transferred to locked wards

Not referred for psychotherapy

Given high doses of medication

Sent to psychiatrists by courts

Suffer from unmet need

Figure 1.4 Racial and cultural issues: British findings

The extent of discrimination in diagrosis and treatment is overwhelming yet difficult to pinpoint. Figure 1.4 gives a list of the main issues identified as 'Racial and cultural issues' in the British context today and detailed in recent publications (Fernando, 1991; DoH and Home Office, 1992). Power is still carried to a large extent by the psychiatric (medical) establishment, backed by clinical psychology. Although reluctantly and belatedly acknowledging (at least in an interview given by Dr Fiona Caldicott, President of the Royal College of Psychiatrists (Gorman, 1994)) that cultural differences must be addressed and that racism in psychiatry is a fact, the psychiatric establishment sees cultural and racial issues as largely peripheral to the main subject matter of psychiatry – 'mental illness'. As community care becomes established, power relationships are likely to change. It is in this context that some hope can be maintained for improvement through training.

SUMMARY

A historical view of psychiatry shows the power of illness models in determining current approaches to mental health. An analysis of the ethnocentric nature of Western psychiatry, with the permeation into it over the years of racist ideologies, shows the nature of the problems faced by professionals and service users. The dominance of medical thinking in Western society ensures that at present research into mental health problems, even when they are not defined overtly in terms of illness, tends to be influenced by the medical model of defining these problems. Inevitably, medical interest, while not rejecting social, psychological and political aspects of 'illness', concentrates on biological systems as opposed to other systems that human beings are involved in. Further, the medical approach in general is to reject the central importance of racial and cultural issues in what is seen as a question of illness identification.

The history of psychiatry illustrates the way in which ethnocentric and racist thinking has permeated the discipline. However the real problem lies in the fact that these ways of thinking have affected popular thinking – the world view of Western societies – and so have become incorporated into what we call 'Western culture'. The British legal framework reflects this thinking – institutionalising it in successive Mental Health Acts. The training of all professionals takes it on by not questioning its basic premises even if minor aspects are challenged in (say) anti-racist training. The 'common sense' of the person in the street reflects it. It is not a matter of reforming psychiatry (as a medical discipline) but of a cultural change that will affect society in general. Yet limited advances aimed at improving community care can be made by modifying or redefining concepts we all use, the major one being that of 'mental health'.

The confusion about the meaning of mental health inevitably results in service providers turning to traditional models, usually based on the illness model of psychiatry. Clearly this is not sufficient to society as a whole, but in the case of multicultural societies, the continuing use of the medical model carries serious dangers. In the field of race and culture the dangers are seen in the discriminatory processes evident in diagnosis and treatment (e.g. the high degree of schizophrenia being diagnosed among black people), the muddle between social control and therapy, the abject failure of psychiatry to address the cultural variation in perceptions of illness and, most of all, in the firm conviction held by many service users that psychiatry and clinical psychology no longer provide useful bases for professional practice in mental health care.

Chapter 2

Professional interventions: therapy and care

Suman Fernando

The history of Western treatment for mental health problems identified as 'illness' goes back to the origins of psychiatry and psychology. As the concept of mental illness developed and expanded in Western Europe, both disciplines developed *pari passu* – psychiatry as the medical approach to mental health problems perceived as 'illness', and clinical (medical) psychology as the application of academic psychology to people deemed (medically) 'mentally ill'. In both cases, the approach to mental health problems is to devise therapies, i.e. essentially a medical approach. Although the boundaries separating the two disciplines now give rise to rivalry and dispute, both psychiatrists and psychologists usually work together in community mental health teams and both disciplines are influential in determining the ethos of multi-disciplinary teams. More importantly, the viewpoints underlying professional practices that are involved in community mental health care are dominated by the thinking within psychiatry and psychology, and rooted in the history of these disciplines.

Clearly the training of psychiatrists and psychologists are different, or at least have different emphases – the former a somatic bias and the latter a psychic bias – corresponding to the soma–psyche split inherent in Western thought. Both disciplines have an interest in behaviour and thought processes which are perceived as determining behaviour. However, both disciplines, being 'scientific', exclude from their considerations questions identified in Western thought as being religious or spiritual in nature. Not surprisingly, the difference between a psychiatrist and a psychologist from the point of view of the general public (or more particularly the user of mental health services who is interested in what practitioners actually *do*) is very unclear. The difference may be seen largely in terms of power; the psychiatrist, for example, being the *only* professional who is able to prescribe medication as well as other treatments, to recommend compulsory removal to hospital and who is qualified to be designated as the Responsible Medical Officer under the Mental Health Act (Chapter 3).

This chapter will begin with a historical appraisal of clinical psychology and psychiatry from the point of view of race and culture and will then attempt to explore the *nature* of what is done, can be done, or needs to be done, when people present to services with mental health problems. The meaning of 'therapy' will then be considered from a cross-cultural perspective by discussing cultural differences in the way interventions are conceptualised in practice, the dimensions of power, and the 'magical element' in the interactions between professionals and service users. Finally the chapter will discuss the nature of 'care' and 'need' as seen from a cross-cultural perspective in a context of racism.

HISTORICAL PERSPECTIVE

Psychology and psychiatry developed about the same time – about 300 years ago, in seventeenth-century Western Europe, although various ideas within the disciplines hark back to Greek philosophy, poetry and medicine (Simon, 1978). Although they at first developed in parallel largely as academic pursuits, they became linked as practical applications emerged. From the nineteenth century onwards both clinical psychology and psychiatry developed in close association. The former has maintained its basis in academic psychology but has drawn inspiration from medical, philosophical, and more recently, sociological insights. The latter, while remaining basically medical in its orientation, especially in its adherence to the 'illness' model for evaluating human problems, has been influenced by clinical psychology, as well as sciences such as biochemistry and physiology. Both disciplines have been influenced greatly by social and political forces in society at large however, especially those in Western Europe.

Psychiatry developed from two main sources. First, from a medical interest in matters to do with the mind and medical influence over the care and control of the insane. In 1632, a medical governor was appointed to the Priory of St Mary of Bethlem – an institution which had been taking in lunatics since 1403. However it was with the establishment of asylums in the early nineteenth century that a rapid growth in psychiatry took place. Psychiatrists, who were then also called Alienists (i.e. those who decided who was alien to society), became as much custodians as physicians, responsible for controlling and 'putting away' lunatics who were disturbing social order in European cities, one way or the other.

In *The Historical Introduction to Medical Psychology*, Gardner Murphy (1938) traces the origins of (academic) psychology to Descartes, who wrote in the seventeenth century about the 'passions of the soul'. Descartes' main contribution to posterity however, was the concept of 'dualism'- the basis of modern Western thinking in terms of Mind and Body, the Psyche and the Soma (Chapter 1). Descartes set the style of (Western) psychology in dissecting human nature and reducing complex systems of emotional and intellectual life in order to 'find' laws, basic 'facts', natural tendencies, etc. This is the reductionist approach to gathering knowledge. Viewed through the insights of cultures with holistic bases to their thinking, such an approach may promote piecemeal understanding but loses the awareness of the human condition that comes from a philosophy that sees human life as an indivisible 'whole'.

The rise of the biological sciences in the eighteenth century led to physiological psychology largely based on study of the sense organs and, later, to neuropsychology based on the anatomy and physiology of the brain alone. In the nineteenth century, Francis Galton, 'the greatest of Darwin's immediate followers in the field of psychology' (Murphy, 1938: 123), applied Darwinian principles of variation, selection and adaptation to the human species. When Galton (1869) published *Hereditary Genius*, showing that individual greatness followed family lines and was unrelated to environmental influences, *individual differences* between human beings became the legitimate subject for psychological study. Psychology was then set to study *individuals* deemed to be mentally 'ill' (i.e. a clinical study), linking up with medical study of such people by psychiatrists. Therefore, in a real sense, Francis Galton was the founder of modern clinical psychology.

In the mid-nineteenth century, psychiatrists developed various concepts for describing alleged thinking patterns of people deemed insane, and identified various 'illnesses' in the lunatics that they were in charge of but without much agreement on a standard classification. Then Kraepelin in Germany differentiated 'manic-depression' from 'dementia praecox' in the 1880s. And in 1911 Bleuler coined the term 'schizophrenia' to indicate a split between the emotions and intellect. As psychological studies came to the fore, the concept of 'neurotic' illnesses was formulated and fashioned: in the 1890s, Janet and Charcot in France popularised 'hysteria' as an illness of women and in the 1920s, Freud developed the concept of anxiety in 'anxiety-hysteria', as distinct from 'conversion hysteria'. The concept of depression, which goes back to Hippocrates (as 'melancholia'), was given a new impetus by Freud when he linked it to guilt – and depression soared in popularity after the war when anti-depressant medication was powerfully marketed. More recently, various other 'illnesses' have been identified, and collected together in two rival systems – the (European) International Classification of Diseases (ICD) and the (American) Diagnostic Statistical Manual (DSM).

Ideologies and pressures in Western society have always permeated the disciplines of psychiatry and psychology fairly freely. So as psychiatry and psychology confronted other cultures and races, ideologies within the disciplines reflected to a greater or lesser extent Western thinking about black, brown, yellow and red people (so-called). Their 'mind', and hence their propensity to illness of the mind, was identified as inherently different to that of white people. Some experts (e.g. Pritchard, 1835; Tuke, 1858, and Maudsley, 1867) saw them as 'savages' who lacked the capacity for mental 'illness' – the 'noble savage' idea of Rousseau; and in the USA, epidemiological studies were used to support the claim that black people became prey to mental illness if released from a state of slavery (Thomas and Sillen, 1972). Francis Galton (1869) extended his theories of family inheritance of individual characteristics to group differences between races which he attributed to to heredity. 'Social Darwinism' identified different races at different positions on a ladder of social and psychological evolution, leading to the eugenic movement (founded by Galton) which aimed to select out 'superior' races (carrying the best 'genes') by controlling human breeding. This became the 'scientific' basis for genocide in Germany during the 1940s but even before then had been used to justify genocidal policies in other parts of the world, such as Tasmania (Australia).

From the mid-nineteenth century onwards until the present day, racism has appeared consistently in psychiatric and psychological writing and also surfaces in practical work. When John Langdon Down (1866) surveyed residents of institutions for people excluded from society because of alleged 'mental deficiency', he concluded that they were 'racial throwbacks' to Ethiopian, Malay and Mongolian racial types. A well-known textbook on adolescence by Stanley Hall (1904) described Asians, Chinese, Africans and Indigenous Americans as 'adolescent races'. And when Kraepelin (1904), sometimes called the 'father of psychiatry', observed that guilt was not seen in Javanese people who became depressed, he concluded that they were 'a *psychically underdeveloped population*' akin to '*immature* European youth' (Kraepelin, 1921: 171, emphasis in original). J. C. Carothers, a colonial psychiatrist writing in a monograph commissioned by the World Health Organisation (WHO) in the 1950s, *The African Mind in Health and Disease*, claimed to have found the 'absence of a sense of responsibility' among Africans (Carothers, 1953), having repeated a few years earlier his astounding finding of a 'resemblance between the African and the leucotomized European' (Carothers, 1951: 12).

In his *Totem and Taboo*, Freud (1913) saw similarities between the 'mental lives of savages and [European] neurotics' – and to him savages were 'primitives' who included Melanesians, Polynesians, Malayans, the native peoples of Australia, the indigenous people of North and South America, and the 'Negro' races of Africa (Hodge and Struckmann, 1975). When instinct theories became popular, McDougall (1920) postulated the concept of 'group minds' attributed to 'different peoples such as the Negro, the White and the Yellow' (p. 111): Nordics he said showed a propensity for scientific worth, Mediterraneans for architecture and oratory, and 'Negroes' an 'instinct for submission' (McDougall, 1921 cited on p. 15, Thomas and Sillen, 1972). A few years later, Jung postulated that the Negro 'has probably a whole historical layer less' in the brain (quoted in Thomas and Sillen, 1972: 14) and when he found apparent psychological deficiencies among white Americans, he attributed these to 'racial infection' from living too close to black people (Jung, 1930: 196). Although blatant racist ideas about instinct and contamination are not usually voiced in modern psychological and psychiatric literature, the underlying racist ethos is often evident in judgements – for example about black people being 'demanding' – or in suggestions about the provision of separate services. And often these judgements and suggestions are couched in language that claims cultural sensitivity.

The perception of black people as immature (or in modern terms, 'underdeveloped') (white) Europeans still persists in the thinking of practitioners trained in Western modes of thought. It may appear (for example) in the form of paternalism underlying stereotypical explanations for clinical 'findings' of psychiatrists. For example, researchers from the Institute of Psychiatry (Bebbington *et al.*, 1981), on finding that the incidence of depression amongst black people was lower than that amongst Whites, observed that 'they [black West Indian Immigrants] respond to adversity with cheery denial' (p. 51). When Leff (1973) studied data from international studies, he concluded that people from underdeveloped countries and black Americans (i.e. the politically 'black') are less developed in their ability to differentiate emotions when compared to Europeans and white Americans. The assumption he made was of the type invariably made by professionals trained in a Western setting, namely that a *Western* style of emotional differentiation or expression is the norm against which 'other' types are to be judged. Such assumptions are inherent in the adherence of most professionals to illness models based on Western thinking whatever the context and whatever the cultural background of the service user. In clinical situations, such assumptions often lead to a pathologising of the culture of black people (Browne, 1995).

Explanations in the psychiatric literature for differences in rates of diagnosis of categories of 'illness' are invariably concerned with biological difference between racial groups, whether resulting from genetic or environmental influences; the socio-political context (carrying racism in it) in which the diagnoses are made are never considered, and the explanations are sometimes somewhat far-fetched. For example, a recent postulate seriously proposed in discussing the relatively high rates of schizophrenia being diagnosed among black people in Britain is that virus infections contracted by pregnant immigrant women who *may* have been unprotected by antibodies (having not been in contact with the viruses of the host country) *may* have resulted in brain damage to foetuses leading to an added risk of adult schizophrenia. In examining the basis for this theory, the only positive data are from two studies of the 1957 influenza epidemic (Mednick *et al.*, 1989; O'Callaghan *et al.*, 1991) which found an association between maternal viral infection and a diagnosis of schizophrenia in the offspring, while data from another similar study (Kendell and Kemp, 1989) had failed to detect such an association. This tenuous evidence is then linked up with the *possibility* (no more) that perinatal virus infection *may* lead to an immunological dysfunction (King and Cooper, 1989) leading to brain damage leading to schizophrenia – all speculations! The number of researchers who quote this immunological/virus theory or a variation of it (e.g. Wing, 1989; Harrison, 1990; Eagles, 1991; Wessely *et al.*, 1991) in order to explain away the relatively high likelihood of young British-born black men being diagnosed as 'schizophrenic' suggests that institutional psychiatry, represented by its journals and researchers who obtain support for the study of racial groups, has a powerful need to protect its current ways of thinking (and hence working), even at the expense of perpetuating the racism which it has inherited from the past.

Although eugenics itself died out after the Nazis applied its theories systematically by genocide, the racist IQ movement of Jensen and Eysenck (Billig, 1979) surfaced in the 1970s, and then, in the 1990s, the world of psychology found Rushton (1990) expounding similar ideas – claiming that 'mongoloids, negroids and caucasoids' differ in terms of their IQ, 'reproductive strategies', etc. (p. 196). Described by some psychologists as 'palpable nonsense' (Howitt, 1991:100), this theory repeated racist stereotypes about sexual permissiveness, size of genitals, criminality, etc., but was considered a suitable topic for 'scientific' debate in a prestigious journal – the official medium of the British Psychological Society. The perception of black people as lacking innate intelligence dies hard in psychiatric and psychological arenas.

So, the study of the 'psyche', set on the road in the seventeenth century by Descartes when he applied 'scientific' methods borrowed from physics to the study of human feelings, emotions, intellects, etc., led, in the nineteenth century, to the *clinical* study of individuals – clinical psychology. Psychiatry, developing from a medical interest in emotional disturbances such as melancholia, achieved power and status once it assumed control over vast numbers of 'lunatics' committed to asylums in the early nineteenth century. The two disciplines have grown together in an uneasy relationship, jointly underpinned however by the traditional Western approach to human beings – described in Chapter 1 as the 'culture of psychiatry' – influenced and permeated by ideologies in society at large. In short, both clinical psychology and psychiatry are ethnocentric and racist.

The variable nature of racism was explained in the Introduction, when reference was made to the existing confusion between culture and race. The term 'cultural racism' is applied to several somewhat different concepts. In terms of Gilroy's analysis of current British racism (Chapter 1), cultural racism would represent racism articulated through the language of culture – discriminatory processes being applied without (necessarily) implying a hierarchy of races or cultures. But cultural racism is defined by Jones (1972) as the individual and institutional expression of the superiority of one race's cultural heritage over that of another. And Howitt describes cultural racism as a process 'whereby the racist assumptions of a culture/society are transmitted from one generation to the next through its institutions and folklore' (1991: 102).

The racist ideas in both clinical psychology and psychiatry (as illustrated in the examples given above) demonstrate a mixture of 'biological' and 'cultural' racism (using the latter mainly in the sense given to it by Gilroy), with a gradual shift from the former to the latter over the years. In a context in which 'illnesses' such as depression were seen in biological terms, it was natural that Kraepelin (in the 1920s) would have seen the 'immaturity' of Javanese as biologically determined. Carothers, in his racist conclusions about Africans and black Americans, referred consistently to African 'culture' but then applied his conclusions to black Americans, indicating a confusion (in his mind) between culture and race. The work of Leff in the 1980s demonstrated a similar confusion but since he assumed (in his theory of emotional differentiation presented as fact) that people from underdeveloped countries were likely to change their ways of emotional expression as they 'evolve', the racism in his theory was more in line with a cultural racism that implied superiority of Western culture over all others. The IQ movement demonstrated biological racism since the IQ differences were seen as inherited genetically. However, in concluding that (white) Americans became psychologically 'infected' by Blacks, Jung was clearly promoting cultural racism, where different cultures were seen hierarchically and were linked to racial categories.

Apart from its inherent racism, clinical psychology and psychiatry have other serious problems in being adapted to serve the needs of community mental health care in a multicultural society. Sinha writing from India and calling for a psychology that confronts social issues, states:

Psychology, as such, suffers from certain inherent constraints. Being modelled after mathematics and the physical sciences, its methodology tends to insulate it from the complexities of social problems. It has certainly produced a vast amount of research impressive for its neatness and precision, but often having no external referent. Methodological refinement seems to have be-

come an end in itself, frequently leading to artificiality and
triviality.

(1993: 40)

In addition to having the same drawbacks as clinical psychology,
psychiatry is hampered in a multicultural society by its tendency to
adhere to an illness model and a definition of therapy that is
constricting. The fundamental cultural issue for psychiatry hinges on
its dependence on 'diagnosis' for the evaluation of people presenting
with mental health problems. The model currently used allows full
rein to racism and limits the possibilities for cultural sensitivity in
practice.

TREATMENT, SELF-HELP AND NEED

The relative nature of the validity of interventions to maintain or
establish mental health – generally referred to as 'treatment' – is self-
evident once the tie to an ethnocentric definition of mental health
is recognised. In taking a broad cross-cultural view, it is possible
to generalise (for the sake of comparison) between interventions
for promotion of mental health ('treatment' for mental illness in
the traditional Western nomenclature) by considering Eastern and
Western approaches (Figure 2.1) in line with the comparison made
in Chapter 1.

EASTERN	WESTERN
Acceptance	Control
Harmony	Personal autonomy
Understanding by awareness	Understanding by analysis
Contemplation	Problem-solving
Body–Mind–Spirit unity	Body–Mind separate

Figure 2.1 Treatment/liberation East and West

Clearly there are vast individual differences between people
within the broad cultural categories 'East' and 'West', and the
allocation to categories may also be unclear in the case of any one

individual. However, most readers will appreciate that assumptions inherent in society (that affect professional training) would naturally promote certain attitudes towards the aims of interventions in general. If the reader examines his or her reactions to Figure 2.1, it will be evident that most professional training will naturally contain assumptions that give problem-solving, control (of disturbing feelings) and understanding by analysis greater emphasis than the aims listed as 'Eastern'. The cultural arrogance involved is not unlike racism, if not identical to it. Thus, a consideration of cultural differences in interventions for mental health ('therapy') must address racism too.

Traditionally, a (Western) 'therapy' is given by a professional (or groups of professionals) to people identified as requiring the 'therapy'. However, the matter is rarely as simple as this, and, in a multicultural setting, it is even more complex. Clearly, what we call 'therapy' is not an absolute entity with a universal meaning identical for all cultural and social settings (Littlewood, 1992a). Indeed the concept of 'therapy' itself – in the sense of being a 'remedy' for a sickness – represents a Western (ethnocentric) attitude to a mental health problem, although the original meaning of 'therapist' referred to one who assisted in the healing process, rather than actually doing the healing (Capra, 1982). In other cultures the approach to such problems may be very different, depending on the problem. Therefore, there is often a large gulf between the perceptions of professionals and those of service users in a multi-ethnic society. Strategies for breaking away from the impasse are required (and these are discussed in Chapter 12).

The degree to which a particular intervention is something done *for* someone else, and the degree to which it enables a person to help herself or himself (i.e. promotes 'self-help') is never clear but cultural differences may play a significant part in determining it. Indeed, cultural differences in the quality of interventions by professionals can be evaluated in terms of a therapy–self-help dimension, looked at from the service user's point of view. For example, if depression is seen as a spiritual matter to be handled with meditation or prayer, the 'remedy' is not so much 'therapy' as 'self-help'. If hallucinations are seen as a form of communication which is welcome to (or at least not resisted by) the person experiencing them, neither therapy nor self-help may be appropriate but perhaps the person concerned may need understanding and acceptance – therapy or self-help for society perhaps. To a person whose main reason for seeking help is to 'get rid of' some unwanted feeling such as early morning depressions, it is 'therapy' that is needed. It will be seen that there are major difficulties in mental health care becoming 'user-led', as the rhetoric goes. Even if a professional aims at evaluating the 'need' or the perceived need of the service user, the judgement of such need is based on her or his expertise, derived from training. Further, the traditional 'professional' approach usually reflects the ethos of Western ways of thinking strongly influenced by (Western) psychiatry's medical model of therapy. From a (traditional) professional's point of view, 'depression', or any other feeling or group of feelings identified as symptoms, requires active interventions aimed at suppressing them or, at least, undermining them in some way, even if it does not go all the way to attempting a 'cure'. And the perceived role of the professional is to provide the means for doing so if not actually carrying out the process of 'therapy'. The ground for misunderstanding between professionals and service users in a multicultural setting is clearly evident.

In traditional Western thinking, therapy is seen as a process apart from either therapist or client. In the extreme versions of this medical model, therapy is something got out of textbooks or training that does not even involve experience with the people being 'given' the treatment. For example, I recall speaking with a psychiatrist who had arranged to visit China to carry out 'family therapy'. She was well versed in family therapy developed in a Western setting but had never even met a Chinese family nor did she feel that she needed to know anything about Chinese families. 'Therapy' was seen by her as something she had learned about and was now ready to 'practise' irrespective of setting, in the way she might have given a drug or performed an operation. Clinical psychologists and psychiatrists tend to describe psychotherapy or 'cognitive therapy' in similar terms – as unrelated to the culture of the person 'receiving' (or being 'given') the treatment.

Another important dimension along which the concept of therapy differs cross-culturally is that of the 'magical' element in it. To many clients, therapy in a Western setting is often a magical process, 'with its own logic, acting in a manner which cannot be disclosed except in an "oversimplified" way' (Banton et al., 1985: 86). In a different cultural setting, an intervention (such as fortune telling) for a mental health problem may be seen as a matter of evaluating interactions around and within persons involved – very matter-of-fact, not 'magical' at all. The recent attempts to 'demystify' treatments by explaining them to clients in simple terms is to be applauded, but sometimes lead to even more mystification being added by theoretical hypotheses being given as 'fact'.

An example of professional experts imposing ways of thinking by defining problems occurs in the case of explanations about the treatment of 'schizophrenia', where unproven biochemical theories, for example that schizophrenia is a brain disorder correctable by a drug, are presented to 'patients' and their relatives. (See pp. 13–14 for justification of the statement that the biochemical nature of schizophrenia is unproven.) A more subtle type of this approach is the method of psycho-education where ethnocentric explanations for mental health problems or even social problems are used to justify 'teaching' relatives of 'schizophrenics' to withhold certain types of emotion. Although this is quoted as an educational approach in mental health care or even as 'family work' (Kuipers et al., 1992), it is basically a socio-culturally insensitive way of working that should have no place in mental health care which aims to confront racism and take account of culture.

Ideally, most professionals would see all interventions as co-operate ventures between professionals and service users, but the perception of users is often very different (see Chapter 6). Nearly always, the professional is in a position of power over the service user. In a culture where the person with a mental health problem expects the work done by a professional to be (say) akin to arranging a ceremony with supernatural significance, the power is not located in either the 'user' or the professional. In this context therefore, professional help for a mental health problem would be perceived by the 'user' in a very different way to how therapy is perceived in the West. This illustrates the way 'culture' is involved in the nature of an intervention ('therapy' in Western terms).

The element of 'care' in mental health care, whether in the community or hospital, is not simple. In a strict Western approach, care is something like the context in which 'treatment' is provided. But like therapy, care is provided by a person, or group of people, for someone else in a detached ('professional') sort of way, separate from pre-existing family support systems or community networks. The historical tradition of independence in self-help ventures that characterises the black voluntary sector is referred to in Chapter 5. A similar tradition of independence from (what may be seen as) state support characterises the approach to care of many people from black and minority ethnic communities, who are conscious of the need to maintain their identities in the face of invalidating experiences in society. In their case, being cared for in hospital does not automatically remove the person from the family nor does it absolve the family from its position as the main supporting network for the individual. This continuing involvement of family networks while 'care' is provided by 'others' is even more important in the case of community care than it might be in the case of hospital care. In effect, 'care' and family support (or community networks) are not understood in all cultures in terms of compartmentalised, separate systems but (as it were) as mixed up together – a fact often not appreciated by many professionals trained in the Western illness mode of treatment provision.

In the changing scene today, the move is towards organising services to meet needs. Here the question of needs assessment becomes crucial. A 'needs-led service' is attractive rhetoric but the experience so far is that *in practice* it may mean 'no-change', at least as far as user participation and medical domination of service provision are concerned. Stevens and Raftery (1992) describe three types of needs assessment: the epidemiological assessment, the comparative assessment and the corporate approach to needs assessment. The epidemiological system would use survey information on prevalence rates of 'illness', since it is assumed that all – or nearly all – appropriate types of care are being supplied. It makes no allowance at all for the fact that most ethnic minorities, and many others too, do not see the current psychiatric services (whether hospital based or community based) as appropriate. The comparative assessment derives information about needs by comparing utilisation and provision of services in one district with those in another. The result of using this approach would be to average out services towards a 'norm', the validity of which cannot be assessed. In the corporate approach to needs assessment, various interested and informed parties including service users and professionals, would be consulted about needs, styles of service preferred, etc. Anecdotal reports of such an approach indicate that relatively powerless ethnic minority organisations are often included within the consultation process but find it difficult to influence the final decisions since they are poorly represented on decision-making bodies.

It is perhaps significant that Stevens and Raftery – both medical authors – voice their preference for the epidemiological assessment as 'the ideal for purchasers' (1992: 48). In this approach, a mental health need is defined as 'the population's ability to benefit from health care' (ibid.: 48) representing the traditional view of the institutional era when communities and service users had no say at all about service provision – they could simply 'take it or leave it'. In spite of this (or perhaps because of it) it is the epidemiological approach to needs assessment that is gaining favour with purchasers, especially at centres of excellence (*sic*), perhaps because the sort of information they think they require (i.e. rates of diagnosed 'illness') is easily available (though of doubtful validity) and the process is likely to be backed by powerful forces – those that have dominated psychiatry for the past 300 years. Needs assessment as a basis for service provision is a good idea – just as (perhaps) providing 'asylum' for people in trouble may have been a good idea in another era. It is in the implementation of these ideas that the 'goodness' often gets lost

CONCLUSIONS

Both psychiatry and clinical psychology, based exclusively on Western thinking about human beings and their problems, provide a dubious basis for professional interventions in mental health in a multicultural society. Cultural differences in the understanding of 'therapy' and 'care', and in the assessment of 'need' in a multi-cultural setting result in serious conceptual and practical problems for professionals involved in providing mental health services. Inevitably these difficulties must be reflected in deficiencies in service provision. Unless they are addressed during this time of change from hospital-based services to those based on community care, the injustices and inequalities of the past will certainly continue. There is no easy resolution but the subtlety and extent of the difficulties indicate that professionals need to work closely with service users, their families and the wider community in the course of providing interventions and 'care'.

Chapter 3

Law and guidelines

William Bingley

As mental health services enter the age of community care in a multi-ethnic society, it is important that all those involved in their delivery have an understanding of the relevant legal framework; its opportunities and limitations. This chapter does not aim to provide details of mental health legislation but to indicate in broad outline the legal framework within which professional work in the mental health services is carried out.

The law plays a central role in the provision of mental health care and the making of other arrangements when an individual is regarded as suffering from mental disorder – especially if that 'disorder' is considered to render the person incapable of making decisions. Powers over the property and financial affairs of a person under (what the law calls) a mental disability, probably first arose in the early years of Edward I, who reigned from 1272–1307. From that time the legal framework has grown increasingly complex as it reflected the growing involvement of the state in response to the needs of people with mental health problems. In addition to specific mental health legislation, mental health services are subject to more general legal provisions that are targeted at different social concerns. In a multi-ethnic community, the provisions of the Race Relations Act 1976 are important. This Act defines two types of racial discrimination:

Direct discrimination arises where a person treats another person less favourably on racial grounds than he treats, or would treat, someone else.

Indirect discrimination consists of treatment which may be described as equal in a formal sense as between different racial groups but discriminatory in its effect on one particular group.
(Home Office and the Central Office of Information 1977: 4)

The Race Relations Act, amongst other things, outlaws discrimination in relation to the provision of goods, facilities and *services* and it is clear government policy that health and social services should be planned and provided in a manner which takes into account the needs of black and minority ethnic communities. Delivering such a service is altogether another matter, one that requires a complex range of activities in which the law may have a part to play.

What is it that the law can be asked to do in the field of mental health? While any global retort is almost by definition bound to be inadequate, one response that is helpful was provided by Gostin (1986). He argued that the law could be asked to address the following issues:

- the provision of services;
- the setting of limits on the exercise of compulsory powers, and
- the enhancement or maintenance of the civil and social status of those described as experiencing mental health problems.

Without wishing to minimise the limitations of this model, it does provide a useful and flexible overview that can be helpfully developed when seeking to understand the place of the law in mental health. Any review of the law has to identify what it has to say (if anything) about the various current critiques of mental health services; for example service users' challenge of current orthodoxies and the dissatisfaction of black and other ethnic minority groups with the way that mental health services are developing, which many regard as largely irrelevant to their needs. Whether the law can or should take the lead in addressing these issues or whether it tends to trail behind until a consensus has emerged cannot adequately be addressed here. However, in seeking an answer to that question it is important to understand what the law does in this particular field.

THE LAW AND SERVICES

The provision of services to people with mental health problems remains primarily the business of the state, although with the passage of the National Health Services and Community Care Act 1990 (the 1990 Act), opportunity for the non-government sector to contract to supply such services has greatly increased. The legal framework encompasses two types of service for people with mental health problems:

1 Those services (in the broadest sense of the word) that are not

confined to people with mental health problems. For example, entitlement to income support and the provision of housing in certain circumstances (although under the Housing Act 1985 mental illness is a specified ground for establishing a priority need for accommodation).

2 In contrast to these more general services there are those more specifically targeted at people with, what the law often describes as, a disability.

With the refocusing of the provision of mental health care in the community it is appropriate to identify first the legal framework encompassing the provision of relevant services by Local Authorities and the health services.

Local Authorities

The 1990 Act places a general duty on a Local Authority, where it appears to that Authority that any person, for whom it may provide or arrange for the provision of community care services, may be in need of any such services to:

• carry out an assessment of his or her needs for those services; and
• having regard to the result of such assessment then decide whether his or her needs call for the provision by it of any such services.

The 1990 Act defines 'community care services' as those provided under any of the following provisions:

• Part III of the National Assistance Act 1948 (provision of accommodation and welfare services for blind, deaf, dumb, crippled and mentally disordered persons).
• Section 45 of the Health Services and Public Health Act 1968 (promotion of the welfare of old people).
• Section 21 of and Schedule 8 to the National Health Service Act 1977 (care of mothers and young children, prevention, care and aftercare, home helps and laundry facilities).
• Section 117 of the Mental Health Act 1983 (aftercare for certain categories of persons who have ceased to be detained in hospital and then leave hospital. This particular obligation is shared with health authorities).

As Richard Gordon (1993) points out, the provision of home helps under the National Health Service Act 1977 and the aftercare obligations under section 117 of the Mental Health Act 1983 are duties rather than powers and, ostensibly, nothing in the 1990 Act operates to convert such duties to powers, although 'the interrelationship between a duty to provide services and the discretionary service provision regime under the 1990 Act is not wholly clear' (1993: 137).

As can be seen, the group of people for whom a Local Authority has a duty to assess under section 47 of the 1990 Act is wide. Similar obligations also arise in relation to people who are disabled, and at law (although in practice there is much overlap with the above) there is a distinct need-assessment regime for services by disabled people set out in the Disabled Persons (Services, Consultation and Representation) Act 1986. Disabled persons are defined at law as those 'who are blind, deaf or dumb, or suffer from mental disorder of any description and other persons who are substantially and permanently handicapped by their illness, injury or congenital deformity' (Disabled Persons Act 1986, section 16). The services to which this Act applies are those referred to in the so-called welfare enactments, that is:

• Part III of the National Assistance Act 1948 (see above).

• Section 2 of the Chronically Sick and Disabled Persons Act 1970 (the provision of practical assistance and facilities in their home for recreation, travel, leisure, meals and communication).

• Schedule 8 to the National Health Services Act 1977 (see above).

Health services

Under the National Health Services Act 1977 it is the duty of the Secretary of State to continue to provide a comprehensive health service designed to secure improvement in the physical and mental health of the people of England and Wales and the prevention, diagnosis and treatment of illness (which includes mental disorder within the meaning of the Mental Health Act 1993). The 1990 Act created new health service structures to pursue these objectives. Under the 1977 Act and the Mental Health Act 1983 the Secretary of State has a number of specific functions including the duty of supervising and the power to direct local social services authorities in the arrangements which they make for the prevention of mental disorder and the care and aftercare of persons suffering from such a disorder.

It is unnecessary to outline the full complexity of the statutory framework for services. The message is reasonably clear: there *is* a statutory framework and practitioners need not only to be aware of it, but also to be in a position to enable service users to consider whether the law could empower them to make more effective demands on the service.

While it is wrong to exaggerate the potential of the law to enable beneficiaries of services in question to enforce their delivery, it is crucial not to forget this possibility either. The 'customer' is said to be king (DoH, 1993a) and therefore the proper use of enforcement procedures can only be said to accord with the prevailing ideology of the provision of mental health services. Again, this is not the proper place for detailed exposition, but it is possible to divide such procedures into three.

Complaints procedures

Section 50(1) of the 1990 Act, for example, empowers the Secretary of State to order Local Authorities to establish procedures for considering representations about any failure in relation to any of the functions that flow from section 47 of the Act (see above).

In relation to the health service it is important to note that the Health Service Commissioner is appointed under Part V of the National Health Services Act 1977 for the investigations of complaints of injustice or hardship caused by maladministration or by some failure in the provision of health services. More specifically, in relation to mental health, the Mental Health Act Commission under the Mental Health Act 1983 is statutorily entitled to investigate certain types of complaint from people who are or have been detained under that Act (DoH and Welsh Office, 1993). The NHS Complaints Procedures have recently been the subject of major review (DoH, 1994) and recommendations for a streamlined procedure have been put forward.

Default powers of the Secretary of State

The Secretary of State in many of the relevant service statutes is given default powers. For example, if, on complaint or otherwise, the Secretary of State is of the opinion that a Local Social Services Authority has failed to carry out functions conferred or imposed on it under the Mental Health Act 1983, he or she may declare the Authority in default and order it to remedy the defect. If it fails to do so, the Secretary of State may then make an order transferring to him- or herself such of the Authority's functions as is appropriate. Similar powers exist in the relation to the health service, although it has to be said that they have rarely been used.

Judicial review

Judicial review is a specific legal remedy whereby the High Court exercises control over the means by which public bodies perform their statutory duties and powers (see Gordon, 1993 for a full discussion in relation to the 1990 Act).

Judicial review is concerned with legality rather than merits. As Lord Hailsham LC stated in *Chief Constable of North Wales Police* v *Evans*:

> It is important to remember in every case that the purpose is to ensure that the individual is given fair treatment by the authority to which he has been subjected and that it is no part of that purpose to substitute the opinion of the judiciary or of individual judges for that of the authority constituted by law to decide the matters in question.
>
> ([1982] IYWLR 1155 at 1160)

In general terms the grounds for obtaining judicial review are *illegality* (e.g. has the authority taken into account matters which they ought not to have?); *irrationality* (e.g. have they come to a conclusion so unreasonable that no reasonable Authority could ever have come to it); and *procedural impropriety* (e.g. non-observance of the rules of natural justice). There are a number of possible remedies available to the Court, including quashing the decision of an Authority or prohibiting an Authority from acting unlawfully. Whilst it would be unwise to exaggerate the potential of judicial review in these circumstances, it is fair to say that the courts have, in the last decade, shown a greater willingness to scrutinise the decision of public authorities in this way (see, e.g. *R* v *Ealing District Health Authority, ex p Fox* (1993) 3 All ER 170, for a case involving section 117 of the Mental Health Act 1959).

PROTECTING 'VULNERABLE' PEOPLE

If a characteristic of a particular group of people renders them vulnerable to particular consequences that are not experienced by others who do not share that characteristic, then one way of addressing such vulnerability is by way of the law. The Race Relations Act 1976 and the Sex Discrimination Act 1975 address various forms of unlawful discrimination on the grounds of race and sex.

In relation to vulnerability consequent upon mental health problems or learning disability, it is possible to identify various legal interventions that attempt to address some of those vulnerabilities. For example, if an individual is rendered incapable of managing their property and affairs by reason of mental disorder then they can be placed under the jurisdiction of the Court of Protection. The Enduring Powers of Attorney Act 1985 enables an individual to put their affairs into the hands of a friend or adviser whose authority will not be revoked by the donor's subsequent mental incapacity. Alternatively, the Department of Social Security has power to appoint an appointee to receive and administer income support or social security benefits payable to someone who is 'unable to act' and who therefore cannot manage their affairs.

A different type of vulnerability is recognised by the Police and Criminal Evidence Act 1984 whose Codes of Practice (Home Office, 1991) make elaborate provision for particular safeguards when a person who is suffering from 'mental disorder or is mentally handicapped' is in police custody.

A not dissimilar vulnerability (the inability fully to exercise individual rights) is recognised by the law in relation to the provision of services. The Disabled Persons (Services, Consultation and Representation) Act 1986, in a provision that still awaits enactment (sections 1 and 2), provides a legal framework whereby 'disabled people' would be entitled to appoint 'authorised representatives' (another name for advocates), who would have the same rights of access to information and to make representations (as provided elsewhere in the Act) about services provided by health and social services as the person they are appointed to represent.

The adequacy of such legal provisions will always be the subject of debate. In this particular context however, it is sufficient to note that there is a history of legal responses to some of the vulnerabilities experienced by disadvantaged groups. At the same time it is appropriate to point out that there has never been any legal provision that addresses unacceptable discrimination arising out of any form of disability, including mental health problems or learning disabilities, similar to the provisions to the Race Relations Act and the

Sex Discrimination Act in relation to certain forms of discrimination arising out of race and gender.

COMPULSORY ADMISSION AND TREATMENT

One of the characteristics that marks off mental health care from almost all other types of health care is the possibility, in some circumstances, of a person being compelled to enter hospital and stay there, and to be forced to receive certain medical treatments for mental disorder. Regulating the use of compulsion is what the Mental Health Act 1983 is primarily, but not exclusively, concerned with. This Act provides four principle ways into hospital care:

First, 'Informal Admission' where the patient either agrees, or at least does not object to admission, is technically under the Mental Health Act 1983. This accounts for approximately 93 per cent of all admissions to a mental hospital, psychiatric unit, learning disability unit or mental nursing home. Second, there are 'Civil Admissions' which are compulsory, resulting from the decisions of professionals (approved social workers and doctors or, in one particular circumstance, the police) without involving the Courts. Third, there are admissions from court to hospital on a compulsory basis. The Act contains a range of provisions empowering the criminal courts to direct that persons appearing before them be admitted to hospital on account of their mental disorder. Finally, a person may be transferred from prison to hospital. In certain circumstances the Home Secretary is empowered to direct the transfer of prisoners to hospital on account of their mental disorder.

Discussion

The 1983 Act, which in many ways preserves the principles of the seminal piece of mental health legislation this century – the Mental Health Act 1959 – is premised on a perception of mental health services that prevailed in the 1960s and 1970s: the large mental hospital which provided the focus of mental health care. The 1983 Act is therefore primarily about providing the legal authority to detain a person in a physically defined place and regulating certain aspects of what happens during his/her detention. The use of compulsion in this context is by definition contentious, involving as it does, not only an acceptance that it is right to do so in pursuit of what might be termed welfarist (as opposed to justice) objectives, but also the necessity to balance up the interests, which are often in conflict, of the individual, their family or supporters and society at large. The challenge posed by this process is exacerbated by the fact that mental disorder is not exactly over-defined and that one person's disorder is another person's rational response to the inequities of society.

Mental health legislation will always be controversial and the subject of continuing debate and, in a multi-ethnic society, it is inevitable and desirable that part of that debate should centre on the use of compulsion in relation to people from black and minority ethnic communities. The current debate draws many parallels between the criminal justice system and what might be termed the compulsory mental health system. If it is right to conclude that black people are more likely to be apprehended by the police on suspicion of committing a crime; more likely to be charged with a criminal offence rather than be cautioned; less likely to received bail; and more likely to receive a custodial sentence, then there are some uncanny parallels with the mental health system. A recent discussion document (DoH and Home Office, 1992) summarises research over the last twenty years as showing that black people who come to the attention of psychiatric services are more likely than white people to be:

- removed by the police to a place of safety under section 136 of the Mental Health Act 1983;
- detained in hospital under sections 2, 3 and 4 (Civil Admission Sections) of the Mental Health Act 1983;
- diagnosed as suffering from schizophrenia or other form of psychotic illness;
- detained in locked wards of psychiatric hospitals; and
- receive higher dosage of medication.

At the same time the report concluded that black people are less likely than white people to:

- receive appropriate and acceptable diagnosis or treatment for possible mental illness at an early stage;
- receive treatment such as psychotherapy or counselling.

The response to such findings has to be multi-faceted and involves the consideration of many issues that are way beyond the scope of this chapter. It may also be the case that the contribution that the law itself can make is less clear than that to be made by appropriate service developments, changes in professional attitudes and the distribution of power within and without mental health services in relation to the groups which they are meant to serve. Having said that, it is where the law most overtly gets involved (i.e. where individual liberty is removed), that the keenest discontent is felt. If the law is about the regulation of the relationship between the state and the individual and also the relationships between individuals then, arguably, it can only make a contribution once those who frame it have determined the social policy they wish to pursue in this regard and also whether its achievement will be assisted by further legal provision.

Any review of the Mental Health Act 1983 has to take into account and develop the recent debates about its adequacy in relation to people in the community. Notwithstanding the fact that mental health legislation has primarily been concerned with detaining people in hospital, it has always contained provisions for applying certain controls to people with mental health problems in the community. Under the current Act, guardianship is the little used community power. Since the Mental Health Act 1959 was introduced, several proposals have been put forward to establish a new form of compulsory supervision or treatment order in the community (DoH, 1993b). In the last twenty years reports making recommendations in this regard have emerged from the Department of Health and Social Services, (DHSS, 1976), the British Association of Social Workers (BASW, 1977) and the Royal College of Psychiatrists (RCP, 1987, 1993).

This debate has culminated in a proposal (DoH, 1993b) for an amendment to the Mental Health Act introducing a new community power entitled Supervised Discharge Arrangement. Such an order could be applied to non-restricted patients who have been detained in hospital under the Mental Health Act and who would present a serious risk to their own health or safety or to the safety of other people unless their care in the community was supervised after discharge. It is unnecessary to go into detail, especially as the proposal still has to find a place in the legislative programme. It is important to note, however, that the order will not include the power to compulsorily administer medical treatment in the community. If this is thought appropriate, then in the absence of the patient's consent it will be necessary to see if the current admission procedures under the Mental Health Act are applicable in each particular case. In some ways this hints at one core issue that lies at the heart of this debate: that controlling people in the community is very different from controlling them in a clearly defined place such as a hospital. In the final analysis, whether or not any community control will be effective will depend almost entirely on the quality of the relationship between the mental health services and the person concerned, rather than on the nature of the order itself and its sanctions.

The debate about community powers is a fundamental one, focusing as it does and will do in the future on the desirability of compulsorily admitting somebody to a service rather than to a place (DHSS, 1993). There are more immediate concerns about the adequacy of the Act. For example, while the Act establishes an elaborate system of safeguards in relation to compulsory treatment for mental disorder, it is silent about the use of seclusion. Recent public concern about its use was expressed in the Orville Blackwood Inquiry (Prins et al., 1993) and the Ashworth Inquiry (Blom-Cooper et al., 1992).

In addition to the various statutory regulations made under the Act there is also the Mental Health Act Code of Practice (DoH and Welsh Office, 1993) which contains the Secretary of State's guidance about the admission of patients under the 1983 Act and also about the provision of medical treatment to people with a mental disorder. While such guidance does not have the same legal weight as statute it is persuasive and should it be the subject of legal consideration in any particular case, it is clear that any professional who ignores this guidance would need to produce a very good reason for doing so.

The guidance in the Code of Practice (the Code) is set out in such a way as to follow the career of a person detained under the Mental Health Act – starting with assessment prior to possible admission under the Act and concluding with the patient's departure from hospital. Its guidance is underpinned by fine guiding principles, one of which makes clear that people being assessed for possible admission under the Act or to whom the Act applies should 'receive respect for, and consideration of, their individual qualities and diverse backgrounds – social, cultural, ethnic and religious' (para 1.3). In the body of the Code there is reference to the crucial importance of not making false assumptions based on a person's sex, social and cultural background or ethnic origin. As far as seclusion (solitary confinement of a patient in a locked room) is considered, the Code contains detailed guidance which is used as the basis for many local seclusion policies. This example does, however, raise the question as to whether the legislation that authorises the use of compulsion should contain more detailed regulation of such matters or, as is the current position in general, it should set a broad relatively undetailed framework, many of the details of which are filled in by a code. One fundamental difficulty of making legislation too detailed is that it can become outdated and inappropriate long before there is a realistic opportunity of amending it.

CONCLUSIONS

It is very difficult to calculate exactly the dimensions of any contribution that the law can make to maximising the chances of ensuring that mental health services provide what their users want. The mere fact that part of its involvement is by way of providing the authority for deprivation of liberty and, therefore, has very specifically to serve other interests, may hint at certain limitations. Having said that, it would be unwise to underestimate its contribution. It is probably not far from the truth to conclude – especially in the context of a plural society – that if the legal framework is wrong then society has a potential disaster on its hands. If it is more right than wrong, then society is some way down the road, but any further steps in the right direction are dependent not only on further legal development but also, perhaps more importantly, on adequate and appropriate administrative arrangements (e.g. more effective use of contracts and service agreements between health service commissioners and providers), professional development and the constructive and effective realisation of the contribution that must be made by those who use the services, their supporters and their families.

Chapter 4

Sectioning: the black experience

Deryck Browne

> When structures of domination identify a group of people (as racist ideology does black folks in this society) as mentally inferior, implying that they are more body than mind, it should come as no surprise that there is little societal concern for the mental health care of that group.
>
> (bell hooks, 1993)

Sectioning is the term commonly used to describe the process whereby an individual is *compelled* to enter a psychiatric hospital (including a secure hospital) under the Mental Health Act 1983 and detained there against his/her expressed will. Black people's experience of sectioning – and indeed of psychiatry as a whole – has been and continues to be, a negative one. Notwithstanding the above quote by bell hooks, almost all of the available research into the black experience of psychiatry, and more specifically compulsory admissions, confirms this (see Chapter 1). Studies in Birmingham of hospital admissions between 1979 and 1984 showed that in addition to there being a general over-representation of African-Caribbean people, they were more likely to be detained under the Act (i.e. sectioned), and to receive treatment in secure facilities. The proportion of black people detained tended to increase as the focus of study shifted to higher tariff points, from informal admission to the use of the civil sections and finally to the use of the forensic sections via the courts (see below). This kind of study has been replicated across the country with similar findings. The question that needs to be addressed is about the context in which compulsory detention is used resulting in what amounts to a crisis for black people with regard to mental health care. This chapter will provide an overview of the sectioning process as it affects black people, by referring to findings of a recent survey of decision-making during the process of sectioning, and a study of practices at a magistrates' court, both carried out by the author. In doing so, the debate around race and compulsory detention and treatment will be pursued, placing these issues in context by exploring various related issues, such as the persistence of negative stereotyping of black people within psychiatry and related professions.

CIVIL SECTIONS

Although the evidence is that the criminal justice system is a major route by which black people present to psychiatry, there is a body of evidence which suggests that the forces at play within the civil sectioning process have similar effects. Not only do black people find themselves being admitted to hospital at higher rates than do white people, but many factors that accompany this 'over-admission' – the attitudes of personnel involved, the manner of admission and the kinds of diagnoses and resulting treatments – are very different for black people compared to Whites.

Moodley and Perkins (1991) found that pathways to psychiatric admission, as manifested in a London borough, were different for black people to that for Whites. Those under 30 years of age were usually brought into hospital by the police or presented directly to psychiatric emergency services; those over 30 tended to present via medical/surgical hospital services, domiciliary psychiatric services or psychiatric outpatients; finally, higher proportions of African-Caribbeans were given a diagnosis of schizophrenia, were compulsorily detained and, interestingly, considered themselves to have nothing wrong with them, while higher proportions of Whites were diagnosed as depressed and tended to consider themselves to have physical rather than psychiatric problems. With regard to sectioning, the authors found that it was *ethnic status* rather than diagnostic category that accounted for the higher rates of compulsory detention of black people. A study in South London (Pipe *et al.*, 1991) in 1986 found an over-representation of African-Caribbean people amongst those detained (by the police) under section 136 of the Mental Health Act. This was accounted for by young men under the age of 30 (who had relatively high rates of arrest under section 136) being perceived as threatening, incoherent and disturbed but with an unclear 'diagnosis' of mental illness.

Such general research findings provided the impetus for a detailed study of the impact that the race (of the prospective patient) might have on decision-making involved in the application of the civil sections of the Mental Health Act (Browne, in press). In this work, perceptions about race (*vis-à-vis* the sectioning process) held by professionals were explored using semi-structured interviews with a range of personnel involved, people working in relevant voluntary organisations and ex-users of the psychiatric services. We supplemented this material with an examination of case records and statistical data (although this was not our primary focus of study). The aim of the survey was to uncover any evidence of deviation from laid-out procedures, preconceived, possibly stereotypical, notions concerning black people and the general attitude to sectioning. The interview data illustrated the accuracy of our opening quote from hooks (1993), while posing further questions about perceptions of dangerousness and the role of race and culture here.

While there existed a range of written guidelines and procedures for social services staff, police officers, nurses and hospital managers in relation to their enactment of the civil sections, there was nothing similar provided for psychiatrists – whether consultants, junior doctors or general practitioners. We concluded therefore that a certain degree of latitude must exist in the way they deal with their patients, in turn allowing for differential procedures to be followed. Results of the semi-structured questionnaires (designed to determine whether or not the race of the patient was having any significant impact on decision-making during sectioning) illustrated that there was a strong association in the minds of many personnel between race and dangerousness, that is, that black people were likely to be seen as such for no other reason than their colour. In the case of fourteen police officers interviewed, the answers to questionnaires showed that the ways in which this perception (of black people being inherently dangerous) manifested itself linked up with (what was seen by them as a necessary) disregard for the written guidelines available. The following were typical statements by police officers:

'The policies do not always work effectively – for example when a person is in a private place you still act for the benefit of that person. If you have to bend the rules then you have to. If a person is in a private place you might lie and say he was taken from a public place. This is in the spirit of the guidelines, and often the families are in agreement.'

'If you can't understand them then they probably won't be able to understand you therefore the more likely you are to find yourself using some form of restraint. Violence is more of a factor because persuasion can't be used – and particular (racial) groups do tend to be more excitable than others.'

Although many Approved Social Workers (ASWs) were aware of the dangers of racial stereotyping, some admitted to a large degree of flexibility in the way that they applied written guidelines. To quote two typical statements:

'There is a false pathology seen in some cultures by the professionals involved – yes the police are guilty but so are many GPs, psychiatrists and social workers. This is bound to affect the way they carry out their assessments.'

'Procedures state that you must interview in an appropriate manner but it does not define that, so I can say what an appropriate manner is.'

Such a stance, coupled with an already negative view of black people, is very likely to result in an oppressive service for black people. In fact 75 per cent of all professionals interviewed concurred that black clients were more likely than their white counterparts to be perceived as 'dangerous'.

An examination of hospital records showed that restraint was used more commonly with black patients upon or prior to admission (16 per cent versus 2 per cent), and that black patients were more likely to be administered medication as a sedative than white clients (24 per cent versus 14 per cent). Although this was a fairly small-scale study – focusing upon two urban hospitals – these findings are entirely consistent with national research. The corollary to these kinds of actions by professionals is that psychiatry is a more dangerous port of call for black people than it is for Whites. Cases such as the death of Orville Blackwood at the hands of staff in Broadmoor (Special) Hospital (Prins *et al.*, 1993) serve to highlight problems at the higher end of the tariff – that is, in the Special Hospitals or Regional/Medium Secure Units. But many cases go under (or un)-reported, such as the death in North London of a young black man (Jerome Scott) uncovered by a television programme. Scott, who had previously been diagnosed as 'a schizophrenic' died after being administered lethal doses of the anti-psychotic drug haloperidol and the tranquilliser diazepam after being held down by police on a London street. In our study we found that, although

ASWs were critical of a police tendency to over-react towards black people deemed to require hospital admission, ASWs also seemed to over-react in the same way in that they appeared to request the assistance of the police more readily when dealing with black clients than when dealing with white people.

As one of the agents of primary care, the role of the General Practitioner is central to the civil sectioning process. Many GPs refused to be interviewed and so the six practitioners who were interviewed, although not a representative sample, were likely to have been supportive of our study and aware of race issues. In fact, we found serious insensitivity to the danger of racial stereotyping. One GP whose patient list was 55 per cent African-Caribbean said:

'It seems there is something in the physical make-up of black people which predetermines the presence of schizophrenia. They (black people) would require higher doses of sedative drugs than white people as they don't respond to normal measures.'

Racist views such as these sit uneasily alongside the fact that GPs have some considerable role to play in the civil sectioning process.

An examination of case records and interviews with hospital staff suggested that the experience of people from black and ethnic minority communities is often very different from that of white people. There was little evidence that doctors considered issues of race and culture in any depth and considerable evidence that the treatment and care of black patients on one or other of the civil sections depended very much on the subjective notions of the practitioner involved. Doctors conceded that black patients were more likely to be screened for drugs use than other groups, yet hospital records showed that white patients were more likely to have a history of cannabis use than other ethnic groups (21 per cent versus 7 per cent). Doctors concurred that they attached a good deal of weight to information contained in case files and that these notes come to be seen as medical facts. Although 'cultural factors' were noted much more frequently in the case of black patients than in the case of Whites (50 per cent versus 6 per cent), 'culture' was viewed as something belonging solely to black people or applying to them only. This is all the more worrying as we found that there was a tendency in some notes for doctors to regard certain 'cultural' characteristics as pathological. One doctor noted the following about a black patient: 'She tended to talk past the point; it is difficult to tell whether this was a sign of psychosis or because of her culture.' Another said:

'The typical black admission is young, in his twenties, loud paranoid, resisting strongly – you need to get him sedated to restrain him, and the doctors don't know what's going on – he's usually brought in by the police, therefore the doctor hasn't got a clue as to his history – and as with men generally they would be more aggressive, you would be more frightened of them and you would put them on more medication.'

Although the study did not examine medication in detail, black patients were perceived as being on relatively high doses. One nurse on a locked ward said:

'Most of the white patients are on medication three times a day; all of the black patients are on (medication) four times a day. Black patients are more susceptible to PRN and restraint.'

(PRN is the term used to describe a prescription of medication, the administration of which is left to the discretion of nursing staff.)

Conclusions

The way in which the thread of perceived dangerousness of black individuals runs through the civil sectioning process is not peculiar to that process. Historically, Western psychiatry, and indeed, Western culture, has portrayed black people as having some increased propensity to dangerousness and risk. Current psychiatric diagnoses carry their own images which in turn connect up with other images held in the mind (Fernando, 1991). A painting by Tam Joseph (1984) encapsulates the argument succinctly. The black youngster's passage through the British education system is punctuated by excerpts from three of his school reports. In the first caption the youngster is, stereotypically, 'good at sports'. As an adolescent the report focuses on his liking for music, and finally, as a school leaver in the third portrait the youth has made the transition to the other side of society and is deemed to 'need surveillance'.

To be young and black, particularly for males, is to be deemed a greater risk and in need of increased surveillance and greater control. This fictitious example is, of course, no different from the view of the psychiatric services which, as far as many black people are concerned, are agents of control. Our own research, as well as much of the existing body of work, tells us that when black people come into contact with the policing agents in the generic sense (thereby including psychiatry) we are seen as requiring control as opposed to care, and custody (or physical restraint) as opposed to cure; preconceptions are more often of madness than of sanity and as Joseph's picture illustrates, the focus is on the body rather than on the mind. The link with the sectioning process is implicit. The crisis for black people with regard to mental health is not one of large numbers of black people breaking down with psychiatric disorders, but one of large numbers of black people coming to psychiatry forcibly (i.e. on one or other of the sections), receiving more serious diagnoses compared to other groups, and receiving greater doses of medication and greater restraint in settings of greater security (Fernando, 1991; DoH and Home Office, 1992).

FORENSIC SECTIONS

The arguments around the processes involved in the use of the civil sections of the Mental Health Act 1983 hold good for the forensic sections. In fact it may be the case that arguments around the inappropriate projection of that quality of dangerousness on to black patients and individuals are even more relevant here with the joining of these two formidable systems of control – criminal justice and psychiatry – with black individuals being overrepresented in each.

As with civil sectioning, the evidence here too is that the experience of black people is a negative one. Black patients in a Regional Secure Unit were found to be significantly more likely to be referred from the prison system while on remand (Cope and Ndegwa, 1990), differing from white patients who were more often admitted from National Health Service and Special Hospitals. An investigation into the psychiatric remand process at magistrates' courts (Browne, 1991) carried out by the author between 1988 and 1990 gave some insight into the way in which some of the forensic sections, and processes leading up to the use of these, impacted on black defendants (although this was not a study of the forensic sectioning process *per se*). The study showed that the experience of black defendants deemed to be mentally disturbed was markedly more negative (when being passed through the courts) than their white counterparts. For example, 37 per cent of white defendants were granted bail compared with only 13 per cent of black defendants; black defendants were more likely than Whites to be detained for longer periods when remanded in prison custody, and 39 per cent of black defendants were diagnosed as suffering from mental illness following remand for reports compared with 22 per cent of white defendants. When it came to disposal, 43 per cent of black defendants received psychiatric probation orders compared with 29 per cent of Whites and more black defendants received hospital orders than their white counterparts. Studies of real cases are presented below to further bear out these inequalities.

Case study: George

George was a single, 25-year-old African-Caribbean male who was unemployed and of no fixed abode. He appeared before the bench at a magistrates' court on a charge of attempted theft, for which he pleaded guilty and consented to a summary trial. At the request of the duty probation officer, George was remanded for social inquiry and psychiatric reports, to be presented on his next appearance in three weeks. He was remanded in custody.

George's psychiatric history dates from when he was 18 years of age. At that time he underwent a psychiatric 'crisis' and was subsequently admitted to hospital on five occasions to be treated for 'schizophrenia'.

When George was brought back to court three weeks later, the psychiatric assessments had not yet been done. Sentence was deferred for four months and George was duly released. On his return to court four months later, the magistrates were not happy with his recent behaviour and remanded him in custody for a week (so that the previously requested reports could be prepared?). He was not brought to his hearing – for reasons not given – and was remanded for a further four weeks.

Thus began a cyclical process of George being remanded again and again and either not being brought to hearings or reports not being available for a period of almost three months. When the reports were eventually completed and made available to the court, it was discovered by magistrates that George had, during the course of his last remand, been taken to a different magistrates' court for a previous offence of robbery and sentenced to twelve months' imprisonment. The reports for which magistrates at court A had waited so long were of no use, and it is unknown whether or not the second magistrates' court had any such assistance in making their adjudication.

Case study: Keith

Keith was a 27-year-old African-Caribbean man who came before a magistrates' court on a charge of criminal damage. He was unemployed and had previous convictions for criminal damage, assault, possession of soft drugs and possession of an offensive weapon. On this particular occasion he was charged with smashing the windscreens of five police vehicles. Upon his arrest he said that he did this 'to go back inside'.

The defendant had been receiving psychiatric treatment since 1982. He was diagnosed on three occasions as having drug-induced 'psychosis' and once as suffering from 'mental retardation'.

There were clearly difficulties in the relationship between the probation service and the prison medical service. While on remand in prison, Keith's probation officer found it impossible to interview him because he was so heavily medicated. Consequently, there was no recommendation from the probation service.

The only other report to be submitted was that of the prison medical service. The senior medical officer informed the court: 'From what I know of him I would say he suffers from faults of character and personality of a psychopathic sort and these are not amenable to medical treatment. I have therefore no medical recommendation to make to the court. He is fit to plead and for any disposal which the court may decide'.

Without any positive recommendations, magistrates sentenced Keith to five months' imprisonment – three times, to run concurrently. Later records showed that he had been moved to Broadmoor (Special) hospital.

Conclusions

The case studies illustrate how defendants can become involved in a prolonged cyclical process from which it becomes increasingly difficult to escape. They also show how the shortcomings of a prison assessment and the overmedication of remandees can militate against black defendants. A series of interviews conducted with various personnel (including magistrates, probation officers, solicitors, court clerks and psychiatrists) confirmed this. The picture that emerged was that the decision to remand is largely intuitive, and that such subjective assessments permit prejudicial and discriminatory practices to develop. Decision-makers appeared more likely to err on the side of caution with black mentally vulnerable defendants and to be affected by a heightened perception of dangerousness with regard to this group, thus mirroring the actions of their civil section counterparts.

DISCUSSION

When considering the issue of mental health in a multi-ethnic society we cannot avoid the historical factors which have led us to the present situation. Western psychiatry and psychology were developed during an era where racist white supremacist thinking was also becoming more clearly defined. When Europe was busying itself with a colonialist agenda, accompanying racist philosophies were necessary to justify these actions. One of the ways in which this was done was quite deliberately to link concepts of madness with race, and to link irrationality with Blackness. Examples of this abound in the psychological journals of the time (Fernando, 1988) and consequently any attempt to examine the current impact of sectioning on black people must be placed in its historical context. Suffice it to say here that not only was psychological sanction given to slavery but also to a range of racist practices and philosophies during more recent history. The current overadmission of black people on compulsory orders cannot be divorced from all this.

The diversion of mentally disordered offenders from the criminal justice system to supportive and caring settings provided by the health services and social services is a fashionable and apparently humane policy being pursued vigorously by the Government. But given the crisis that already exists for black people wherever they come into contact with the mental health professions – be that in hospital, in the community or other therapeutic (*sic*) settings – we have to register the question, can the equation be this simple? Is diversion from one system (i.e. criminal justice) to another (i.e. mental health) a justifiable and good thing when in fact both systems are negative and oppressive for black people? Clearly where people do suffer some mental health problem and are simultaneously, or consequently, caught within the coils of the criminal justice system, every effort should be made to divert them from this system. The available research (e.g. Dell *et al.*, 1991) points to prison being an 'inhumane' place for the mentally disturbed. But at the same time attention must be paid to the nature of the so-called 'humanity' of the facilities to which diversion is proposed.

Our own work confirms fears that the sectioning process militates against black people, in keeping with other aspects of the psychiatric system. This encompasses both the civil and forensic sections and would appear to be linked to a persistent and unjustified view of black individuals (with or without mental health problems) as having some increased propensity to dangerousness. Although there are historical reasons for this development, its current manifestation tends to be in the ways in which sectioning procedures are carried out and the simultaneous creation of a climate within psychiatry (and related professions) which has almost come to sanction the 'need' for the *compulsory* treatment of black people. This then opens up a series of possibilities, any of which might be taken up, and most of which are disadvantageous to black people – (over)medication, increased surveillance, greater restraint, increased security and so forth.

Chapter 5

Voluntary groups

*Tanzeem Ahmed and
Amanda Webb-Johnson*

The traditional voluntary sector in Britain is composed of a variety
of organisations, ranging from large institutions such as the National
Association for Mental Health (MIND) to small groups staffed by
one or two people. Historically, they derive from Victorian phil-
anthropy and charitable works of the last century, but they are now
well established and accepted as institutions that are often heavily
supported financially by state funds. However, voluntary groups
serving the needs of ethnic minorities are generally modest, small-
scale organisations composed mainly of local people, and focusing
on providing practical help together with religious and cultural
activities for their communities. They arose largely during the 1950s
in response to a need for self-help, coupled with a feeling of
communality in the face of discrimination (Institute of Race Relations, 1993). Therefore there is a strong tradition of independence
from government among black voluntary groups, although many are
now funded by the state or by large 'white' grant-giving agencies.

During the past ten to fifteen years, the social, economic and
political context under which mental health services operate has
changed and voluntary organisations have had to adapt. The require-
ment of compulsory competitive tendering under the 1988 Local
Government Act brought market forces to bear on the provision of
social and welfare services. Grants are now being replaced by
contracts, leaving little room for advocacy and campaigning. Currently, Local Authorities are changing their roles from providers to
enablers, and the voluntary sector is being incorporated into the
state's commercial delivery mechanism for purchasing care from the
cheapest provider. In this contracting culture of the 1990s, the
voluntary sector, traditionally seen as the centre for innovation and
independence from government forces, has had to lose its vibrancy.

And the rapid growth of the ethnic minority voluntary sector during the 1980s is being eroded as many groups disappear almost as rapidly as they started.

This chapter considers the problems faced by voluntary groups serving black and ethnic minorities by focusing on Asian groups. In doing so, the authors draw on research conducted by workers at the Confederation of Indian Organisations (CIO).

BACKGROUND

Ethnic minorities (in Britain) are derived largely from migrants who came to Britain in the 1950s to take up employment in unskilled trades with poor work conditions and few opportunities for promotion. As the number of people in these communities increased, the problems of housing, employment and general social issues became more prominent. The experience of this largely working-class population to bring themselves out of their low socio-economic status has been stifled by racism, feelings of dislocation and uncertainty over immigration status. Traditional voluntary agencies, set up to serve the (white) indigenous population, did not meet the needs of ethnic communities and the communities were forced to look towards themselves rather than the mainstream services to provide answers to their problems. It was in this context that small self-help groups were established, offering social and welfare services as well as advice and support to members of ethnic minority communities. These groups relied on the support of internal community networks and the goodwill of committed individuals; their organisational structures were poorly developed and the resources available to them were minimal. Many groups operated from individuals' homes.

The majority of ethnic (voluntary) groups in London were in inner London areas and were encouraged and financially supported by the Greater London Council (GLC). The GLC established an ethnic minority unit with grant-giving powers and the black and ethnic minority voluntary sector prospered in the 1970s. The funding policies of the GLC towards ethnic community groups inspired other Local Authorities to pursue similar policies and gave legitimacy to central government to fund initiatives through schemes such as section 11 of the Department of the Environment's Urban programme (see Haughton and Sowa, 1993). After the inner city riots of the early 1980s, funding for black and ethnic minority projects increased and many organisations moved away from financial self-help towards dependence on state funding.

Confederation of Indian Organisations (CIO)

In 1975, a number of Asian voluntary groups providing services to the Asian community together set up the Confederation of Indian Organisations (CIO) as an umbrella/support system for their work. Initially the work of CIO was to help those people from within the community who had recently arrived from the countries of East Africa, but it has developed into an organisation that promotes voluntary work within all Asian communities and campaigns for changes in legislation both nationally and locally. CIO is typical of many groups set up by ethnic minority communities in that it was initiated by people from within a minority ethnic group, starting initially without any premises or financial resources. As CIO developed, it secured grants from the GLC for many of its projects, particularly its outreach work, and found premises. It then concentrated on helping other organisations to set up and deliver services locally, CIO itself providing training and carrying out research.

VOLUNTARY GROUPS AND MENTAL HEALTH

Each community has its own norms and values and individuals within that community are socialised into regarding their own culture as the norm and viewing other cultures, in relation to this norm, as different. In Western European society, however, the norm of the majority population is reinforced through the education system and institutional practice. Hence the values and assumptions of the majority population become the norm and underlie standard practice and policy. Services which are provided by statutory bodies and mainstream organisations are based on these values and norms and the values of other cultures are viewed negatively or else ignored.

Such norms and prevalent belief systems are used as a basis of theoretical models that guide treatment and care. The use of Western models for diagnosis and treatment of people with mental health problems clearly illustrates how constructs that are universally applied are not tenable. Knowledge of what is normal and what is pathological is shaped by cultural definition of personhood, social identities and role expectation. For example, Western constructs assume the distinction between mind and body. Research carried out by CIO (Beliappa, 1991) found that Asian people facing emotional difficulties were less able to compartmentalise emotional experiences as affecting the individual psyche as opposed to the body, social roles, etc. Instead, they used a holistic model and linked emotional experiences within a normative structure of roles and expectations. Emotions that are private experiences located within the inner self in individualistic cultures are often externalised in traditional cultures and located in the relationship between the subject and the object of the feeling (Pina, 1986).

Responses to treatment of mental health problems will vary in different cultures. In some Eastern cultures, where there is a greater emphasis on spiritualism, the techniques used may be more spiritual than clinical. If individuals believe that the cause of their emotional problems has been the product of sorcery, they may find it irrelevant to talk to a psychiatrist about their childhood experiences and would find it more relevant to go to a religious healer who specialises in taking away the effects of sorcery. Similarly, people from cultures that recognise the existence of spirits or *Jinns* may believe that certain experiences such as hallucinations or indistinct communications are the result of spirit possessions. In Western psychiatry such beliefs may be seen as symptoms of schizophrenia.

These few examples highlight that Western medical models grounded in white middle-class ideologies may have little real meaning to communities that do not share these ideologies. The inappropriateness of diagnostic tools, added to the problems of communicating in different languages, has led to several cases of misdiagnosis. This has serious implications for the treatments offered to these communities. Lack of understanding of the meaning of symptoms in different cultures has led to mental health workers basing their diagnosis and treatment on stereotypes and assumptions about the different ethnic communities. The main stereotypes relating to the South Asian communities relate to the alleged stigma attached to mental distress in the Asian communities, a view that Asians 'look after their own' when problems do occur, and a perception of Asians as not psychologically minded and therefore lacking the capacity for (psychological) insight necessary for certain therapeutic interventions.

PERCEPTIONS OF USERS OF SERVICES

A community study based on ninety-eight randomly selected Asian people conducted by the CIO (Beliappa, 1991) during 1989–1990 drew some significant conclusions about mental health needs of Asian people, including the following.

The stereotypes about the stigma of mental distress were not supported by that study. A relatively high percentage (23 per cent) of people in the sample reported experiences of mental distress suggesting that that they were prepared to talk about emotional distress as long as the context is safe. Only 13 per cent of the sample saw the family as a viable means of support and then only for concerns over health and child care. Hence, though the family was traditionally seen as a source of support it was not accessed in times of emotional distress. The findings relating to somatisation illustrated the significant differences that existed between the conceptualisations of mental health problems within the (Asian) communities and the perceptions of (Western trained) professionals. Contrary to the common assumption that Asians cannot psychologise emotional distress, our findings suggested that emotional difficulties were recognised but were not classified as pathological. One woman in the sample described her condition as follows: 'I am fit now, but for years I was suffering with aches and pains, sleeplessness and lack of appetite . . . . I could see that all this was caused by stress. I had three miscarriages because of this . . . my experiences in my marriage led to physical ailments . . . they [doctors] would treat me for physical problems, gave me pain killers, but never bothered to find out what the problem was.'

The majority of (Asian) people experiencing distress had consulted GPs but it appeared that primary care workers were ill-equipped to recognise symptoms of distress and make suitable referrals. This research also investigated the coping mechanisms used and the knowledge and uptake of mainstream services. The findings revealed that a large proportion (45 per cent) of those with mental health problems used prayer, or other internal mechanisms such as crying (36 per cent) as coping mechanisms. What is important is that a significant number of people wanted to talk to someone about their problems but there was no-one appropriate. On the whole there was little awareness of where to go for social and emotional problems. Nearly one-third (32 per cent) of the total sample were unaware of services provided by the statutory sector and only 6 per cent were aware of social workers. A mere 3 per cent had sought help from the statutory services, while 32 per cent had approached the voluntary sector for assistance.

It was clear from this study that there appeared to be an alarmingly high rate of undetected distress in the Asian community. The people in this study had few outlets for expressing their emotional distress and had few resources to turn to. They lacked awareness and confidence to use existing statutory services, yet expressed a desire to be able to talk to someone about their problems. It is reasonable to assume that Asians who reach statutory services often bypass traditional mainstream preventative care, reaching services at a point of crisis. However, the need for preventative mental health services is recognised by the community; although statutory or other mainstream bodies are not accessed for help, Asian voluntary organisations are approached. The question as to whether the (Asian) voluntary sector is equipped to meet this challenge was investigated by our next study described below.

ASIAN VOLUNTARY SECTOR

During 1991–1992, a project was undertaken to research the activities of Asian voluntary organisations (Webb-Johnson, 1993). The main purpose of the study was to establish the nature of health promotion activity and access to information about health services within the Asian voluntary sector. It was based on a sample of thirty-two voluntary groups operating in eight geographical locations. The findings of the study included the following.

Reasons for setting up (Asian) services

It was found that all the groups studied had been set up in response to local demand from the community and sought to fill gaps which resulted from the failure of statutory services to provide for needs well recognised by the communities involved. Most of these groups were set up by committed individuals from within the community. On the whole, they were started with volunteers and developed organically as funds became available. For example, the women's groups started as self-help groups to provide mutual support and assistance for women who were isolated, experienced language barriers or suffered from racial discrimination. The youth groups were generally set up to respond to the particular needs of young people, providing social, cultural and educational activities. One of the youth groups in the study was formed as a result of a response to racist attacks against Asian communities by (white) 'vigilante' groups. Elderly groups had been formed to serve those isolated from existing statutory services, such as day care provisions, because of language barriers. One elderly group described the plight of Asian elders: 'There is a stereotype of Asians looking after their own families. The elders are often forgotten about. They expect a return from the younger generation, but are often living in isolation, and are not aware of social services facilities. This centre was started to cater for their particular needs'. Groups for refugees had been set up in response to the needs of Tamil refugees and asylum-seekers. In this case, as no community structures existed to represent them, they needed organisations to help newly arrived refugees with problems related to accommodation, immigration and advice for asylum-seekers. These groups also identified the need for supportive services for people with mental health problems resulting from the effects of torture or displacement.

It was clear from our study that most groups were set up to address unmet needs for various sections of the community, especially the elderly, women and the disabled, because these people were identified as experiencing isolation and were finding it difficult to access services for reasons such as language barriers and cultural/religious inappropriateness of statutory and mainstream voluntary services.

Nature of Asian voluntary groups

One of the important differences between these groups and those serving the indigenous population was that all these groups provided generic rather than specialist services and often acted as referral agencies for other statutory and voluntary bodies. Hence the range of activities provided by any one organisation would include general information, advice on welfare rights, housing, family and personal issues, health information, interpreting, translation, language classes (both English and Asian languages) as well as a range of user activities. Approximately two-thirds of the organisations in this study also offered immigration advice, assistance with employment, outreach work and home visits. In general, the work of many Asian voluntary groups in the sample centred on providing advice and information on a broad range of personal and family issues and on meeting the social, cultural and emotional needs of their communities.

Organisation, staffing and funding of the groups

The organisations had common structures, which consisted of an Executive Committee, Management Committee, coordinator, staff, members and/or users. In most cases the Management Committee was responsible for the organisation's overall strategy and policies and would meet on a regular basis, usually every month.

Staffing levels within these groups were minimal; the number of full-time staff ranged from one to six with an average for any one group of between one and two full-time staff. The groups relied heavily on part-time workers and volunteers; the number of volunteers working in each organisation varied from between one or two up to fifty, with an average of ten. The majority of groups reported that they were understaffed compared to the level of service provision expected of them. Staff shortages affected the quality and effectiveness of the services the organisations were able to deliver to members of their communities and put tremendous pressure on existing staff to provide an increasing level of services.

Despite the staff shortages, these groups reported serving between ten and 300 users per day. Within this sample of groups, the organisations for the elderly served the largest number of users, (an average of eighty-seven per day), with youth groups serving a similarly high number of users (sixty-three). The disability and women's groups were serving a smaller number of users (thirty-two and twenty-one respectively). These figures reflect the nature of services provided by the groups in the sample. For example, the elderly and the youth groups were more likely to provide activities in which a large number of people participated, whereas women's and disability groups provided a more personal and specialist service.

Funding was the main source of concern and insecurity for these groups. Within this sample eight out of ten groups relied on their Local Authority for their core funding. In addition eight out of every ten grants received were short-term, one-off grants with no guarantee of extension or were subject to annual review.

Discussion

The voluntary services studied were not specifically designated for people with mental health problems but services geared to general needs seen holistically. Therefore the people involved were not trained to provide individual counselling or anything approaching specific 'therapy', and indeed were clearly unable to deal with mental health problems in a way that could be thought of as comprehensive or sophisticated. The different needs of the users of the voluntary services were met by providing specific activities which catered for age, gender, religious and cultural variations. For example, some

groups provided women-only activities, or for celebration of religious occasions, or catering geared to different diets depending on
religious requirements. Also, the organisations were able to meet
different language needs of their users. The staff employed by them
usually had language and literacy skills in various Asian languages.
These provisions make their services more accessible to the local
communities.

Our study serves to illustrate some basic details of voluntary
organisations working for the Asian community. It is crucial to
understand that the groups were set up by the community to work
for the community, providing services which took account of the
norms and values existing within these communities. They responded
to the needs in the community in a culturally appropriate manner,
using languages which rendered their services accessible. As they
were based at the grass-roots level, they were in touch with the
changing needs in the community and hence were in a good position
to fully understand problems of the community and to plan an
adequate response to their needs.

It was striking that all the Asian voluntary groups faced extremely
serious problems arising mainly from the interrelated issues of
funding and staffing. Similar findings to ours were reported in a study
of African-Caribbean voluntary groups in London (Hinds, 1992).
The researchers observed that the effect of understaffing on service
provision ultimately 'undermines the credibility of many organisations in the eyes of the community, and makes it difficult to attract
or retain community support . . . . [and] helps to create negative
stereotypes about the competence of both the organisations themselves and of the staff they employ' (ibid.: 43). Also in that study
Hinds found that Local Authorities were the main source of funding
for 63 per cent of African-Caribbean groups in London and the sole
source of funding for 44 per cent of the groups.

Given an overreliance on Local Authorities for funding, the
future of voluntary groups serving ethnic minorities has become
inextricably linked to the funding policies of Local Authorities. The
cuts which have been introduced by many Local Authorities have
therefore had drastic effects on the survival of these groups. The
demise of the GLC had left a great vacuum in the availability of
funding for ethnic community groups which has not been filled by
any other major funder. Many of the groups which were totally
reliant on the GLC for funding ceased to operate. As revenues
received by Local Authorities dwindled and they were forced to

make significant cuts (especially at the time of the introduction of the community charge in 1990), the voluntary sector was targeted for these cuts and smaller community groups suffered the worst casualties.

A large number of organisations in the CIO study had experienced cuts or tapering in their Local Authority grants. In a recent study by Latimer (1992), *Funding Black Groups*, over half of the ethnic community organisations (53 per cent) reported cuts in their statutory funding and over one-third (39 per cent) specifically to their Local Authority funding:

> As the black voluntary sector as a whole is relatively new and many groups are small and inexperienced, and come from particularly disadvantaged communities, the effects of these cuts is probably more pronounced, with longer-term effects, than in any other part of the voluntary sector.
>
> (Latimer, 1992: 52)

The new commissioning role of Local Authorities poses a real threat to the future of black voluntary groups, as grant aid is replaced by service level agreements and contracts which jeopardise the advocacy role and innovative work of community groups. In addition, reduction in the revenues available to Local Authorities has led to cuts in service provision. This has had a two-fold effect on Asian voluntary groups. On the one hand, cuts in statutory services have meant that voluntary groups have an increased demand on their services. On the other hand, this increased demand is not met with resources but instead by a cut in grant aid.

Our study showed that Asian groups operate under very insecure conditions in terms of staff, premises and grant aid; inevitably, they would find it very difficult to compete for contracts since the lack of a secure managerial base and structure does not lend itself easily to service level agreement. The situation faced by the Asian voluntary sector is likely to apply to the black voluntary sector in general. Therefore it is likely that contracts will go preferentially to national, White-led, well-established charities. As these national charities apply for contracts to provide services to members of the ethnic communities, the relatively 'weak' black voluntary sector is likely to get squeezed out, because efficiency and reliability are overriding factors in the commissioning process, while accessibility and appropriateness take a secondary position.

We have observed that, as many groups serving the ethnic

communities have had very short life-spans, grant donors have interpreted this as a reflection of poor management. Our analysis has shown that when applying for funding, ethnic community groups apply only for basic project expenses. The funding they receive is on the whole short term, and as shown by a recent study by the African Caribbean Development Unit *Funded to Fail – Nuff Pain No Gain* (Wenham, 1993), their funding arrangements are such that failure is an inevitable consequence for most of these groups.

The question then arises whether large traditional voluntary groups can provide services for members of the ethnic communities. In a recent report, Haughton and Sowa (1993) argue that:

> having consciously or unconsciously excluded black communities from their remits for long periods of time, it is now proving difficult for such organisations to adapt their policies and practice sufficiently to gain access to black networks and to offer appropriate and effective provision. The experience of racism that black communities have been subjected to has led to these communities becoming justifiably suspicious of white groups who claim or attempt to change their policies, practice and provision within a relatively short span of time.
>
> (1993: 3–4)

The fact that (as our research has shown) services provided by voluntary groups serving ethnic communities are qualitatively different, have developed the trust of the local communities and are culturally appropriate by being based on the norms and values of the communities for whom they are provided, does not seem to carry much weight in the contracting culture.

CONCLUSIONS

Given the findings of our study of voluntary groups and the earlier study of mental health needs, it is necessary to consider whether mainstream organisations can provide appropriate services to members of the ethnic communities. In the area of mental health, it is clear that the models on which statutory services as well as those provided by the mainstream voluntary sector are based are not appropriate for all communities. Our research has shown that there is a very low take-up of preventative services, resulting in a greater incidence of crisis admissions. In this context, we need to look into some of the reasons why members of the community do not access available services. Some of the barriers identified in our earlier study (Beliappa, 1991) included:

- lack of awareness of existing services;
- lack of awareness of what services can offer;
- language and communication barriers;
- lack of appropriate and accessible information about existing services;
- lack of confidence in the ability of services to understand and meet their needs;
- perception of services as not user-friendly;
- fear that confidentiality will not be preserved;
- negative past experience of services.

Individuals from the community wishing to make use of services confront various barriers therefore. Some of these barriers arise from the lack of accessible information about existing services and the communities' perceptions of the services as alien and often racist. However, problems relating to inappropriateness of traditional services are probably more important. Black and ethnic communities find that their problems are misconstrued because of differences in language, culture, beliefs, diagnostic models and racism. Language barriers are a particular issue for members of the South Asian communities. If there is no common language at the point of initial contact with services, it is extremely difficult to be able to request the services required. Language barriers become more significant in mental health as the process of diagnosis is dependent upon communicating feelings and experiences. It is difficult to achieve this communication effectively through the use of an interpreter. Members of the South Asian communities also fear that as certain problems arise within a cultural and religious context, they may be misinterpreted by people who do not share this understanding. This leads to inappropriate recommendations being made for how individuals might resolve their problems.

So far, it has been shown that mainstream bodies have certain limitations and shortcomings which make their services inaccessible to members of the South Asian communities. It is likely that other black and ethnic communities feel the same. Given these limitations, should we then be looking at Asian groups and professionals exclusively to provide services for their communities? The limited number of therapists and counsellors from the South Asian communities would make it very difficult to respect individual choices. Matching individuals and therapists on culture, language, religion and gender becomes extremely difficult under these limitations. In some cases it has been shown that, even when individuals are matched in this way, if the therapist has been trained using Western medical models the theoretical models they are working with confine them to offer explanations which are based on these models. The absence of alternative models of therapy which are part of the mainstream school of thought has meant that mental health professionals, whatever their ethnic background, are restricted in their professional practice.

The strength of community organisations that provide general services lies in their ability to offer innovative approaches and meaningful services, operating at a grass-roots level. However, despite their flexible approach and accessibility, the constraints operating on these groups means that we have to be cautious not to treat these groups as dumping grounds for all of the community's problems. It is clear from our study of voluntary groups that such groups have limited resources. They operate under very insecure conditions which results in high staff turnover. In addition, the limited number of staff employed who have to deal with a wide variety of issues and cater for the different needs of their many users, means that the time required for any long-term individual therapy is simply not available in these organisations. The staff are also ill-equipped to deal with some complex issues surrounding mental health due to the lack of training available to them in this area. Hence although community groups remain in the best position to be able to provide such services, they are not resourced to be able to do this. On the other hand, although mainstream organisations are well resourced and more likely to have secure structures, their services are neither accessible to, nor appropriate for, all sections of the community. The obvious answer is that ethnic community organisations should be resourced to provide appropriate services. In the current contracting culture adequate resourcing is unlikely to be available.

Suggestions for change

The voluntary sector has an important, perhaps crucial, role to play in the provision of mental health services in a multi-ethnic society. However, if this is to happen, changes will need to be implemented, both in the way mainstream groups provide services as well as in the way funding is awarded to ethnic community groups. Service providers will need to make room for different approaches to the provision of services, ensuring that their services are more accessible, appropriate, sensitive, flexible and accountable. Particular emphasis will need to be placed on training, so that key workers are able to recognise limitations in their approach and accept alternative approaches and models. It must be recognised that services for ethnic communities can only be effective if they are planned in consultation with the communities they are designed to serve.

Responsibility must be placed on the authorities awarding grants and contracts. They need to recognise the strengths of the voluntary organisations operating for ethnic communities and that their services cannot be effectively replicated within mainstream settings. Funding policies must be designed to secure their structures and ensure their stability and growth. It must be appreciated that the approaches adopted by these organisations are different but relevant to the needs of the communities. By attaching unrealistic conditions to grants and service level agreements these organisations are more likely to change in a way which satisfies the needs of their funder rather than the community. As has been shown, many organisations operating in the black voluntary sector are already underresourced and deprived of the secure managerial and financial base required to attract more funds. If these groups are to tender successfully for contracts they will have to change dramatically – a change which is neither feasible nor desirable. As one of our reports states: 'Concerted effort will have to be made to ensure that this contract culture which is now part of health and welfare provision in Britain does not work to the detriment and further disadvantage the Asian and other ethnic communities' (Webb-Johnson, 1993: 89).

Part II

Confronting issues

The effectiveness of a mental health service depends on the quality of professional training of those who run the service (as well as the resources needed to keep it going) but the final arbiters (of effectiveness) must always be the users of services and the potential users, especially those who need the services but who are excluded by various means. Indeed the interaction between users, potential users and professionals is a crucial element in the equation that measures quality. In this second part of the book, questions are raised about the involvement of service users – especially black users – the role of training for race equality is discussed, and some imaginative approaches to mental health care in a multi-ethnic society are explored in some depth.

Chapter 6

Consulting and empowering Black mental health system users

Mina Sassoon and Vivien Lindow

The psychiatric system can be disempowering for many of its recipients. Users of services have increasingly been resisting and challenging this disempowerment by speaking out against the system as it exists and by working towards the development of alternatives. Such action, aimed at empowering users of the mental health system to take more control, has come to be termed the 'user/survivor movement' – a collection of area-based action groups and individual users promoting often dissenting explanations and responses to emotional distress.

For African-Caribbean people and those from other minority ethnic communities, racism, in various guises, permeates the psychiatric experience. This chapter will explore the user/survivor movement particularly in relation to the experiences of Black communities, specifically those of African-Caribbean and Asian origin who form the largest 'minority' group in the UK. Both groups have not, on the whole, been involved in the movement's campaigning aspects. The fact that they are less involved implies that the philosophy of empowerment in some respects may have been constructed in line with dominant White values and that many Black users may prefer alternative routes to making their voices heard.

The Black voluntary sector and many Black mental health workers within mainstream service provision have made significant contributions in setting up Black support groups and other culturally sensitive initiatives that collectively challenge racist practice by their very existence. We will return to these later in the chapter. However, while the largely White survivor movement has developed in particular ways and is a regular contact point for informing the debate on the user's perspective, there is, as yet, no national Black service user movement collectively having its views heard.

INTRODUCTION

We are aware that discrimination within the psychiatric system affects many groups in various ways. Irish people fare badly in the British system; lesbians and gay men have a bad deal; working-class people from all cultures receive different and inferior treatment to that received by middle-class people. Women have a harder time compared with men. Disabled people and people with sensory impairments are discriminated against, often having no access to mental health services at all. While we regard the situation of all these groups as serious, here we will particularly focus on the voices of Black recipients of a system that is both racist and that oppresses on the grounds of mental and emotional difference. We use the term 'Black' in this chapter to refer to African-Caribbeans and Asians in general terms, but will refer to specific groups when appropriate.

There is no agreed language among people who have experienced psychiatry about how to be described. Indeed, there are many terms imposed: patient, consumer, client, user, sufferer, victim, each one reflecting the power of psychiatry – a power which undermines individuality by assigning personal and emotional distress a psychiatric label. Here we use the terms 'mental health service users' and 'psychiatric system survivors', and combinations of these interchangeably, to refer to current and past recipients of the mental health services.

VOICES OF THE SILENCED: EXPERIENCES OF BLACK USERS

Other chapters in this book have made clear the huge impact of institutional racism on the lives of Black people in the UK, and the effect of this on mental health. In addition, statistical and research evidence has been cited which makes it clear that the mental health system itself is racist in its workings, with African-Caribbean people over-represented in the most coercive aspects of the system and in receiving major psychoactive drugs, and seldom referred for counselling and community services. Conversely, Asian people are discriminated against both by having limited access to appropriate mental health services and by being marginalised into certain aspects of it; for example, being over-prescribed anti-depressants. Indirect racism, whereby service providers base types of services on common stereotypes and assumptions about both communities is still common.

We reflect below on psychiatric experiences of Black users that are representative of statistical findings. First, two African-Caribbean people, speaking on the video 'We're not mad, we're angry' (Multiple Media, 1984). To begin with, Peter:

'For the first two years of me going into psychiatry I was deemed to be a schizophrenic, but in the last nine years I have been deemed to be a manic depressive. Which says a lot for the hospital's ability to give you whatever title they choose and treat you accordingly. Because psychiatry is just about drugs, it's not about anything else. It's about suppressing people with drugs and controlling people's behaviour with drugs.'

Shirley has similar experience:

'They would always want to say to me that I was suffering from post-natal depression, and they would recommend tranquillisers. And I would always seem to say "No, I don't need them, I don't believe in them". But being in this hospital I was forced to take them. I had no choice, I had to take them.'

Such experiences can start early, as this woman describes. Having been thrown out of school at 13, and put into the hands of a psychiatrist:

'I was sent to the adolescent unit, and there were people there for reasons like they couldn't get on with their parents or had problems at school .... It was a place where, if someone was crying, they put them in a strait-jacket and put them in a room with no windows .... They used to drug us up all the time. They gave me some sleeping pills every night and some other tablets during the day.'

(quoted in Bryan et al., 1986: 117)

Such a start can lead to a lifetime in institutions and for Black people this is more frequently prison and secure psychiatric institutions than for their White fellow citizens:

'The prison system treats all women prisoners as if they're mad because they can't see how women would be in prison unless something is wrong with them. They've got this belief that Black women are violent or "savage", as they'd put it, and that therefore we are mad. When I was in prison in the ordinary block, I'd say that more than half of the Black girls were being given largactil.'

(Bryan et al., 1986: 123)

Indeed, stereotypes of Black people abound:

> 'Because we talk loud and we laugh out loud – our behaviour is more loud than White people – they think it is mental illness.'
>
> (Hyacinth Dale, quoted from the video 'From anger to action' produced by Mental Health Media, 1992)

> 'When the police have taken you to hospital once, that's it. They will always be watching you and stopping you to ask stupid questions and find out your business . . . . You start to know which areas to stay away from to keep out of their way. They never forget that you have been in hospital. . . . Any chance they get they'll put you back there.'
>
> (African-Caribbean man quoted in Frederick, 1991: 9)

For Asian communities the issues are somewhat different. Research in this area has tended to focus on why Asian people do not use certain services rather than their actual experiences of them. The results from such studies are often used to provide a framework on which to develop culturally appropriate services. However, the few pieces of research that have been carried out bear witness to the utter despair expressed by many, especially speakers of other languages unable to speak English in times of distress:

> 'When I went into hospital I felt more anxious. I kept thinking, what sort of jail have they put me in. The doctors and nurses would come and give me tablets. I don't remember very much about being in hospital, only that I wanted to go home. I didn't have anyone to talk to at all there.'
>
> (Asian woman quoted in Fenton and Sadiq, 1993: 35)

Equally important are the feelings of second generation Asians for whom stereotypical assumptions and judgements from psychiatric professionals damage self-esteem and identity – even when feelings can be articulated in English. Take this extract from a poem:

> Valium, psychiatrists, falling more into the abyss
> of white man's medicine.
> Hospital, enforced activity, consistent cajoling
> to fit their categorisation of me,
> All the time denying me *my* pain *my* confusion,
> Reinforcing my 'badness' at feeling these things.
> Isolating me, alone with 'my' problems.
>
> (Trivedi, *Untitled*, 1992: 82)

The above experiences show how damaging and long-lasting the effects of being in a psychiatric hospital can be. This spiral of control can have far-reaching consequences.

THE VALIDATION OF THE USER VIEW

In recent years, in recognition that mental health services have a long way to go before they can truly relate to people's human distress, there has been an increasing interest in hearing the user view as a means to provide more user-friendly services. Numerous studies eliciting the views of users have cited more counselling, supportive housing, twenty-four-hour survivor-run crisis centres, women-only spaces and less emphasis on medication and chemical treatments. In an attempt to show that treating emotional distress with medication is just masking the issues that caused it in the first place, research has also been pursued on the lived experiences of those involved rather than academic, medical theories of 'mental illness'.

However, a Black perspective is usually missing from such literature. For example, although MIND's research document *Experiencing Psychiatry* (Rogers *et al.*, 1993) is an excellent source and reference point for information about survivors' experiences generally, only eighteen of the 516 people interviewed were of African-Caribbean or Asian origin.

Separate reports of Black user views initiated by members of the Black community highlight some of the key differences in grievances between Black and White service users. Although housing, unemployment, poverty and so on are endemic to all society and obviously play a large part in the creation of mental distress, Black people are subject to racism which is too big an oppression for other grievances to be seen as completely separate issues. One such report (Sadhoo, 1990) relating to African-Caribbean people's experiences of mental health services, surmises:

> Afro-Caribbeans are the victims of racism and their total ideology addresses not only the acts of discrimination to which they are exposed but all those other social problems which are common to the experience of both blacks and whites. Racism is thus experienced not as an additional problem but as an interpretative schema through which all problems are to be understood.
>
> (1990: 14)

It is a fact that Black people's lives have controls imposed on them in the form of racism and discrimination within all societies' institutions including housing, social services, health services, employment, the legal system, schooling and higher education. Oppressive practices within psychiatric institutions can be seen as part and parcel of the overall discrimination faced in the wider society. The many campaigns led by Black communities fighting against a multitude of oppressions reflects the part that campaigning plays in Black people's lives: there are campaigns against racist attacks and murders, wrongful imprisonment, racist asylum and immigration laws to name a few. Equality and equity has to be fought for.

THE EMERGENCE OF A PSYCHIATRIC SYSTEM SURVIVOR MOVEMENT

Before looking at the racial issues within the survivor/user movement, we outline its activities for readers unfamiliar with its development. Service user groups undertake various types of action. While groups of people who have experienced psychiatry often engage in many varied activities, they tend to focus on one or more of the following:

* pressure and campaigning to change psychiatry and mental health services: this often includes training workers, and activities under the heading of user consultation, participation and involvement;
* self-advocacy and collective advocacy about individuals' difficulties with services;
* looking at alternative ways of understanding emotional distress;
* user-controlled alternatives to mental health services.

Such activities are to be found internationally wherever there are psychiatric services. For example, countries such as the USA, Canada, New Zealand, Australia and Japan all have extensive mental health service user movements. Different forms of action tend to predominate in different countries. In the USA and Japan, for example, user-controlled alternatives feature much more strongly than in the UK, though the picture is beginning to change here. These alternatives take the form of clubs and day facilities, housing and work cooperatives and many other activities. The point about them is that they are entirely controlled by the people who use them, including the whole budget and the employment of any workers. One key feature is independence from mental health service providers of all kinds. These are not mental health services; they are alternative forms of support to give independent lives to people who experience emotional and mental distress.

In the UK, although there has been user-led protest from the last century, the movement burgeoned from the mid-1980s. Survivors Speak Out, a national network of service users, allies and action groups, was formed in 1986. This is a new movement in its early years of formation, and as with any group of powerless people protesting against the establishment, funds are very difficult to secure. In 1994 Survivors Speak Out has had an office for a year and has one part-time worker.

One complaint of many mental health service users is that psychiatry and allied professions exist to suppress their feelings and behaviour. Mental health workers go through training that makes them diagnose or analyse instead of listen to people. Because of this training, professional people constantly act and speak as though they know more about what is best for distressed people than they do themselves. In general, the longer a person has been receiving mental health services, the less they are deemed to know what is best for them. Many people who use mental health services have been taught to believe this is so. This is a deeply disempowering state of affairs and has led to service users getting together and reevaluating and revaluing their experiences. Survivors Speak Out has held several conferences around such issues as eating distress and self-injury.

So far, most energy in the UK has gone into attempting to reform psychiatry through self-advocacy schemes and user involvement in planning, running and monitoring existing provision. One form, imported from the Netherlands, is the Patients' Council, a support group of ex-patients going into hospital wards to enable in-patients to meet without staff present and formulate and take action about their grievances. A national network of these more system-focused groups, the UK Advocacy Network (UKAN), was formed in 1992.

Another import from the Netherlands is the Hearing Voices Movement. Started by two Netherlands professionals, people who hear voices have themselves taken up the activity of learning from each other to understand the personal meanings of their voices and different ways to live with this experience. There is a national Hearing Voices Network which publishes a regular newsletter, and increasing numbers of local Hearing Voices groups.

A different sort of creativity is found in artistic activities. Survivors' Poetry, initially a London-based organisation but spreading fast, published a successful book of poetry in 1992. Local survivor groups often produce newsletters that contain both creative and protest writings.

This element of protest is at the core of the world-wide psychiatric system survivor groups. This is a liberation movement that takes its inspiration from activities of other oppressed groups, not least the Black civil rights movement. An example of its activities has been to oppose any increase in the coercion of survivors through the introduction of 'Community Supervision Orders', proposed by the Royal College of Psychiatrists and the mental illness pressure group SANE. The Government appears to have listened to survivors' counter-lobbying, and new legislation – which proposes registers of people in the community considered 'at risk' if they stop taking medication – falls short of some of the more reactionary proposals. This particular struggle is ongoing. The survivor movement also works with the wider disability movement in an attempt to get anti-discrimination legislation to protect the rights of people who have seen a psychiatrist to equal treatment in health, housing, employment and other facets of their lives.

In the case of mental health, the oppression takes the form of society's discrimination against people who have seen a psychiatrist and the additional harmful and disempowering treatment received within mental health services. This oppression is sometimes called 'mentalism', in parallel with racism and sexism. People who are deemed mad have experienced centuries of oppression in a wide variety of countries and cultures. By working together, psychiatric system survivors hope to redress the power imbalance a little in their favour.

There is no doubt that the survivor movement has had a significant effect on curbing some of the most abusive practices within the psychiatric system and that these have helped everyone, Black or White. However, while there are a few user groups that have positively sought to involve both Black and White users, on the whole, issues around racist practice have not been pursued in a significant way at national level.

In an attempt to redress this, concerted efforts have been made to explore the issues around race and discrimination within some pockets of the survivor movement. Survivors Speak Out members have listened to what Black mental health workers, and when given the opportunity, Black survivors, have had to say about racism. There is an understanding in some quarters that joining a mainly White group may not be attractive to Black survivors, and although many members wish to be part of a multiracial organisation, they respect the wishes of Black survivors who may prefer to explore issues related to the psychiatric system with other Black people.

In this, the survivor movement has something in common with women's liberation. Many women of different classes and cultures, both Black and White, have recognised oppression on the basis of gender. But racism and classism were found to exist within the women's movement, so that Black women and working-class women, for example, have formed their own groups and perspectives, while working together on issues in common.

Because of this, at least some White survivors have been very wary of any attempts to 'recruit' Black survivors to the movement by introducing them into groups in a tokenistic way. Rather, they hope to work alongside Black survivors when issues coincide.

White survivors sensitive to their place as part of a racist society have come up with a few solutions, some of which are:

To follow the lead of Black survivors and other Black groups, attempting to help as assistants in issues that they raise, for example, the Orville Blackwood community campaign, a Black-led campaign fighting for justice for the death of a young Black man in Broadmoor. Here, White survivors have been involved by, for example, helping to organise fundraising events and generally supporting its aims, while being sensitive to the focus of the campaign – the particular oppression faced by African-Caribbean people in the psychiatric system.

To adopt the issues of Black survivors in campaigning, and always to include as a high priority the fact of extra discrimination in the psychiatric system due to racism, plus the extra mental and emotional stress of experiencing racism.

To undertake anti-racism training. Individual White survivors have done this, but we have not heard of groups doing so. This may be partly lack of will, partly lack of the human and financial resources many groups need in order to do more than respond and survive.

Having said this, there is still an immense amount of work to be done in working towards, exploring and appreciating the diversity of ways in which we are affected by our unique experiences, and to work collaboratively to ensure all issues are taken up.

RELATIONSHIP BETWEEN BLACK SERVICE USERS AND THE MENTAL HEALTH SERVICE USER MOVEMENT

Informed by our different Black and White perspectives, we explore some of the issues within the survivor movement and the ideology of 'user involvement'. The experience of having control taken away from our lives in a psychiatric context to some extent unites the disparate collection of people who use mental health services. However, there are differences – both in cultural and political terms – in what 'empowered' actually means in practice.

The developments outlined earlier have provided a kind of 'empowerment model': campaigning for changes in the psychiatric system via action-type groups; involvement on planning and development committees with services providers; promoting alternative interpretations of emotional distress and creating more appropriate, survivor-led support. How far does this process of 'empowerment' – currently grounded in various forms both within the survivor movement and the current ideology of 'user involvement' within service provision – take into account the variety of belief systems, class structures, gender issues and cultural values that exist side-by-side in this country? Who dictates what is going to be empowering for an individual or group? And equally important, how are differences in dealing with the effects of the psychiatric system to be judged? Below we cite some issues for consideration.

Inequality of power and the consequences

The fact that different groups of people are accorded varying amounts of power depending on their race, culture and class has far-reaching implications for potential involvement. For example, what impact does the experience of racism have on speaking out against oppressive psychiatric practices? The fact (established by research) that African-Caribbean people are given disproportionately excessive doses of debilitating major tranquillisers (itself a racist act) mitigates against meaningful involvement while in hospital. Additionally, African-Caribbeans are less likely to speak out against unfair treatment for fear of recrimination by, for example, being sectioned under the Mental Health Act or given even larger, sometimes life-threatening, doses of medication while a voluntary patient. For Asian people in hospital – who may be unable to communicate in their first language or who fear being misunderstood or having their cultures ridiculed – it is hard to complain. Both communities are likely to steer clear of anything to do with mental health services once out of the system.

Ideology

The largely White survivor movement is presently influenced by an ideology governed by a Western value system. One line commonly taken by survivor groups is that 'empowerment is seen as gaining control over one's life'. For a person with Western beliefs, control is perceived to be attainable from an individual stance and often separate from culture, society and environment. In contrast, the focus in Eastern cultures, for example, is that control is sought in harmony, and in consideration of the family and community. Traditional beliefs such as the belief in 'Karma' – the universal law of cause and effect whereby every action, both good and bad, has a consequence – affect ways in which people may accept their lot in life, which in turn affects the nature of empowerment and the strategies which can be used to achieve it. Empowerment models must be able to coexist with beliefs and traditions fundamental to a culture – for example, its family structure – in order to achieve success within it and not only at its margins.

Stigma

For some Black people, in common with others who have experienced multiple oppressions, involvement in the mental health system on both recipient and activist levels is an added threat to an already vulnerable status. Respect within one's own community, which itself is already subject to judgements and racism from wider society, may be jeopardised.

There has been increased value attached to surviving the psychiatric system, particularly amongst White survivors, evident in survivor-led forums for sharing and validating mutual experience and for the nurturing of creative talents, for example, initiatives such as Survivors' Poetry. The increase in the respectability of having used psychiatric services is reflected in the way in which some more progressive organisations actively encourage users or ex-users of mental health services to apply for jobs, viewing such experience as positive. In contrast however, qualities asked of candidates for jobs within Black mental health projects are language skills, familiarity with a particular culture, and personal experience of discrimination. This may reflect the different paths to empowerment appropriate for a diversity of needs.

Racism

Another, obvious reason why there has not been much involvement of Black people in the user groups is that White survivors are a cross-section of society and as likely to be racist as any other White group. Within the system Black people may have experienced racism from their fellow patients:

> 'I found the patients even more racist than the staff. One of them had the habit of calling me Sambo. I couldn't believe it, even mad people hate us.'
>
> (quoted in Westwood *et al.*, 1989: 30)

Of course people with such experiences will be wary of White service user groups unless these can demonstrate anti-discriminatory policies and, more importantly, put them into practice. Some user groups are beginning to formulate equal opportunity policies citing that racism will not be tolerated, but there is still a long way to go before the implications of having such a policy are understood in terms of tackling both direct racism *and* indirect racism. Some well-intentioned survivors who would probably describe themselves as non-racist, see the issues around being a survivor of the mental health system as the central and most important issue whatever your colour or religion. The 'we're all in the same boat' attitude, however, can be alienating for some Black users who may feel unable to articulate ways in which they feel discriminated against in a mixed group. In the same way that White survivors want separate space from workers to reevaluate experiences and shared histories, Black survivors might draw strength from a shared history with other Black people. The following are the views of a Black user speaking about the values of being in a Black patients' group:

> 'I feel secure here. We talk about things that I want to know. Like the discussions about racial issues and talks about African and Caribbean history. I don't think I would have talked about race

and my Caribbean history if the group had White people in it. I
always have problems talking about these things with White
people. I don't think they can understand discrimination.'

(quoted in Wilson, 1993: 15)

Even if Black survivors decide to join in some actions in mixed
groups, they might also want to meet separately to explore the
experiences and effects of racism and marginalisation in the mental
health system and in wider society at the same time as examining
their experiences of mentalism in the psychiatric system. There are
a range of ways in which people draw strength to seek control.

Internalised oppression

Some Black people experience oppression about their identity that
may have been internalised, that is, denied. The effects of psychiatric
treatment can serve to increase this internalisation. It is not un-
common to hear a lone Black user in an otherwise all-White group
outwardly reject the idea of Black-only groups. When this happens,
White users, unaware of the way in which Blackness can be rejected
and who may also feel more comfortable with someone who denies
difference, can unwittingly serve to further disempower Black users.

Black users and workers

Conversely, Black mental health workers who in common with Black
users have experienced racism, may well share this experience with
users on a personal level, but in some instances, be unaware of how
its affects are further compounded by mentalism. It is often said that
any Black person is potentially likely to find themselves entangled
with the mental health system because of the experience of racism
in causing distress and the way in which Black people's behaviour
is negatively stereotyped and interpreted. In some quarters this line
of thought leads to Black professionals speaking on behalf of users,
which can prevent some Black users telling their own stories.

To draw a parallel with the disability movement, Hill (1994)
writes about the experience of being disabled and Black, in response
to a Black non-disabled woman who suggested that she should
always see race as the most important facet of her identity, and
therefore racism as the most important issue:

'I am cursed by continually having to explain why it is that I am a
Black disabled woman and not a Black woman who 'just happens

to be disabled'. Most people who have little or no understanding of simultaneous oppression have difficulty in coming to terms with this notion . . . my race, my gender and my disability all inform who and what I am and all in equal measure.'

Addressing non-disabled Black women, Hill advocates a 'process of collective consciousness to make sense of our shared experiences [as Black disabled]' and that the community 'accept our right to do that and allow us the space in which to do it, instead of . . . trying to impose your views about who you think we are, or more precisely what you think we should be' (1994: 14).

This corresponds to the experience of some Black mental health system survivors even though arguably racism has more of a causal relationship to distress than to other disabilities.

BLACK EMPOWERMENT MODELS

Whereas in the survivor movement considerable importance is placed on the creation of user-only spaces and meetings without professionals, for Black groups, if there is mutual understanding between Black staff and Black users, user-only space is apparently less of an issue, although this could change in the future.

There are a growing number of Black-led projects and organisations that have empowered Black users in variously creative ways. While mainstream mental health services have traditionally been set up with little or no consultation with users, Black mental health groups were established and developed alongside what Black users were saying about their experiences.

Campaigning for changes in services for the Black community has largely come from Black workers and others concerned with the plight of their particular community. The motivation behind getting something done arises from a sense of despair and anger about the injustices evident (but not personally experienced) in the treatment of Black people, be it the over-diagnosis of 'schizophrenia' in young African-Caribbean men, or the way in which Asians are judged inappropriate for psychological treatments on the basis of a perceived lack of insight.

There have been two strands to empowerment of Black users. We have called these 'reactive' and 'innovative'. By the former we mean the response to the impact of inequality upon people's lives and subsequent initiatives to enable Black people to have more control on an immediate, individual basis to combat the effects of racist psychiatric treatment. This includes advocacy, legal representation and provision within Black training projects to build users' consultancy skills, enabling them to comment on and criticise from a recipient perspective. In short, activities that would not be needed if the services were not so bad in the first place.

Innovative developments veer away from trying to reform psychiatric practice from within. In common with the survivor movement that has developed perspectives of distress through collective consciousness raising, innovative Black projects have provided a safe base in which consciousness around Black identity and its relationship to the psychiatric experience can be explored. The acknowledgement and reclaiming of traditional cultural practices as bearing positive healing properties is also pursued. These have been described elsewhere in this book. Here we look at two initiatives that particularly focus on campaigning for a better deal within mental health services, but which also have a self-help and consciousness raising role.

BLACK USER PROJECTS

Two projects supported by paid workers but essentially steered by the users within them are the Black Carers and Clients Project in Brixton and the Awaaz project. The former is a recent development under the auspices of the Afro-Caribbean Mental Health Project. It aims to explore the needs of Black carers and clients, evaluate the most appropriate forms of support, and campaign for more resources and better services for Black people, while exploring ways of empowering the people it aims to serve. Its primary purpose therefore is to empower from a Black perspective. As the project's literature states, 'without dealing with the effects of racism, Black empowerment in any service, is an impossibility'. Its wide range of activities includes: individual casework; a support group; a training course on welfare benefits; seminars on Black history and the long-term effects of racism on the Black mind as well as creative, activity-based classes. Project members have been actively involved in steering the work of the project, and after pursuing consultancy training, have acted as consultants to the London School of Economics, Brunel University, Southwark Social Services, West Lambeth Community Care Trust and the King's Fund. Members of the group have also gone on to form their own support groups in the community.

The Awaaz group is an initiative within a self-advocacy project aimed at supporting user groups in the North Manchester area. It was formed to share experiences of using mental health services from an Asian point of view. Awaaz have their own office in a building where other Black community groups meet. It provides a resource offering information and advice on a range of mental health issues, including drugs, alternative therapies, rights under the Mental Health Act, and it also offers other sources of help in the community. Support is offered in relevant Asian languages. Both men and women are involved with Awaaz, but the women also meet separately. Although the group is consulted about, and involved, in the planning of future mainstream mental health services, there is a feeling in the group that the onus ultimately falls on the community itself to take the lead role in providing a culturally appropriate support and information base. Ideas for mainstream mental health services to become more sensitive to minority ethnic needs have been voiced in planning committees, only to be told that there is inadequate funding to put ideas into action. The group is involved with the area-based Black health forum and sees a way forward in the contract culture as a viable way of overcoming obstacles of short-term funding.

CONCLUSIONS

The mental health service user movement has features in common with other oppressed groups. Where the initiative has been started by members of a dominating White culture, racism and other Black issues have not been seen as key factors affecting empowerment. As a result, Black members of that group have started to meet separately and to form their own organisations.

To take the disabled people's movement – which in this country has perhaps five to ten years start on the psychiatric system survivor movement – we see such organisations as the Asian People with Disabilities Alliance and the Black Disabled People's Group (Power). In the field of learning difficulties, Black People First members have started to make their voices heard. At the beginning of this chapter we observed that there is, as yet, no Black psychiatric survivor movement. However, now that a base of Black support groups has been established, Black users are increasingly speaking publicly about their experiences. Many individual Black mental health service users are now working extremely hard to protest about existing services, and to empower other Black survivors. Many of these are in the Black voluntary sector, others forming a minority within White survivor groups. Some Black service users are talking about forming their own user-controlled Black survivor groups: by the time this book is published there will certainly be such groups in existence.

SOME ADDRESSES

World Federation of Psychiatric Users
c/o Mary O'Hagan
PO Box 46018
Herne Bay, Auckland
New Zealand

European Network of Users and Ex-users in Mental Health
Rene van der Male
The European Desk
PO Box 4006
1009 BB Amsterdam
The Netherlands

Survivors Speak Out
34 Osnaburgh Street
London NW1 3ND
(tel.: 0171 916 6991/5472)

Scottish Users' Network
SCVO Box SUN
18/19 Claremont Crescent
Edinburgh EH7 4QD
(tel.: 0131 556 3882)

US all Wales User Network
c/o Jeff Williams,
80 Ynyswen Penycae Ystradgynlais
West Glamorgan SA19 1YX

Hearing Voices Network
Creative Support
Fourways House
16 Tariff Street
Manchester M1 2EP
(tel.: 0161 228 3896)

UK Advocacy Network
Suite 417
Premier House
14 Cross Burgess Street
Sheffield S1 2HG
(tel.: 0114 275 3131)

Survivors' Poetry
34 Osnaburgh Street
London NW1 3ND
(tel.: 0171 916 5317)

Chapter 7

Training to promote race equality

Peter Ferns and Mita Madden

Training has a central role to play in the promotion of race equality in services. However, it cannot in itself bring about real change in services without being an integral part of a strategic approach to promote race equality. Figure 7.1 represents a coherent model for the development of race equality in services.

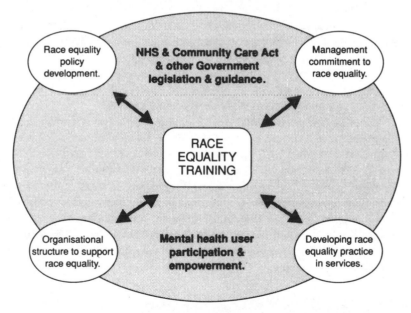

Figure 7.1 Model for race equality training

Policy development and supportive organisational structures are essential for race equality training to be instrumental in producing good quality services. If race equality training is undertaken in isolation it can easily become tokenistic and counter-productive. This chapter will focus on the central role of training in the development of race equality, and highlight the need to inter-link training with some key elements of services in order to achieve effective change. Race equality training will be defined and put into a context of wider changes in services, such as the shift from institutional to community care and the developing concept of user empowerment. Finally, the role of managers in relation to race equality training will be examined.

Race equality training is a challenging activity for both trainers and participants. The complex influences of institutional racism in services are sometimes difficult to discern and harder to challenge. Race equality training must not only set up a constructive challenge to participants' personal values and attitudes but also help to develop new ideologies to support and promote equality in practice. Training has to be practice-orientated so that participants have clear indications about what is good practice, and consequently, personal behaviour that is free from racism. (It is usually easier to change and monitor people's behaviour rather than their attitudes.) Since many workers, without a professional qualification have a big impact on the day-to-day quality of life of service users, race equality training should be made available to all workers involved in mental health services and not just to professionally qualified staff.

Although the process of training is important, this should not be the primary measure of successful training. Its effectiveness must be linked to outcomes in terms of better quality service provision to users. The reduction of unwanted institutional attitudes (measured by their effects on service users), changes in staff behaviour, improved procedures and services that promote the quality of life of users should also be important criteria for judging successful training. These principles for the evaluation of training often require new or adapted approaches in methods of evaluation and in following up training in practice.

DEFINING RACE EQUALITY TRAINING

Race equality training is concerned with promoting race equality in a productive and creative way, adapted to the needs of individual participants in the training, so that they go away able to tackle both personal discrimination as well as institutional racism. Although awareness-raising on a personal level is often part of race equality training, it is not the main focus. Identification of patterns of institutional racism, removal of barriers to race equality and the creation of accessible and appropriate services for Black and minority ethnic users are the most important aims. These aims would require a strategic approach to changing services, not just reliance on personal commitment and action of individual course participants.

Race equality training should offer definitions of racism on structural, institutional and personal levels. However, the most important part of the training is the development of personal understanding of institutional processes that perpetuate racism, through exploration of individual feelings about issues and (more importantly) about personal professional practice.

Inevitably, questions about cultural differences arise during race equality training. It is a common fallacy to take the view that if professionals have adequate knowledge about the cultures of Black people they would naturally be non-racist – or even anti-racist. Researchers in Leicester found that they were often asked for 'a key to Afro-Caribbean and Asian cultures as though they could be written on index cards and called up when required' (Westwood et al., 1989: 65). We believe that training on race must actively avoid a cultural approach and take an overtly anti-racist approach. The fundamental problem of a cultural approach without an understanding of the effects of racism on the lives of Black people is that an erroneous assessment of their needs is very likely to result. It is often the emphasis on a cultural understanding (to the exclusion of con-sidering racism) that leads (for example) to services not being offered to Asian families because they are believed to 'look after themselves' through extended family systems. A study of Asian people in Haringey showed that only 13 per cent of the sample (out of 98) regarded the family as 'a viable support structure and only for concerns relating to health and child care' (Beliappa, 1991).

The point that needs emphasising in considering culture and race, is that concepts of culture are never value free in a racist society and professionals need to get hold of this fact before 'culture' can be looked at. Cultural considerations may sometimes be used to create divisions between Black communities through (racist) assumptions of one Black culture being 'better' or more 'advanced' than another.

Historically speaking two important sets of ideas came into psychiatry from the basic sciences. First, the view that Black people are born with inferior brains and limited capacity for growth, and second, that their personalities tend to be abnormal or deviant because of nature (genetic endowment) and/or nurture (upbringing).

(Fernando, 1988: 17)

These manifestations of racism should be addressed during training, allowing professionals the opportunity to vent and examine their own feelings about them so that they may develop an understanding of the differences between a cultural and an anti-racist approach to practice. Figure 7.2 shows the key characteristics of race equality training.

Raising awareness of institutional and personal racism

Analysing service provision from a race equality perspective

Constructive criticism of professional practice

Examining current good practice

Empowering of Black users and carers explored

Quality and standard of training reinforced

User and carer participation in training encouraged

Action planning to implement race equality in practice

Local consultation with Black people promoted

Integrated multi-agency approaches reinforced

Taking a holistic approach to assessment and service delivery

Your personal responsibility for promoting race equality emphasised

Figure 7.2 The process and outcome of race equality training

CONTEXT OF RACE EQUALITY TRAINING

Various studies have shown that there is a tendency for Black and minority ethnic people to be over-represented in the 'social control' and 'compulsory' aspects of mental health services and under-represented in their 'welfare' and 'preventative' aspects. Race equality training must analyse the influence of racist stereotyping and institutional racism that creates this situation in order to identify strategies to eliminate such practice.

There are some general trends in the development of mental health services which are potentially more positive for Black and minority ethnic communities. For example, the trend towards more generic and multi-disciplinary services has the potential to promote a more 'holistic' approach to services, rendering them less inappropriate for Black and minority ethnic users by taking into account their individual life experiences, cultural and religious needs.

The shift to community care from institutional care provides opportunities for improvements in services to Black and minority ethnic communities as well as risks. Better planning procedures in the form of published 'Care Plans' by authorities means that there is potential for more accountability to service users and indirectly the community itself. Training should clarify and highlight the needs of Black communities – needs which are different in many ways to those of the majority community. Practitioners who identify needs in ways that are sensitive to both culture and race can contribute to the pressure being put on authorities to develop appropriate and accessible services for Black communities.

Black people are over-represented in various institutions, particularly those concerned with control or compulsory treatment. Institutions are generally impersonal systems and Black people admitted to these institutions are disadvantaged as a result of discrimination and culturally inappropriate forms of care given *en bloc*. The individual needs of Black users are more likely to be recognised and met through a needs-led approach to assessment and greater flexibility in the use of money to purchase care packages. So training should promote needs-led assessments and emphasise the importance of strengthening and utilising informal community networks.

The lack of equity in service provision has resulted in less choice for Black users. The generation of a greater variety of services can benefit Black users if authorities work in partnership with Black-led service providers and work to adapt mainstream services to better meet the needs of Black communities. Training should encourage creativity in the construction of care packages and positive action in commissioning services from Black-led agencies for Black users.

The emergence of users and carer participation as a key issue in the legislation should be reflected in training. The concepts of advocacy, including self-advocacy, should be explored as well as the need to redefine the role of professionals in empowering users and carers and enabling greater participation in service delivery. Empowerment of Black users in mental health services is a particularly difficult challenge for professionals in light of a long tradition of institutional racism in these services. Changing the balance of power between Black users and professionals can only be achieved if those with more power begin to analyse their position and remove discriminatory barriers for the less powerful. Training has a crucial role to play in this process through self-analysis, personal challenge, education and information and in identifying practical ways forward.

RACE EQUALITY TRAINING PROGRAMMES

The Central Council for the Education and Training of Social Workers (CCETSW, 1993), outlining the purpose of training for Approved Social Workers (ASWs), points out: 'Training will need to ensure that in fulfilling their role and discharging their responsibilities, ASWs effectively challenge and combat racism and other forms of discrimination which may disadvantage mental health service users, relatives or carers'. Even though the Paper is directed towards ASWs it applies to all workers in the mental health field.

Race equality training is most effective when it starts from the understanding that practioners have of race issues and helps people to develop their understanding and skills from this viewpoint. Analysis of skills, knowledge and training needs should identify what is required for race equality practice. This information can then be used in designing an appropriate training programme. Training courses should consist of the following broad processes:

- presentation of an acceptable value-base for race equality;
- identification of patterns of discrimination and barriers to equality services;
- clarification of key race issues in practice;
- formulation of problems and areas for development for specific services;
- generation of action plans to improve practice and implement learning.

These broad processes must take place in a context of healthy group dynamics which supports risk-taking by participants, constructive-challenging and a stimulating learning environment. This would obviously include the careful facilitation of difficult feelings often raised by racism to avoid paralysis of action through feelings such as guilt.

Training programmes should include a historical perspective of psychiatry and offer an explanation of racism in psychiatry. Without a historical perspective it would be difficult to understand the existence of racist practices in mental health work at the present time. In view of the over-representation of Black people in institutions in general, including secure psychiatric units, it is important for professionals to have some knowledge of forensic psychiatry, the criminal justice system and the processes by which people come into contact with such services.

The reasons for over-representation of Black people among those compulsorily detained in hospital must be analysed in race equality training. The influence of institutional racism and stereotyping must be thoroughly explored along with personal experience of these issues. The effect of the changes in hospital and the community services on their delivery in an equitable manner needs to be analysed and observations and conjecture related to personal experience.

Issues around user and carer empowerment in general must be fully discussed, especially in relation to Black people. Users and carers need to present their views so that professionals will get a feel for what the user struggle and the responsibilities of carers are really all about. Obviously training should explore a Black perspective – emphasising strengths, rather than the weaknesses in Black family life. Race equality training should include positive examples of Black-led services working with Black people, directly involving these workers. Professionals can then learn to identify ways of working with the strengths of Black families and individuals, counteracting an approach in training which tends to pathologise Black communities.

Race equality training can help to shape organisations and make them more accessible and representative of Black and minority ethnic interests. Mental health services are particularly resistant to any form of user participation and empowerment because of the nature of the stigma attached to mental illness. Due to racism, it is likely that Black users would have even less credibility than White users. Organisations would have to take positive steps to encourage Black user participation – not merely be 'willing to listen' to Black users. Race equality training could support user-led approaches by training practitioners and managers in working with Black user-led groups.

It would be necessary to enable Black users to have a separate space within organisations to create their own power base. The training can lead to action planning that improves user participation and representation, creates new posts or adopts existing ones and develops appropriate services for Black users.

Black user and carer involvement in training itself should always be encouraged. Trainers need actively to seek out Black users and carers through organisations led by Black people. Care should be taken by trainers not to exert undue pressure on users and carers to take on a training role. It would be good practice to offer training and support to users and carers who are involved in training. In the absence of Black user and carer trainers, trainers should present views of Black users and carers through the use of appropriate video materials or statements gathered from interviews with Black people.

Professionals need to recognise and understand support systems available to Black people in the community, including family, friends and local Black organisations. In this context, alternative ways of working with Black families and individuals should be explored. 'Racist views that Black people are incapable of experiencing depression and that their under-developed linguistic and intellectual faculties renders them unsuitable for psychotherapeutic treatment will result in the "absence of the appropriate use of these resources" and will put Black patients "at a disadvantage"' (Francis, 1991: 87).

Similarly, claims about Asian people communicating their distress in 'somatic terms' has led to mental health professionals stereotyping Asian people as not being 'psychologically minded' and therefore lacking in 'capacity for psychological insight necessary for certain therapeutic interventions' (Webb-Johnson, 1991: 13). Race equality training should therefore equip professionals to take a holistic approach to assessment which explores alternatives and offers choices.

Professionals must be able to offer services to Black and minority ethnic communities, particularly those for whom English is not their first language. Training should include some exploration of the issues relating to working with interpreters. They should be able to identify good practice guidelines in the use of interpreters in health and social work situations.

Training programmes should always facilitate the participants to consider how their learning can be put into practice. Exercises should help participants critically to analyse their practice in a way that leads to specific suggestions for improving their practice on individual and team levels. Action plans should be devised in sufficient detail and with time scales to increase the likelihood of these plans being implemented. Follow-up days could be a useful way of reviewing and evaluating plans that are devised.

EVALUATION AND FOLLOW UP

The evaluation of race equality training should be based on outcomes in terms of changes in practice, with a focus on improvements for Black and minority ethnic users, as well as subjective views of participants. It is important that Black trainers should not be exclusively used for training around race issues only. It should be recognised that Black trainers can also contribute on many other topics and must be enabled to do so. This is a much more creative approach and also avoids stereotyping and restricting people – recognising a person's full range of knowledge, experience and skills.

Race equality training courses should be followed up by trainers and managers with action plans and practice-based projects resulting from the training. This may well require some kind of monitoring arrangements that are linked into existing supervision systems. The evaluation of race equality training should always be based on practice outcomes. Judgements about practice outcomes and criteria for quality of practice should be defined from Black user perspectives. Training evaluations should encourage practitioners to build in feedback from Black and minority ethnic users in gauging the effectiveness of their own practice. Practitioners need adequate resources, tools and work structures to be able to engage in race equality practice. Training cannot substitute for good management in providing these prerequisites for practice which promotes race equality.

CHECKLIST FOR TRAINING COURSES

Process

- Course publicity should reflect race equality principles and venues should be accessible to all participants, including those with a disability.

- Importance of societal values in diagnosis and treatment of mental distress should be emphasised.
- Alternatives to a medical model for mental health should be presented such as social models.
- Power dynamics between professionals and service users should be explored.
- Presentation of a Black user perspective should be incorporated in the training.
- Positive images of Black users should be presented wherever possible.
- An understanding of institutional racism and its impact on mental health services should be put forward in the training.
- Organisational and agency practices should be analysed in a constructively critical way and areas for development should be highlighted.
- Participants should be encouraged to take a critical approach to their own practice with a view to eliminating personal discriminatory practice.
- Participants should feel able to admit their needs in relation to race equality practice and explore how their learning needs could be fulfilled.

Course organisation

- Trainers should adopt a practice- and action-orientated approach to their training.
- Trainers should model race equality and anti-discriminatory practice in their own practice.
- Trainers should not set themselves up as 'race experts' (or allow others to do so) and should ensure that they value and respect everyone's contribution and efforts in tackling discrimination and promoting race equality. In short, they should empower others to deal with racism effectively.
- There should be Black trainers involved with race equality courses and a gender, disability, sexuality and age mix should be sought out as much as possible.
- Trainers and course organisers should ensure that there is a varied participant group and should take positive action measures to achieve representative groups of workers.
- Empowerment and affirmative training should be offered to Black people in courses specifically designed for them.

IMPLICATIONS OF TRAINING FOR ORGANISATIONAL DEVELOPMENT

The importance of a strategic approach to achieve real change in services was highlighted earlier. A strategy is not possible without a clear commitment to race equality by managers, and strong leadership in translating commitment into actions. Institutional racism operates in a way that sets up barriers to change and improvements in services for Black and minority ethnic people, and these barriers require active responses rather than passive stances or the expression of pious hopes by managers. A public statement of commitment to race equality should be made by senior managers linked to any existing equality policies of the organisation. The statement of commitment is only a first step and not an end in itself, as it appears to be in some authorities where equality is nothing more than a paper exercise.

The next step is to translate statements of commitment and policies into a strategic plan with concrete, achievable targets and a clear plan of implementation with responsible managers including time scales (and sanctions, if necessary). The resource implications of such plans will, of course, need to be identified. If plans for race equality are regarded as integral to good practice and incorporated into other ongoing strategic plans of the organisation, resource allocation should not be the biggest hurdle to implementation: where resource issues are presented as a barrier, this may indicate a lack of understanding of how race equality is truly integral to good practice.

Managers may well require training and consultancy themselves in formulating race equality strategies. The training needs of managers should have the highest priority in any race equality training strategy as so much depends on their quality of leadership for successful change. A key training need of managers, apart from the formulation of the strategy itself, is supervision and monitoring of staff to carry out implementation. All staff should be supervised in an anti-racist way and Black and minority ethnic staff should be empowered to use their potential skills fully and enabled to develop a Black perspective to their work. The role of Black workers in a White-led organisation should be explored in training, and the danger of Black workers being thrust into an 'expert role' on race issues should be carefully analysed.

Communication between managers and practitioners is a crucial factor in successful implementation of the strategic plan. Training should aim to facilitate and improve channels of communication between managers and practitioners and help to create a flow of information from the 'bottom up'. In this way managers can receive more up-to-date and relevant information, allowing them to be more responsive to practice issues raised by implementation. A simple device of asking workers in training courses about the key issues and problems they are facing can be a powerful way of giving practitioners a means of feeding back to managers.

Training should always be closely linked with policy development, as all policies cannot be implemented properly without consideration of their training implications. People need the appropriate skills and knowledge to bring any particular policy into their everyday practice. Race equality policies should always be formulated with the participation of Black and minority ethnic communities and practitioners. Policy formulation groups should have Black and minority ethnic representation and training can play a facilitative role in this process of participation by helping Black and minority ethnic users and carers to develop skills in understanding the issues for themselves and contributing to meetings.

Race equality policies are essential for training. Race equality training in a policy vacuum is at best tokenistic and at worst counter-productive as it often leads to practitioners feeling exposed and frustrated in dealing with racism. Policies help to provide a supportive work environment for race equality, and co-ordinate initiatives on race, leading to more efficient use of resources. Some authorities never get beyond starting race initiatives and do not follow through with consistent action; consequently there is often very little long-term progress. Race equality training without a policy framework can lead to piecemeal and individualistic approaches which are dependent on specific individuals staying with the organisation.

Race equality training could make a valuable contribution to the process of policy development. Providing up-to-date and direct information from practitioners to managers has been mentioned earlier. Race equality training can also help to identify new practice issues and create pressure for new policies to respond to these issues. Politically, race equality training should not be regarded merely as a tool for management but as a means of facilitation for practitioners and practice issues and as a safeguard for users' rights and quality of services. An ethical and campaigning approach to training is essential for progressive and responsive services.

CONCLUSIONS

We are facing a period of rapid change in mental health services at present, with the closure of hospitals and the development of community-based services. The new community care arrangements offer us an opportunity to ensure that future service provision is more accessible and more appropriate for Black and minority ethnic people than it has been in the past. We must acknowledge racism and social injustices of the past if we are to understand and deal with the legacy of history. Black and minority ethnic users and their communities will not develop a trust in mental health services unless institutional racism is identified and rooted out in services. The challenge of race equality training can contribute to the creation of new and dynamic alternatives in mental health services for Black and White users. Race equality training is at the forefront of analysing mental health services and redefining good practice and professionalism in terms of equality and empowerment of service users. Training has a vital role to play in translating concepts of equity and fairness into everyday practice, and firmly establishing equality as an integral part of good practice. The political impact of training has not been fully recognised in the past. There is an enormous potential through training either to collude with or challenge oppression in society and discrimination in services. Trainers, managers and practitioners must each take personal responsibility to ensure that training does not become marginal to change, but is a potent force for equality and progress.

Chapter 8

Reaching out

Parimala Moodley

Traditionally, mental health services have been institutionally led but, more recently, there has been a major shift towards the provision of care outside the walls of large institutions. The reasons are numerous and include the beliefs that people are better served in their own homes and that it is more humane to keep people in familiar surroundings that are non-institutional. Institutions are faceless, heartless and careless, and large institutions have contributed to the disabilities experienced by patients with long-term psychiatric problems. Political opinion has also swung in favour of care in the community, largely driven by economics. It was believed that the money tied up in the large Victorian institutions on prime sites would be released easily to provide better care, more cheaply, in the community. While most clinicians believe that community-based care is the best way of providing care, it is government policy that has determined the rapid shift into the community – often without sufficient resources to ensure adequate reprovision. As the quality of a service is as important as, if not more important than, its location, particular care needs to be taken to ensure that the quality of service is not compromised in the process of relocation. Provision in the community has meant the creation of smaller, local units, people being looked after in their own homes for longer periods, and the closure of hospital beds. The reduction in the number of available beds has made people think more about those patients who are heavy users of beds. One such group comprises the 'revolving-door' patients. These are people, usually with long-term and severe mental health problems, who come in and out of services usually in crisis. These may be people who, in the past, would have spent long periods in institutions. In the inner cities the majority of these appear to be black.

The traditional structure of mental health service provision has been relatively rigid and inflexible. This has been relatively satisfactory for some people in that they have either fitted into the structure quite easily or been flexible enough to adapt themselves to the service provision. They are a good fit (see Figure 8.1). However, there remain a proportion of patients who cannot (or will not) adapt themselves to the relatively rigid service provision – *they do not fit*. Consequently they either receive no services, or if they come to the attention of the public in any way, they collide with services. People of all backgrounds may fall into this category. This problem may account for at least some of the homeless mentally ill. Also, it may explain the relatively low incidence in rates of recognised 'mental illness' in certain communities; in other words, people with significant levels of distress in some communities may not come to the attention of services because they do not 'fit' the service based on traditional models of 'illness' and treatment. In the case of people who *do* come to the attention of the public and collide with services, they often become the recipients of the more custodial forms of care. These are the people seen as suffering from severe and long-term mental health problems, who come into services in crisis, and then keep clear or fall out of the service until the next crisis. These are the people referred to as 'revolving-door patients'.

Looked at in terms of 'fit', the task of a mental health system that aims to provide care for all groups in the community is to provide services that fit the clients rather than ones that force the clients into a predetermined mould. Outreach services are one way of providing services that have a good fit. Reaching out to provide services to people in the community serves both to improve the quality of life as well as to proactively prevent revolving-door admissions in crisis. Outreach is particularly appropriate for minority communities because they are much more likely to lose out in the existing systems (as discussed in Chapters 1 and 2).

COUNTERACTING RACISM

Most institutions are constructed in a manner that is racist. These debates have occurred elsewhere and do not warrant repeating. Suffice to say that as a result the care provision by these institutions is viewed with considerable suspicion. All institutions have a responsibility to examine themselves and seek ways of changing their institutional practices. If changes are to be made and sustained

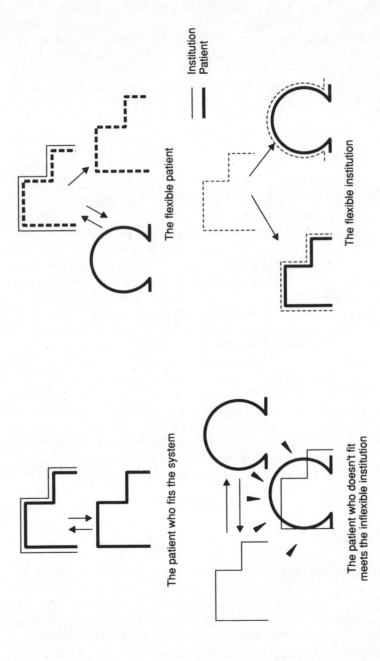

Institution ——
Patient ——

The flexible patient

The flexible institution

The patient who fits the system

The patient who doesn't fit
meets the inflexible institution

Figure 8.1 The patient and the institution

it is essential that the whole organisation is seen to be attending to issues of race and racism and that it is not left to the isolated endeavours of individuals.

When setting up or providing any services for black people considerable attention has to be paid to counteracting racism. That racism exists is self-evident. Establishing the impact of racial discrimination on individuals is extremely difficult. Certainly, the available evidence would suggest that for a proportion of our patients at least, there are significant and long-standing issues of race that have never been resolved. The reluctance to discuss these issues openly with all but a very few, if that, would suggest that there is conscious refusal to discuss racial issues with people they do not trust and/or there is unconscious denial of this very painful material. Whatever the reason, if it is not dealt with, it festers like a sore and pours out when the person is less in control – as when their mental state is deteriorating.

At an individual level practitioners have to be aware of their own racism in order to counteract racism. This is not easy. Issues involving race (especially when racism is to the fore) are very emotive wherever people are in the debate. As mental health workers we have an obligation to rid ourselves of any bias as to what kind of treatment patients should get. If we regard black people as bad and dangerous, we may decide that certain modes of behaviour are not of psychiatric concern when they do in fact reflect mental illness – hence the ongoing debate of 'mad' or 'bad'. On the other hand, failure to take account of particular circumstances may lead to judging normal behaviour to be pathological. While some clinicians have ignored issues of race altogether others have argued that it is the central core of all black people's distress. Neither position is acceptable in the author's view. Blackness is as much a part of the individual as is their gender. As such it may be a major or minor factor in their problems. It cannot be ignored.

It is necessary to be aware at all times of how social circumstances, including the environment, may influence behaviour. The danger in this lies in the fact that an acute awareness of the extremely negative circumstances that many of our clients live in, may lead to the adoption of the stance that it is hopeless to treat people who are going to return to or remain in such a pathogenic environment. This belief – that the cause of mental illness is racism – and that white authority, including psychiatry and its institutions, are responsible, may lead to the conclusion that the only solution is to get rid of racism and one should not apply first aid when radical surgery is required.

Unfortunately this attitude neglects the needs of people who already have, for whatever reason, serious or major mental health problems. It is important to remember that not all mental health problems are the result of racism. Some mental problems have a genetic base, others have a biochemical base and still others an interpersonal base. Discrimination and poverty may exaggerate these problems. It is insulting to black people to suggest that their problems are only due to race. Whatever the cause, the task is to devise the best possible interventions.

The mental health worker has the dual responsibility of fighting racism, as do others, as well as ensuring that the individual client has the best possible package of care. The patient in distress seeks relief from that distress and is not likely to appreciate the neglect of that in the pursuit of a common or community good. Anti-depressants, psychotherapy and other treatment interventions may have positive effects even though they cannot eliminate the negative environmental situation in which the problems developed. The call for social action therefore needs to be combined with the provision of accessible and acceptable services.

There is an increasing literature on factors that create and sustain inequality in service delivery and patient care. Much attention is given to language and cultural differences and relatively less to different approaches to service delivery and the eradication of racial discrimination. This may be because language and cultural differences are more tangible and less threatening. It is also a commonly held belief that inequalities in services are mainly due to language and cultural differences rather than the organisation of services and the attitudes of staff towards their work with black and other ethnic minorities. As part of the reorganisation in order to ensure that we make our services more equitable we have also to ensure that the workforce has a positive attitude towards its work with black people and other racial minorities.

Contracting

The changes in the NHS with providers and purchasers, and contracts for service provision, afford an ideal opportunity for the development of equitable services. Unless specific requirements are laid down and targets set, particularly in terms of race equality, for those who manage as well as for those who provide the services, the most articulate and the most vociferous will continue to receive the bulk of the services. What changes do take place will be in the region of the least threatening, that is, language and culture, and services will remain inequitable.

Contracting can play a major role in ensuring equity of services. Equity will be ensured when all corporate contracts – ranging from the NHSE to individual provider units – include within them core race equality standards. The responsibility therefore exists at every level from the Department of Health to the purchasers and providers. Race equality standards, which should be written and made available to staff as well as black patients and community organisations, should include issues of diet, language and communication, culture and religion, written information in different languages, respect for privacy and dignity, preference for female or male doctor/nurse and access to complaints procedures. The specific mental health needs *as well as* social care needs of the local black population should be included in all local health strategies and should be made available to staff, users and the local community.

Race equality strategies should be developed in conjunction with black users, community organisations and black staff. It is necessary therefore to ensure that these groups are represented on all joint-care planning teams. Strategy documents should include a written commitment to race equality in service provision. A senior member of staff should have the lead responsibility of ensuring the development of appropriate strategies, ensuring wide dissemination and regularly amending and reviewing the strategy. Community care plans should include details of how services will meet the needs of black patients. As the actual implementation of strategy is largely dependent on individual members of staff it is essential that all staff are trained to understand and implement race equality policies.

Two extremely important factors which underpin equitable service provision are ethnic monitoring and feedback from black users and the black community. Therefore there should be a written policy on ethnic monitoring that includes the aims and objectives and details the process. Where appropriate, staff should be trained on record keeping and monitoring. In-patient facilities (including the use of locked wards), day-care and after-care facilities should be monitored, as well as treatment decisions such as the use of the Mental Health Act for compulsory admission and treatment and clinical outcomes. In terms of feedback, satisfaction surveys should be designed to include issues that have particular reference to the black community. There should also be a well-advertised complaints procedure in relation to racial abuse, harassment or discrimination.

OUTREACH INTO THE COMMUNITY

Outreach services are locality-based services. Ideally they are part of a total package of service provision so that, as people's needs change, they may access other parts of the service with continuity of care being maintained. The development of outreach services must take account of the heterogeneity of the population. It is necessary to know the locality and the community therein intimately in order to provide appropriate services. Two essential prerequisites for setting up and providing good outreach services are (1) accurate information systems, and (2) extensive local community networks.

Information systems

Accurate information systems have to be set up and constantly updated in order to provide a sound base to inform the development of the service. These have to be of high quality, designed to provide diverse and complicated information across a wide range of areas. These include demographic profiles; geographic distribution; levels of psychiatric morbidity (measured in a sensitive way); mental health and social care needs; availability and utilisation of existing services, and availability of other resources in the community. All districts now have available to them a variety of sources for demographic information. The 1991 census, which for the first time included a question on ethnic origin, is an important basis on which to build more detailed information systems. However, it should be noted that the census data may be an under-estimate of the black population in some areas.

The information system should be designed in a way that provides details of the geographic distribution of the different ethnic communities across the area. Some areas may be selectively settled by refugees or people from certain ethnic backgrounds (e.g. people of South Asian origin). Some areas may have relatively high numbers of homeless families, and other areas (or perhaps the same areas) designate a large number of families as 'problem families'. It is necessary to know as much as possible about people's origins, family and cultural backgrounds and other factors that determine the way people live and interact with those around them – including service providers. It should not be assumed that all the so-called visible minorities or 'people of colour' are the same. There is enormous diversity within the black population and this needs to be recognised and taken account of when setting up services. Further, people who originate from a particular area of the world may have very deep and irreconcilable religious or political divisions (e.g. Tamil and Sinhala Sri Lankans and North and South Vietnamese). There are also differences of opinion amongst black groups as to what is appropriate – as there are differences of opinion amongst all groups. Failure to take this into account will inevitably lead to inappropriate service provision and failure to take up services. Homelessness (or being a 'problem family') is not an affliction but a consequence of various factors, such as the availability of housing, levels of deprivation in society and political policies of Local Authorities. All these must be taken into account in collecting data.

Having established a population and geographic profile it is necessary to gather information on a range of social and cultural norms. While culture is defined as prevailing values within a group or society, it must be remembered that culture is actually dynamic, and communities, groups, families and individuals change and adapt for a variety of reasons. It must also be remembered that there are enormous class differences within all communities which may have a significant effect on presentation of problems as well as utilisation of services. Assumptions should not be based upon popular literature, or after limited contact with members of a particular community. All societies have particular religious practices and customs surrounding birth, death and marriage, particular forms of address and styles of greeting. Prevailing family structures need also to be elucidated in order to be able to work sensitively with any community. Information relating to all of these may now be obtained through written material provided by various organisations. However, information gathered from literature should be corroborated when communicating with people as it may not be universally applicable.

Knowledge of the languages spoken in a particular area is crucial to the setting up of services for a multi-ethnic community. Levels of literacy in English as well as in the mother tongue need to be assessed. Some communities have a high level of literacy in their own language and can therefore utilise leaflets and other written material that is translated into different languages. Other communities that have a low level of literacy in their own languages cannot be accessed in this way and alternative ways have to be sought such as using local radio and discussions held in local community settings as well as material available on videos.

Some people may have extensive family, religious or other community network, while others may be much more isolated. Information needs to be gathered on all sources of support in the community. Most Local Authorities have directories of statutory and non-statutory organisations in the community, and increasingly these are being shared by health care providers. Voluntary organisations provide a considerable amount of care and support to people with mental health problems in the community. Unfortunately many of these organisations are financially reliant on unpredictable sources of support and therefore do not always survive for very long. Nevertheless links need to be made with these organisations in order to enhance the delivery of care and to ensure that the needs of the community are being met.

Apart from an inherent rigidity, existing mental health service provision has the drawback of having been set up against a norm which has probably (but not necessarily) been judged to serve the needs of the majority population. The result has been to neglect the needs of others in the community – minority groups, including ethnic minorities. To provide equitable services for all the community requires detailed analysis of the needs of the different communities and the individuals within each community. It is very important that such 'needs assessment' is meaningful for a heterogeneous population. Although community surveys are expensive, they are the most accurate way of finding out people's attitudes towards services and evaluating why some services may be under-used and others over-used. Most importantly, one can learn from the users and ex-users of the shortcomings of the service.

In a survey carried out on in-patients and out-patients at the Maudsley Hospital we found that all patients believed it was important to be visited at home when they were unwell, that staff should understand their problems and they wished to have full explanations of their conditions and treatment options. While white patients considered the social contacts made through hospitals as being more important, African and African-Caribbean patients rated seeing a member of staff of their own colour, being understood and receiving help with finding jobs as more important. These black patients were also less satisfied about the information they were receiving about their clinical condition, the different treatments including drugs, the respect they were accorded and the opportunity to see staff who understood their cultural background, their problems and the way they spoke. This survey helped to concretise many of the issues that had been thought to influence the engagement of black patients with services. In terms of providing services for black patients it would seem important therefore to have staff who are black and staff who understand people's cultural background as well as the way they speak. It is clearly important to discuss in detail the clinical condition and the treatment, as well as to provide help and support with practical issues like housing, finance and work.

Local Community Network (LCN)

LCN serves a very useful function in establishing open communication lines between voluntary and statutory agencies and the community, and in providing accurate and factual information. When planning and setting up the service it is necessary to form an extensive network of contacts within the local community that includes as wide a range of people as possible; people from different backgrounds, users, carers, religious leaders, community workers, local business people, etc. Regular stakeholders' meetings are necessary, with genuine consultation and active involvement of people in the debate. Entering into a dialogue with the community will also serve to establish credibility with the community that is essential for the development of good services. Establishing credibility takes time. It occurs concurrently with getting to know the community and gathering information. It is important that the entire service is seen to be credible and not just the outreach service. Statutory providers of mental health services have a considerable credibility gap to overcome. The experience of minority communities is that they have been ill-served by the statutory services; they have been given too much or too little; they are not listened to and their needs are not met; they often experience the system as hostile and uncaring. The power invested in psychiatrists and mental health workers to admit and treat people against their will contributes further to the suspicion about mental health services. Acknowledgement of the existing constraints and our limitations in terms of scientific knowledge and understanding is important.

Mental health professionals have great difficulty accepting and acknowledging the uncertainties within the discipline of psychiatry, and have particular difficulty with 'controversial' treatments such as

ECT. We do not understand exactly how it works, but we know that it does work for certain conditions in certain patients and is actually the treatment of choice in certain circumstances. In these circumstances mental health workers quite rightly fear a barrage of criticism and hostility and are therefore not prepared to confront these issues. In the author's experience it is possible to set up meetings with voluntary workers and users to discuss these thorny issues and to survive and continue to provide a good service. Respect for the other point of view is essential if productive relationships are to be built.

Services

Outreach work aims to engage and provide services often where other services have failed. In outreach services there is no one intervention style as there is no 'perfect' community-based service. The type of intervention follows from the mission of the outreach programme. The outreach team must address the totality of needs of people who are fragile and at risk of psychiatric decompensation. People with severe, persistent and disabling mental health problems present a sophisticated array of needs and a multiplicity of difficulties that have often rendered mental health care providers impotent to provide appropriate and adequate services.

Engagement strategies need to be devised based upon the specific aspects of the person's life in that community, so that outreach and networking can be sensitive to the total context of the problems experienced by the patient. A multi-disciplinary team approach is essential in order to engage and monitor those chronically and severely mentally ill patients who are at risk of decompensating psychiatrically and not accessing services except in crisis. A variety of skills are required, and team members have to be flexible about their roles. Every clinician has simultaneously to provide expert psychiatric assessment and treatment while adapting to the people in their own environments – providing them with necessary social and medical services and interfacing with other agencies working with these persons. The work may be very labour intensive. It may require two or more clinicians spending entire days with one patient. During crises these patients will require more intensive intervention with more team members to prevent decompensation and rehospitalisation. Care management services cannot be separated easily from crisis management in work with people who are seriously mentally ill.

It has been said that many of the newer experimental services such as outreach services have succeeded because of the charisma and force of the leader. I would argue that success hinges on the enormous skill of the entire multi-disciplinary team, and its commitment to a new and different way of working, as well as adequate resourcing. If it has not been possible to replicate the work done in certain centres it is as likely to be because there are insufficient resources, insufficient commitment to the task in hand and insufficient expertise as it is likely to be because of lack of a charismatic leader. The commitment and support of the entire mental health service structure is essential if any part of it is to succeed. Accounts of outreach services that provide the detail of the numbers of people seen, and the practical issues that are covered, frequently do not detail the qualitative aspect of the work which determines success or failure. It is about building relationships – with the staff team, the community and with patients. It is about trusting one another. Black patients in particular who have historical, community and individual reasons for viewing institutions and authority figures with distrust will probably find it much more difficult and therefore present a much greater challenge.

The Maudsley Outreach Support and Treatment Team (MOST)

The work of MOST illustrates some of the issues involved in providing an accessible, acceptable and appropriate outreach service. MOST was set up to provide an assertive outreach service to those people with severe and long-term mental health problems, who would not or could not use the services as traditionally provided. These were people who were either admitted repeatedly in crisis and were lost to services between admissions, or who had not come to the attention of mental health services although they were recognised by some people in the community as having mental health problems. The service was designed to be complementary to the rest of the local mental health services and not an alternative. As such it did differ from most other assertive outreach services. The service was offered in a very deprived area with a large minority ethnic population, and it was anticipated that, given the available evidence of relatively higher non-engagement with services amongst the racial minority populations, black people would be the higher users of the outreach service.

MOST was established on the following premises: (1) traditional or conventional services had failed to provide appropriate services for people – *not* that people had failed with the services; (2) people with long-term problems were not *just* patients (i.e. 'sick' people), they were people like all other people – it was their 'personhood' that had primacy and not their 'patienthood'; (3) every individual has personal values and strengths as well as weaknesses; (4) people have a right to make informed choices about their lives without losing our support because they do not choose to conform to our therapeutic endeavours; (5) we would work together with our users to establish common goals; (6) we would make use of every resource available to assist in the process of achieving their goals; (7) people should be assisted and encouraged to achieve their maximum potential and to remain at that level; (8) people should be encouraged to do for themselves rather than to have done for them or to them; (9) people with long-term problems need long-term care; (10) people should be engaged with other services, wherever possible, so that MOST was not the exclusive or main provider of services.

In practice, the principle aim of MOST was to provide a clinical service that would be both accessible and acceptable to the local community, particularly those sections that were not effectively engaged by the current services. The key elements of the service were identified as:

1 Priority to be given to the most severely disabled.
2 Each patient to receive an individualised treatment plan effectively linked to other resources and programmes in the community.
3 Assertive outreach techniques to be used to reach patients.
4 Promotion of cooperative enterprise and eclecticism (i.e. the service would use all the help it could get in responding to the patient population).
5 Responsiveness to local culture, the effects of racism and population needs.

The physical base of the service was a shop-front facility on the local high street. It was very easily accessible for the entire area it served. The office base had an open-plan office on the ground floor from which the secretary acted as the receptionist. Daily and weekly national and local papers were available and patients were encouraged to make their own tea and coffee. The floors above were used as interview rooms, meeting rooms and offices. The office was open from 9 a.m. to 5 p.m. on weekdays, but staff often worked outside these hours as the need arose.

The staff team initially comprised a consultant psychiatrist, three community psychiatric nurses, an approved social worker, a community liaison worker and a secretary. Efforts were made to recruit staff who were themselves of minority ethnic origin and initially the entire staff team were black. As there was staff turnover and further staff were recruited the nature of the staff team changed over time. Getting to know the community was seen as an essential prerequisite for the provision of the service. All the members of the clinical team were required to spend time initially making contact with statutory and non-statutory organisations in the community. The task of the community liaison worker was to maintain the dialogue between the service and the community. She had to seek out and develop and maintain contacts within the community. Information was systematically collected about all the voluntary organisations in the community who offered support, advice and care to people with mental health problems. Meetings were held jointly with staff of these organisations to discuss psychiatry and the delivery of services.

The target group comprised those patients aged between 18 and 65 years, who had been diagnosed as suffering a major 'mental illness' of at least one year's duration, who were not successfully engaged by services and who were believed to be at risk of further episodes of 'illness' as a consequence. The only exclusion criteria were people with primary substance abuse problems and primary organic disorders. Violence was not an exclusion factor and a substantial number of our patients did have a history of violence. Patients were selected through an intensive 'case finding' operation. All hospital consultants and their clinical teams were invited to refer patients who were 'lost to the system' because of their refusal (or inability) to comply with the treatment offered, but who clearly had a need for ongoing care. All the patients who were currently in patients but (it was believed) would not use the usual types of aftercare offered, were also referred. Community psychiatric nurses were also invited to make referrals as were GPs. Our referral criteria were sent to Social Services, Housing Departments, local residential facilities, voluntary organisations, religious leaders and the police. These letters were followed up by visits to the various organisations to explain in some detail what the service was about. Referrals were accepted by all these organisations and self-referrals and referrals by friends and family were also accepted.

Acceptance by MOST was followed by a procedure of engagement which was sometimes very long drawn out. The team operated a 'key-worker with team management' model. The initial contact with a new patient was always made by two members of the team. In-patients were contacted on the wards, the MOST service explained to them and post-discharge arrangements made with them. All others who were referred were contacted by a member of the team, often in writing; this professional then explained MOST, its purpose, way of working, etc., and offered an appointment time. Failure to keep this appointment resulted in the MOST team making unscheduled visits. Friends, family, carers or any other known agency were recruited to help make contact.

The MOST team was very persistent in its efforts to pursue patients and engage them on whatever terms possible. Much time and energy was spent on working out strategies to engage people and putting these into operation. As 'the buck stopped' with MOST, staff took very seriously the fact that failure to engage these particular people would mean that they would continue to come in and out of the system in crisis. There was immense pressure to find some 'currency' and some strategy that would work. The initial aim was to have a face-to-face meeting with the person and to ensure that they heard the case for MOST. We would persist until we exhausted all possibilities of making contact. If our services were consistently refused we had to respect the individual's right to refuse treatment. We then wrote to the patient inviting him/her to contact us if they should change their mind. We also informed the referrer that we would be prepared to reengage the patient if they changed their mind.

When contact was made with the patient our agenda was clearly stated: we were concerned that people had experienced difficulties; that they had spent considerable time in hospital, often repeatedly, and that as a consequence their quality of life had deteriorated. As patients had the same concerns, we had a common agenda – that people should remain well and, as far as possible, out of hospital.

During the sometimes protracted engagement phase, fresh in-formation was gathered on the patient's history and life circum-stances. This was concurrent with finding out what people wanted from the service. Offers of help were made for all areas of people's lives, for example, housing, help with securing the correct benefits, structuring day-time activities, etc. Over time, our users were encouraged to look at their goals and our goals for them were continually made explicit. Goals were ordered and accorded priority. These were translated into care objectives for the clinical team.

On average, patients were seen once a week at home, at the team base, or in any other community setting. At times of crisis, these contacts increased to several times a day. Sessions lasted 30 minutes, an hour or even longer. Patients who failed to keep arranged appointments would have a note left for them arranging another time. Repeated failure to attend would precipitate calls to agencies that people were known to in order to make contact.

Almost all the patients spoke fluent English, but interpreters were involved where there was any doubt with communication. Sessions with the key workers covered a wide range of issues including all aspects of living in the community, such as rent arrears and problems with fuel bills as well as discussions about living with and coping with mental illness. Patients were accompanied to housing offices, the dentist, or to adult education classes if that was appropriate. Others were assisted to use the telephone to arrange appointments or appointments were made for some. Money was managed for people while they were acquiring budgeting skills.

Medication was prescribed by the team or by the patient's GP in the form of oral and/or depot preparations. If medication was refused, while every effort was made to persuade people to take medication, it was clearly acknowledged that it was the patient's decision to take the medication or not. Everything possible was done to ensure that the decision regarding medication was truly informed and the positive and negative consequences in both the short and longer term were discussed with them. Life charts were frequently used to discuss with people the risk of deterioration if medication was not taken. Compromises were often achieved whereby medication would be reinitiated if certain symptoms reemerged. Consistent refusal to accept medication was respected and care was not withdrawn if medication was refused.

An important aspect of the work with each patient was an exploration of the earliest signs of relapse that may be detected by the patient or others. These 'alert signs' were explored on every subsequent contact with the patient. Negotiations were also made with patients about reinstituting medication if alert signs should reemerge when they were off medication. Counselling and supportive psychotherapy were an ongoing part of patient–worker interaction. It was clear that many of these patients, despite having limited education and not being extremely articulate, were able and actually keen to explore their backgrounds and early experience and the impact of this on their lives. Individual sessions therefore often included activities of daily living, as well as exploration of more long-standing and fundamental issues along psychotherapeutic lines. Issues of racism and discrimination were sometimes brought up by patients. Occasionally a black patient requested a white worker and sometimes a black patient insisted on having a black worker. Patients often avoided talking about issues of race even when they were specifically invited to do so. We were aware that there were issues because these were sometimes raised when people's mental state was deteriorating. We found that, at these times, some of our patients began talking about hitherto denied black–white problems and their traumatic experiences with white authority, particularly the police. Some of them also requested to see a black member of staff, or withdrew from contact with their white key-worker at these times.

At the outset it was made clear to patients that while we were aiming to help them to stay out of hospital, should their problems/ difficulties become severe enough, we would facilitate the process of admission, admitting them involuntarily if necessary. The team did not retain responsibility for patients when they were admitted to in-patient care. This passed to an in-patient team for the duration of the admission. MOST staff remained in close contact with the in-patient team and patients during admission in order to facilitate continuity of care when patients were discharged from hospital.

All staff aimed to meet all patients under our care in order to facilitate the team response to people in emergencies and when the key-worker was unavailable. Key-workers were allocated to patients on the basis of existing case mix, particular needs of patients and particular interests or expertise of staff. The average number of patients per worker varied between eight and eleven.

The clinical team met formally twice a week to review treatment plans, to discuss new referrals and emergencies, and for detailed case conferences – where all other agencies involved with a person, such as housing officers, general practitioners, etc., were invited. The total patient caseload was divided into three groups, such that for each group, progress was reviewed on a three-weekly basis. Care objectives were reviewed on a three-monthly basis by the whole staff team. One member of the clinical team was on duty in the office each day of the week to deal with telephone enquiries, people dropping into the office and emergencies that arose. This person also had responsibility for the safety procedures that were in operation.

The nature of the work demands a high level of skill and training. The flexible nature of the work and the relatively autonomous way of working outside the safe environment of the institution may produce high levels of anxiety in the staff. Additionally the intensive nature of the work is likely to produce burn-out in staff. It was necessary therefore to ensure that maximum staff support was available. Every team member received individual supervision from the consultant psychiatrist once a fortnight. Each member of the team also received regular supervision from a member of their own discipline outside the outreach service. Group supervision of casework occurred fortnightly, and was conducted by a psychotherapist and a weekly staff group was facilitated by an outside therapist.

Fortnightly teaching occurred on the unit and material was presented by a member of the staff team or by an invited expert. Initially there were extensive discussions on core value systems. Subsequent teaching sessions included the translation of psychiatric terminology into everyday language, and ways of discussing psychiatric symptoms and diagnosis with patients and relatives in language that could be understood by the average lay person.

Most new services have research built into the design. Ideally, research studies are undertaken with random allocation of patients to the new service or to standard services and analysis of outcome. We chose not to undertake random allocation of patients to the service because we believed that outreach services had already been demonstrated to work. People with mental health problems, particularly those who have serious and long-standing difficulties, often do not accept the additional intrusion of a researcher. People who refused to be interviewed by the researcher were not excluded by the service, because this was a service that was being researched and not a research study with service as a part of it. Clinical staff kept accurate records with standardised assessments that they were trained to use, and these were analysed to reflect the progress that our clients made.

Between September 1989 and May 1993, sixty-nine of the patients referred to MOST were accepted. Of these only 30 per cent were white. Of all those accepted 90 per cent were successfully engaged. There were no violent incidents involving staff or patients and there were no suicides. Given that these were a group of patients who were believed to be unengageable by the services this was a substantial success.

We believe that our success was achieved through attention to various factors which are usually ignored. These include the ease of (geographical) access of our base, the persistence and commitment of staff, and the non-threatening nature of our involvement with the patients referred to us. But most of all, we believe that our success was a result of working *with*, rather than for or at, our patients. Our interventions were always made explicit and nearly always agreed upon between the professionals and service users involved – with compromises on both sides. In other words, our success derived from our willingness to listen to and involve the users of our services – the people we called patients. All this of course occurred against a background of knowledge about the community we worked in, their social needs, the stresses they were under, etc., and an appreciation of the tremendous burden of racism carried by many of our clients.

Chapter 9

Interaction in women's mental health and neighbourhood development

Sue Holland

This chapter describes a method of working with a focal group – depressed women on a multiracial inner city estate, in such a way as to make connections to the wider community – social and political issues which often remain invisible although contributing massively to personal distress. It is described more fully elsewhere (S. Holland 1988, 1990a, 1992).

Essential to the principles of empowerment and liberation which inform mental health promotion is the idea of beneficial movement or change. In this case, the aim was to bring together a combination of techniques drawn from sociological, psychological and therapeutic sources, known therefore as 'sociopsychotherapy' or 'social action psychotherapy', in order to facilitate change. The movement was also described in a conference paper as 'From social abuse to social action via psychotherapy' (Holland, 1990b). The theory and method described here led to the development of an innovative model of psychotherapeutic work with depressed women in their own community setting. The women were residents of a large working-class, multiracial inner London housing estate. The psychological and inter-personal problems they experienced were usually compounded by inequalities and deprivations: poverty, racism, unemployment, lack of childcare facilities, limited educational and recreational choices, to name a few.

In order to address not only their personal psychic pain – which shows itself in the form of depression, anxiety, or phobias – but also their social suffering, a model of mental health intervention was used which confronted both psychic depression and social oppression. The women were encouraged to move through a series of perceptions of themselves, ranging from passive victim/patient to active participant in their own and their neighbours' well-being. In practice this involved a series of steps from brief focal psychotherapy to educational discussions – preferably 'conscientization groups' based on Paolo Freire's (1972) concept of 'conscientization' (p. 142) – to social action around specific local issues or demands. The model of intervention is *dynamic* in that the woman moved through a series of psychic and social 'spaces', each more socially complex than the last. This has proved to be a particularly effective method of therapy with women whose depression stems from childhood abuse, and who later experience the added abuse of economic exploitation, racism and sexism.

FOUR STEPS IN SOCIAL ACTION PSYCHOTHERAPY

The steps in social action psychotherapy are described in non-technical terms so that educational deprivations and inequalities are not allowed to rob people of a means of liberation. A leaflet outlines the 'Four Steps in Social Action Psychotherapy'.

Step one: patients on pills

Women sometimes feel so bad about themselves that they can't face their everyday life. We go to the doctor complaining of 'nerves' and get given pills to calm us down (tranquillisers) or cheer us up (anti-depressants). We then see ourselves as having a 'medical' problem. Sometimes the doctor will send us to see a psychiatrist who continues the regime of, usually stronger, mood-changing drugs. We now see ourselves as a 'psychiatric case', passively expecting to be cured.

Step two: person-to-person psychotherapy

White City Mental Health Project offers women an alternative to pills. Talking to a woman therapist helps us to explore the meanings of our depression and so reveals our buried feelings, such as anger and guilt. We can then take charge of all our painful 'ghosts' from the past.

Step three: talking in groups

Now, freed from our personal ghosts, we can get together in groups and discover that we share a common history (HER-STORY) of abuse, misuse and exploitation of ourselves as infants, as girls, as women, as working-class women, as black women . . . . Now we can see, and say together, what we really want!

Step four: taking action

Having changed ourselves from patient to person, from a state of depression to self and self–other awareness, we can now use our collective voice to demand changes outside in our community . . . in our schools, our health centres, our community centres, our housing, transport, and in anything else that affects our lives.

Issues and obstacles

By using this model of therapeutic intervention, depressed women can move through psychic space into social space and so into political space. 'Finding a space for oneself' thus becomes a series of options, each more socially connected than the last, in a progression from private symptom to public action. This is conveyed diagramatically in Figure 9.1 using the Burrell and Morgan (1979) paradigm map as developed by Whittington and Holland (1985), and elaborated as a therapeutic model by Holland (1988).

Both practitioners and clients will be able to locate themselves

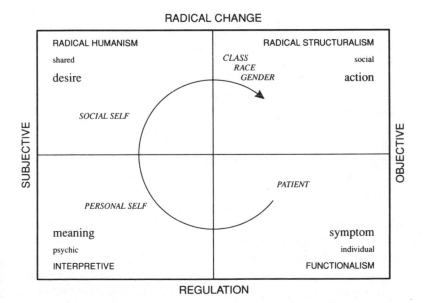

Figure 9.1 Theoretical positions in moving from personal symptom to public action

within these modes/paradigms. Both will have experienced a greater or lesser degree of movement 'around' this framework, and both will express preferences for particular modes/paradigms. For example, the clinical psychologist who is more comfortable desensitising a woman's agoraphobia than exploring her unconscious desires, will have more 'success' with the woman 'patient' who has also internalised a functionalist/mechanistic view of herself and the world. Both practitioner and 'patient' are capable of changing and moving on to other modes of intervention – for example, a consciousnes-raising group based on Paolo Freire's (1972) concept of 'conscientization', which has a significant collective and socio-historical meaning – but both will require retraining in order to move them into this alternative radical humanist mode.

In short it is a *reflexive* model of practice and teaching which assumes that what is so for the client is so for the practitioner. Even more problematic is the move to the radical structuralist position since it demands an active, even confrontational, stance which does not come easily to many practitioners and clients (Holland, 1991).

EMERGENT ISSUES

Since professional people of many kinds are charged with, or lay claim to, responsibility for community mental health, it is necessary to say something about the issues of identifying who can do what to help facilitate this kind of movement.

The work is disrespectful of existing professional boundaries in three senses. First, it challenges the vested, and anxiously protected, interests of the many distinct professional groups involved in community work. Second, it has been necessary to demystify the conceptual language of psychology and sociology, and it is no easy task to put rigorous theory into the local vernacular, without posturing as a member of the working class. Finally, in attempting to use available services it has been evident that the welfare system condones the passive victim but criminalises those who are angry and assertive. It has been necessary to address not only personal loss but also expropriation (having been robbed) and the desire for justice. It challenges the very notion that professional intervention is necessarily better informed and more beneficial than lay action. It challenges the notion of a hierarchy of professional legitimacy and power, usually referred to as 'medical dominance'. This challenge does not obliterate the idea that specialists of various kinds may provide essential services. It objects only to the claim by any group that they always, exclusively, know best. There are some people in all these professions with sufficient flexibility to make a valuable contribution, and part of the work is to identify and relate to these helpers. But what a challenge it is to all professions that there has emerged from this work a completely autonomous group of local women with their own funds and premises, known as WAMH.

WOMEN'S ACTION FOR MENTAL HEALTH (WAMH)

WAMH is a resource for all those women who distrust 'the professional', who might or might not take the prescribed pills, who would like to work but have no confidence or opportunity, as well as those who need advice on how to prevent themselves being robbed, raped, exploited and mistreated in their personal relationships and in their dealings with social institutions and authorities of various kinds. For those who have already suffered some kind of abuse it is also a refuge. WAMH is on the spot and easily contactable during unsocial hours in an emergency. (Ironically their most social hours – evenings, weekends, bank holidays.)

This unit is able to provide services that are acceptable to local people because its workers are members of the community. But acceptability does not merely depend on the location of buildings (Community Mental Health Centres) or with proclaimed 'interest' in a community approach. It is the common bond forged through sharing both the pride and the stigma of the 'council tenant'.

FROM 'FRINGE' TO 'MAINSTREAM'

The White City Mental Health Project started in October 1980 and is still in existence as a mainstream social services resource fourteen years later. The ex-client/users organisation which sprang from it, Women's Action for Mental Health (WAMH) still thrives, and received its grant from Hammersmith and Fulham Council for the twelth year running. This durability and tenacity is an almost unique feature in the present political climate in which small, innovative and radical multiracial, black and working-class projects have not survived longer than two or three years.

Unless such experimental projects can fight their way into the mainstream there will be little prospect of progressive multi-ethnic resources within our community mental health systems. The fact that the White City Project and WAMH have been successful in surviving and influencing other programmes outside their immediate neighbourhood is due directly to a number of features, the most crucial being its coherent therapeutic theory and practice of 'social action psychotherapy'. Its other features show that the project had incorporated in a pilot form almost every characteristic which was later drawn up by social services in 1990 as a blueprint for community care. So by its tenth birthday the project could demonstrate a twenty-point quality audit:

1 'Front line' in an accessible and homely flat on the estate.
2 User-friendly' – encouraging self-referrals.
3 Particularly targeted towards disadvantaged women, 40 per cent of whom were black.
4 Maintains close links with neighbourhood networks, groups and 'key' people, and so can put clients in touch with such resources.
5 Plays an active role in neighbourhood development in general and mental health consultancy in particular.
6 Empowers clients both individually by its distinctive therapeutic techniques and philosophy, and collectively, by facilitating ex-users' mutual help groups. The WAMH unit sprang directly out of this effort, and so set up its own neighbourhood counselling, support and advocacy organisation funded initially by the GLC and then by the Borough Council.
7 Multi-disciplinary and multi-ethnic, staffed by a community clinical psychologist and two social workers, as well as an administrator and sessional staff brought in for group work, research and interpreting.
8 Pays particular attention to skilled assessment in sessions of up to two hours, thus discouraging referring agencies from psychologising women's difficulties merely because there is a psychologist available.
9 Provides a highly skilled, specialist, brief focal psychotherapy service, where appropriate in a relaxed and homely setting and quite separate from the high-status, high-profile medical psychotherapy satellites of local psychiatric units which were not (at that time) reaching black and minority ethnic women. Due to the support networks which the project had engendered, the therapists could now hold in therapy a number of clients who would be considered 'unsuitable' by more orthodox psychotherapy establishments.

10 Uses the goal of empowerment to encourage clients to move on from individual psychotherapy into wider-ranging discussion groups which explore needs, desires and demands.

11 Gives monitoring and evaluation a priority by recruiting a black research worker to be supervised by a member of the council's planning and research staff. A sample of referrers and ex-users were interviewed using a questionnaire drawn up from constructs proposed by a pilot group of referrers and users. Overall, both referrers and users gave positive feedback about the work, which appeared to be particularly successful in meeting the needs of black and national minority women (e.g. Irish) and women in trans-racial marriages.

12 Promotes equality for women and makes known its anti-discriminatory and anti-racist practice. It attracted 45 per cent black clients – which truly reflected the ethnic composition of its catchment area, unlike the medically based psychotherapy services in the regional health authority described by Ilahi (1980).

13 Holds its own budget, controlled by the project manager and with back-up and consultation from a line manager within the social services, it is able to use its funds flexibly and imaginatively. Although never overspending, it was able to improve its facilities and equipment for the benefit of clients, staff and visitors, including audio-visual equipment and a specialist library. It was able to use consultancy fees for clients' leisure/educational activities such as theatre tickets for the Black Women's History Group.

14 Opens office hours and flexi-hours, including late nights and weekends if necessary, it was able to provide an informal emergency service in close collaboration with WAMH, preventing many admissions to casualty departments and psychiatric wards. This is a unique and effective example of professional and voluntary cooperation.

15 Works closely with other mental health services to contribute important service developments such as a self-harm monitoring and counselling programme which it initiated in 1981 and which was later taken up by a local hospital team – extending the catchment area and including men. It was noted that female para-suicides on the estate dropped, whereas the figure for males increased in line with the national rate.

16 By way of teaching, consultancy, workshops and published

papers, reaches a wider audience and thereby contributes to the improvement of existing services and the setting up of new ones. By way of consultancy, the West Lambeth Health Authority was enabled to set up the women's psychotherapy service, *Shanti*. Also, the *Forward Project*, a residential psychotherapy and outreach service for young black people was created by several years of committed work involving ourselves, other professionals and black women carers in the locality.

17 By way of an advisory group made up of people living and working on the estate, keeping in touch with some of the main social issues on the estate and their relevance to mental health.

18 Through close links with the under fives provision on the estate, addressing the needs of mothers and children, and representing mothers whose mental health was at risk. Teaching and consultancy for nursery staff and mothers' groups was given by project staff.

19 Liaises with the local Community Mental Health Team (CMHT) whereby the territorial confusion over clients was resolved amicably. Our emphasis on 'early intervention' gave us a flexibility which the CMHT's remit for working with the 'recovering mentally ill' precluded. Although many of the women seen in the project had psychiatric histories, our emphasis on non-stigmatising language and neighbourhood support networks enabled us to 'hold' them in the community for considerable periods of time. However, it is also important to be able to call on the CMHT's professional support services rather than misuse and exhaust the neighbourhood counsellors.

20 Professional staff work themselves into and out of jobs via development work, therapy, supervision, teaching and consultancy. And since many professions criss-cross the community it may be necessary to devise a job with little or no precedent and no easy career structure. Given that para-professionals are so important to the work, and that professionals may have to break their normal boundaries, there are serious issues as to appropriate training. But what is vital to the kind of collaboration that will be effective is a sense that practitioners and clients move in the same uncertain world of contradictory modes and paradigms.

Now into its fourteenth year and firmly rooted in its working-class and multiracial catchment area, the project can afford to be less exclusive and separatist. Renamed 'Bridge' and shedding the clinical associations with the word 'mental', the service will now project itself as a 'Centre for Women's Emotional Wellbeing', offering counselling, psychotherapy, group-work, family-work, workshops, training, consultancy and a specialist library. The group-work will open its membership to a wider catchment area, forging links between women living on the estate and those outside. The title 'Bridge' conveys the links to be made between women, and also echoes the core philosophy, which is to make bridges between the private/personal and the public/social lives of women. Bridge publicity leaflets, although offering problem solutions, also celebrate the strengths and resources of women, and illustrate this with a triumphant poem by Maya Angelou – *Still I Rise* – the last few lines of which are a fitting metaphor for the therapeutic struggle of all those who have been enslaved – black or white.

Leaving behind nights of terror and fear
I rise
Into a daybreak that's wondrously clear
I rise
Bringing gifts that my ancestors gave,
I am the dream and the hope of the slave,
I rise
I rise
I rise

(Maya Angelou, *And Still I Rise* 1986: 42)

Chapter 10

Culture and family therapy

Inga-Britt Krause and Ann C. Miller

The early development of family therapy was based on two theories; a theory of complex interaction, General Systems Theory (von Bertalanffy, 1962) and a theory about human communication (Watzlawick *et al.*, 1967). The interplay between these ideas and the pragmatic benefits of treating patients or clients in the 'natural setting' of their families, meant that professional understanding and treatment of people's problems was contextualised in ways which, in the West, they had not hitherto been. This shift in theory and practice fitted well with other prevailing ideas about destigmatising and deprofessionalising problems in living, which 'psychiatric' labelling had moved out of the domain of ordinary living and into the domain of 'experts'. Family therapy proposed, in both its theory and practices, a view of the 'patient' as a family member, actively participating in the creation, expression and attempted solution of the family's dilemmas in living together.

This view was held irrespective of whether families were actually domiciled together, but, for the most part, a relatively narrow view was taken of the system in which problem patterns were reckoned to be embedded. The system was frequently deemed to be coterminous with the family, and often with the nuclear family. It did not take into account the wider systems of which both the family and the therapist were a part, and it did not usually address gender, class, ethnicity or culture. Although some authors (e.g. Minuchin and Montalvo, 1967; Auerswald, 1968; Aponte, 1977; Speck and Attneave, 1974) addressed class and cultural issues in different ways power differentials between therapist and family were rarely explored in any detail, and they were certainly not central in the major textbooks.

However, in the 1980s a major critique was undertaken – largely by women therapists – of the structuring of women's experiences both as clients and therapists by the theory and practices of family therapy. The 'heroic innovator' model of therapist behaviour was scrutinised, and the potential power of the therapist to contribute to oppressive practices towards women and girls or, equally problematic, to colonise the family's view of itself, were brought into a wide-ranging debate (e.g. Walters *et al.*, 1988; Goldner, 1988; Perelberg and Miller, 1990). This coincided with the publication of views of family therapy's practices in relation to culture (Montalvo and Gutierrez, 1988; Boyd-Franklin, 1989; Lau, 1984, 1990; O'Brian, 1990; Waldegrave, 1990; Perelberg, 1992), where family therapy came under review as to its cross-cultural applicability.

Although family therapists were interested in what they called 'belief systems' this term tended to refer to what clients believed about the problem(s) they were presenting. What people believed about their circumstances was, of course, closely related to their cultural background, but it was not so much this general aspect of belief which interested family therapists at first. Rather what was emphasised was the way a belief about a problem prevented the persons involved perceiving how things could change (Campbell *et al.*, 1989). What did not receive much attention was the way culturally derived ideologies differed, and how problems, treatments and solutions are all aspects of specific and coherent cultural themes and hence also vary cross-culturally (Littlewood, 1992a). In other words, family therapists could acknowledge that certain ideas might be connected to certain (problem) behaviours, but they did not widen this insight to an understanding of how different ideas might be connected to form a deep and pervasive rationale for existence. They tended to portray beliefs as straightforward non-contradictory bits of information which could be considered out of context and therefore easily changed. It is only more recently that interest in language and language systems (e.g. Anderson and Goolishan, 1988) and the exploration of theories about diversity (e.g. Jones, 1993), shifting identities (McNamee and Gergen, 1992) and coconstructed narratives (White and Epstein, 1990), have helped move family therapy nearer to a position from which it is possible to address the question of cultural relativity rigorously and sensitively.

In this chapter we first discuss some of the more important general themes which arise when therapists work cross-culturally. In doing this we offer our own framework and our definition of 'culture' as a guide to practice. We then describe the development of a community-based service which highlights the importance of the connection between treatment and wider social and cultural issues. Finally we give examples of our clinical practice.

THEMES IN CROSS-CULTURAL THERAPY

The problem about understanding and helping as a therapist when you are not from the same background as your client is a familiar one, shared by all mental health workers whatever their profession. It is also an issue which exists in all types of therapy and all kinds of communication between individuals. In this respect cross-cultural therapy and communication makes overt, what in intra-cultural therapy and intra-cultural communication is hidden, but nevertheless exists. This is because cross-cultural communication usually involves communication between individuals who in some manner cannot avoid acknowledging their differences, whereas in intra-cultural communication it is easier to assume (rightly or wrongly) that the persons involved are the same or at least share substantial chunks of behaviour patterns, thoughts and ideas. In inter-cultural communication it is impossible to blur the distinction between oneself and the other, and this distinction can become the vehicle for many different relationships. Racism is one such relationship. In racism the undesirable aspects of one group of people or one individual may be projected on to another group or individual, so that instead of both groups having both good and bad characteristics, one (the most powerful) is seen as good and the other (the least powerful) is seen as bad (Rustin, 1991). Racist relationships are generally thought of as based on physical characteristics, but the process may be based on any sort of difference: a different way of cooking, dressing, inter-personal behaviour, religious worship, philosophy etc. – all aspects of life which may be broadly defined as part of culture (see Chapter 1).

This ubiquitous quality of cultural material and processes makes it difficult to construct clear and appropriate models for cross-cultural work. In the last few decades there has been a wealth of different approaches in the mental health field designed to deal with this problem and it is only recently that the complexity of the issues is beginning to be appreciated (Falicov, 1982; McGoldrick *et al.*, 1982; Kleinman, 1987; Littlewood and Lipsedge, 1989; Perelberg, 1990; Fernando, 1991; Littlewood, 1992b; Watts-Jones, 1992;

Krause, 1993, 1994; Tamura and Lau, 1992). The different trends
described in the family therapy literature exemplify general trends.

The need for information

An early approach emphasised the need for health professionals to
have more information about their patients' and clients' ethnic
groups and cultures. The simplest version of this approach was the
publication of lists of cultural traits for health professionals to keep
in mind when they were treating patients from different cultural
backgrounds. A more subtle and sensitive version advocated that
clinicians should 'focus on a few groups with whom they have
considerable exposure as a way of training themselves to be more
aware of the cultural relativity of all norms and values' (McGoldrick,
1982: 26). This statement was made by one of the editors of the first
serious volume addressing cross-cultural work in family therapy
generally. The bulk of the volume addressed and described different
behaviour patterns, customs and traditions of many cultural and
ethnic minority groups in the USA. The issues relating to the
therapist herself received less attention (see, for example, Falicov in
the same volume). The book thus became a source of factual
information about various cultures, and for many in the family
therapy field it was the first encounter with different cultural
patterns.

Although drawing attention to cultural variation and differences
between ethnic groups was extremely important – before this family
therapists, although working cross-culturally, had hardly acknowledged this fact or described the difficulties in detail – there are
several drawbacks with an approach which places the main emphasis
on cultural information. First, the status of the information presented
is not clear. We are for example rarely told how the information was
acquired: who said it?; is it the construct of one person?; several
persons?; the therapist herself?; or did she read it somewhere?
In other words information or knowledge for which sources cannot
be traced or documented carries the danger of stereotyping (see
Chapter 1).

A second problem is related to definitions of words and ideas such
as 'ethnicity' and 'culture'. Quite often these words are not defined
– writers assuming that everyone knows what they refer to. This is
a mistake, not only because there may be many meanings, but also
because clarity may help to question assumptions. When terms were
defined in this early approach, 'ethnicity' tended to be considered as

a sense of commonality and identity shared between a group of people, who also shared cultural traits such as how they celebrated certain rituals, what they ate and how they felt about life and death (McGoldrick, 1982: 4). In this way an ethnic group was seen as a group of people who shared a common culture, and 'ethnicity' became synonymous with 'culture'.[1] 'Culture', in turn, was seen as a collection of traits which were discussed as if they existed 'out there' in the world independently of people. Although hardly pursued, the idea that culture dictates to individual persons how they should behave, think, feel and what they should value was implicit in theory, if not always in practice.

Culture, politics and therapy

The approach which emphasises the need for information also assumes that such information can be used by therapists to help client(s). In other words it is assumed that after a while the expert will be able to comprehend the information and therefore do her job better. There are no serious qualms about the inequality of power between therapist (expert) and client in their interaction.

Much more recently approaches have developed which place this inequality and particularly its colonial roots at the centre of the therapy process. Accordingly, the therapist cannot be an expert on how people from different cultural backgrounds think and feel, especially when these people have long been dominated by the group to which the therapist herself belongs. If she is to do her job at all, the therapist can only do so with the help of cultural consultants who will make sure that treatment and interventions are isomorphic with the cultural values of the client(s). In this approach there is great respect for the cultural identity of clients and for the meaning of this identity. The process of therapy tends to be adjusted to mirror, as much as possible, ways of healing and communication found in the practices of the clients' own social and cultural context.

In family therapy, this approach may be exemplified by work carried out in New Zealand with the Maori and Samoan communities there (Waldegrave, 1990). This is perhaps the best example of culturally sensitive family therapy addressing not just processes within the consulting room but also general political processes in the community, and the relationship between the therapy clinic and the communities it is expected to serve. Here, culture is not so much a series of traits, but rather a body of ideas, which people hold and which shape the way they do things. It is defined as history, beliefs and ways of doing things, and is seen as the 'most influential determinant of meaning in people's lives' (Waldegrave, 1990: 15). Despite a difference of emphasis in what actually constitutes culture between this approach and the one described earlier, they both share a view of culture as a regulating device for individuals. Culture moulds and determines the way individuals experience and behave. And when oppressed cultures are treated with respect, it is whole groups of people who are empowered. Culture is a collectivity, to which individual persons adjust and conform. .

This assumption of uniformity in cultural identity and cultural meaning poses problems for family therapy and for mental health professionals generally. There is the danger of stereotyping referred to above and although such stereotyping may carry positive values, it may also violate individual needs and circumstances. A second problem is that while a positive emphasis on culture may empower groups of people it may have the opposite effect on individuals. Cultural values are not held equally by everyone who otherwise would define themselves as members of a given culture. D. Holland (1992) showed that when young American women clearly identified themselves as agents in a cultural system (of romance in this case), this system became salient for them. In other words, for most of the time we hold cultural values and ideas as general themes, which may have a range of meanings but which may not matter greatly to us. It is only when we see ourselves as agents in upholding or destroying such themes that we begin to feel strongly about them and begin to be experts in how to operate them. Thus people are committed to cultural norms to different degrees and therapists should check the precise status of cultural themes with their clients, for example, by asking 'Is this something which is important to you?'.

A third difficulty with the assumption of cultural uniformity is that it may in fact lead to discriminatory service delivery. This has been described for Puerto Rican families (Montalvo and Gutierrez, 1988). Increased cultural awareness easily replaces a sound common-sensical knowledge of basic human needs and wants and of diversity in normative frameworks. Indeed it may become politically correct to place primacy on culture and only secondary importance on general human themes. In this case 'the right to proper treatment, independent of ethnic affiliation, is superseded by the idea that proper treatment is possible only within that affiliation' (Montalvo and Gutierrez, 1988: 183).

Black clients – black therapists

It is often argued that many issues and pitfalls in the provision of services for ethnic minorities can be avoided if therapists and health professionals themselves are members of such minority groups. It is assumed that therapists from ethnic minority groups will have first-hand experience about the way cultural, political and general human themes intertwine. While there may be some truth in this and while it is also true that there are too few therapists and other health professionals from black and minority ethnic groups, there are other issues involved. Problems which arise between black therapists and black clients in a multicultural and multiracial society, both in the therapy room and in health service politics generally, have been well documented (Montalvo and Gutierrez, 1988; Thomas, 1992). But more importantly, if clients from ethnic and cultural minority groups are always treated by health professionals from the same backgrounds, health service management and white health professionals may find it easy to abdicate responsibility; inequality of health delivery may be promoted under the banner of equal opportunity.

If then there is no answer except to persevere with the development of models for cross-cultural communication and inter-cultural therapy, what can white family therapists learn from therapists who are black or from ethnic and cultural minority group backgrounds? In their writing and in their work, black therapists rarely elevate culture to a domain of communalism which transcends the minds and wills of individual persons. Indeed the most striking aspect of the work of black therapists such as Boyd-Franklin (Boyd-Franklin, 1989) and Aponte (Aponte, 1985,1986) is, first, the notion of variation in the normative framework of different families despite a shared cultural affiliation, and, second, the extent to which individual persons change, influence and reinterpret cultural themes. This view of culture as something *created* by persons through their interaction is often lost on white therapists even though it accords well with the practical and general goal of most therapies – namely to empower individual persons and their families to take charge of their own lives. In this view culture ceases to be only a regulating device for how individuals should behave and becomes a flowing body of ideas open for negotiation as well. The point is that culture is both, and that cultural meanings are never completely given or taken for granted. For each individual such meanings are constantly confirmed or challenged and redefined through interaction with others.

A double definition of culture not only allows empowerment of individuals and families, it also encourages therapists to consider general human issues alongside cultural ones, and to acknowledge that cultural patterns may produce dysfunction and unhappiness. It places responsibility on the therapist to strike an appropriate relationship with her clients, and importance on how the therapist goes about this process. Thus Boyd-Franklin advises all therapists working with black families to explore themselves, and to facilitate a careful and respectful joining phase with their clients (Boyd-Franklin, 1989) and Aponte has emphasised the importance of a negotiation of values between therapist and clients in family therapy (Aponte, 1985).

A FRAMEWORK FOR 'GOOD ENOUGH'[2] CROSS-CULTURAL UNDERSTANDING

The approaches outlined above have developed as the interest and awareness of how cultural and racial differences may be manipulated for political ends has increased. At this point in time, with an increasing awareness of the strengths of local communities and persons who given the right contexts are able to solve many problems themselves, it is possible to develop a more subtle model for cross-cultural work.

We do not know for sure where cultural differences between different people and groups begin or end. We know that there are differences, but we also know that it is possible to communicate cross-culturally. We know, too, that cultural differences can become politicised and imbued with power and inequality and that cultural themes may be vehicles for survival of both dominant and dominated groups of people. Whichever aspects of culture we see at work, we have no choice but to communicate with our clients through cultural codes. These codes are not rules and regulations cast in stone however. Rather they have a double existence, on the one hand as ideas handed down to us through our socialisation and learning to become persons, and on the other as ideas which we ourselves reinterpret in the light of the circumstances of our own lives.

There are three main reasons why therapists must find out or check their knowledge about the cultural themes and ideas of their clients *for themselves*. First, because culture is not a thing, but a framework of ideas which persons hold in their heads and which are interpreted and reinterpreted according to a particular context, and particular sequences of interaction with other persons. Most ideas are held abstractly, and only when they are salient to personal circumstances do they become activated. Second, because it is important that therapists and health professionals are aware of the status of the information they hold about other people. Without this awareness it is easy to stereotype and to disregard the variations in normative frameworks of any culture. Third, therapists must find out for themselves because finding out about differences by showing respectful and empathic curiosity is a way of joining and of negotiating a relationship with clients. Cross-cultural communication like any communication is always personal and context dependent.

Because culture is both a blueprint for behaviour, thought and feeling *and* a loosely structured body of ideas open to interpretation and reinterpretation by individuals, therapists – who no less than anybody else are influenced by both – must also adopt different strategies in their finding out about other cultures. They must assimilate information by themselves either by reading books about culture or by experiencing cultural processes at first hand. Such information may serve as a pool from which information about diversity may be drawn (Carrithers, 1992), but it will not provide easy answers. Answers can only be found through the more specific interaction which constitutes personal relationships, because it is only through personal relationships that we acquire embodied experiences of others and ourselves with others. Another strategy is thus for therapists to maximise and consciously learn from their relationships with their clients. Without this specific context the development of empathy and cross-cultural understanding would be impossible since this depends not only on cultural themes but also on gender, status, age or simply on a chance connection.

CROSS-CULTURAL PRACTICE: DEVELOPING A COMMUNITY-BASED SERVICE

The importance for institutions in becoming connected to and involved with the communities they serve has been emphasised by many writers (Chambon, 1989; Aponte, 1990; Waldegrave, 1990). The authors work in a small NHS institution with a multilingual, multicultural but predominately white staff group. It is an all-age referral service which deals with issues usually referred to child psychiatry or child guidance services or to adult outpatient psychiatry. In this institution there were both internal and external pressures to develop services that would reach clients in the community whose needs were not being met. Internally the service was undergoing a transition in raising its own awareness of the effects of institutionalised racism on maintaining the status quo, both in regards to staffing the institution and to the ethnic profile of the clients which the institution served. Externally, NHS management was seeking to increase the amount of outreach work provided to its patients. Despite increasing numbers of Bangladeshi families residing in the area very few had been referred and they had failed to keep appointments. Wishing to address this, one of the authors (AM) and a colleague[3] took up a referral of a Bangladeshi child, determined to learn how to deliver an adequate service.

The first case

Having heard from the referrer that this was a family of eight children under thirteen, the therapists abandoned the idea of inviting them to come to the service and made the first contact in the form of a home visit with the referring social worker and an interpreter (located with difficulty). In the house they met a couple who were very worried about their eldest son's behaviour and were told by the father, who spoke good English, that Abdul (13) had been raiding parking meters and had also been caught shop-lifting. More recently and more seriously he had set a fire in which he had just escaped injury.

During the first interview the mother spent much time out of the room tending to other children and in the kitchen. When she was present she sat on the other side of the room from her husband and questions addressed to her were largely answered by her husband. The interpreter (a man) also appeared to disregard the therapists' attempts to speak to the mother as inappropriate or irrelevant (they were not sure which). There was one daughter only, an 11-year old who appeared to be sharing the child care with her mother.

Using general family therapy principles, an attempt was made to connect with everybody, which included learning their names. The referrer, who had until then been working without an interpreter, called them Mr and Mrs Miah, but their laughter indicated this was not right. The therapists were unfamiliar with the naming system, so, accepting the family's apparent rule that father was the 'gate-keeper', they asked him to introduce his wife by name. The interpreter and family appeared both impatient and embarrassed and the therapists remained uncertain as to how to address the couple.

The therapists tried to include the young children, although talking to the little ones was quickly interrupted by the parents who clearly thought it was very odd. They also learnt that the parents were cousins, the husband was the eldest son of his own parents, and his father had died recently. The house appeared impoverished, but it was difficult to know whether this represented a step down or a step up in the family's sense of their economic position.

Despite the therapists' clumsiness, they empathised strongly with the fear and horror that everyone had felt at the possibility that Abdul might have died as a result of his confusion and foolishness. This, together with their expressed conviction that his parents (and not Social Services) had the key to his future safety, allowed the parents to accept help. The fact that the family's current dilemma had touched the therapists, and that the family knew it, was an anchoring point over the coming weeks and months.

The family work started with a general hypothesis that if the identified child was acting in an 'out of control' way there was a high likelihood of major conflicts between important adults in his life – possibly, though not necessarily, his parents. There was also an idea that his behaviour would be linked to important recent events impinging on the family, either internally or externally, and, since his paternal grandfather's death coincided with the point at which he had started getting into trouble, an initial hypothesis was that his behaviour may have some function in attempting to stir his father out of his deep depression by forcing him to focus on his own naughty behaviour. It also occurred to them that Abdul's behaviour had brought both police and social services to their door, and to wonder if there were any benefits for the family to this otherwise highly undesirable state of affairs, particularly in the light of the urgent nature of his most recent 'symptom'.

Although these ideas and the sympathetic connectedness which the therapists had managed to establish with the family proved to be important (indeed it later emerged there was major conflict between the parents), the therapists were handicapped by their uncertainty about cultural codes. They did not know what to call the couple, whether cousin marriages were considered desirable or not, whether the couple's behaviour with each other (sitting very separately and apparently not conversing or even looking at each other) was considered to be standard behaviour of a married couple in the presence of strangers, or whether it was a sign of their marital conflict. They were also unclear whether an 11-year-old girl taking a major share in child care was a common occurrence, or idiosyncratic to this family. Finally, they had not developed a relationship with the interpreter which allowed mutual understanding about their respective goals. Although all of these issues were subsequently clarified in different ways, the deskilling of experienced therapists when first working in a very different culture from their own has been well documented (Boyd-Franklin, 1989; D'Ardenne and Mahtani, 1989; Messent, 1992). The possibilities of being oppressive or offensive to the family are considerable at this point, as is the risk that the family might therefore reject the therapists' attempts to help.

As the work with the first family continued, the degree to which they were subject to crude racist attacks emerged. On one occasion the husband had just been chased home by a youth wielding a knife, and had only just been dissuaded by his wife not to take up a kitchen knife and turn on his assailant. In one of the many network meetings around the family (they had many problems including the delayed development of at least three of their children and a serious illness in another), there were at least fifteen professionals involved. Information about each child in turn was being shared, and the degree of racial harassment that the family was under was discussed. It looked as though this would be treated simply as yet another piece of information to be shared by the professionals, when one of the therapists started to feel that the potential for using the power of all these professionals to divide and disempower the family was so great, why would it not be possible to think about reversing that process and discuss how they could act to empower them.

Expressing this feeling led to a general discussion about the estate on which they lived – notorious for its degree of violence – and to the idea which was already forming that several of the professionals present, particularly those in the infant and primary schools which many of the children attended, should call a meeting of Bangladeshi residents and other members of the professional and local community to think about how to address the degree of racist violence on the estate. There was a lot of support for the idea, and it was agreed that Abdul's parents should be invited to attend it. It also became obvious that they should be at the next professional network meeting. In this way the individual family/systems work started to impinge on the wider system in ways that could empower the family.

Where much of the meaning of a family's way of being together cannot be taken for granted by the therapist, there is a danger of an interview being overtaken by questions related to understanding basic rules of family life. Perelberg (1992) argues that family therapists' assumption of familiarity with clients of the therapist's own cultural background is often mistaken, and that apparently familiar territory may turn out to be quite unexpected. Similarly, what we view as unfamiliar may have more in common with the therapist's own experience than at first appears. Perelberg argues that careful enquiry and observation within the session will lead to clarification. This fits well with the concepts of neutrality and curiosity described in the family therapy literature (see e.g. Cecchin, 1988), and with the double definition of culture referred to above. In addition, the dimension of the embedded power relations present in the encounter between white middle-class therapists and un-employed Bangladeshi families, means that the therapist needs to be aware of the effect of what can appear to be a therapist's ignorance of, or insensitivity to, basic assumptions of family structure and values. Cross-cultural encounters pose major challenges to therapists to revise their 'knowledge' when it contains mostly Western assump-tions about life cycle developmental tasks, the nature of marital relationships and the marital contract and ideas about personhood (Shweder and Bourne, 1982). It also brings therapists face to face with the impact of racism on the lives of their clients, and challenges them to respond to it.

Building a service

The tolerant forbearance of the first family allowed the therapists, through many trials and errors, to learn about them and their lives. Part of their understanding emerged from the family and another large part of it emerged from their continuing lengthy and wide-ranging conversations with the Bengali interpreters. A short time later, they took on another Bangladeshi family, which increased the scope of their enquiries and increased the circle of people outside of the two families who could help them understand more about the beliefs and practices of Islam, Bangladeshi kinship and naming systems, expectations of relationships between husbands and wives, sons and daughters, mothers and fathers, the history of migration from Bangladesh and the impact of personal and institutional racism on the lives of the families in this community. As their understanding grew, aided also by reading (Aziz, 1979; Kakar, 1978, 1982; Maloney, 1986; Adams, 1987), they decided that the best way to proceed was formally to set up a counselling service for Bangladeshi families and treat it as action research, with a view to establishing how best to meet the community's needs.

Figure 10.1 outlines the stages in the development of the service. Networking with professionals as to why they did not refer Bangladeshi cases to the service revealed several explanations. They included: 'they don't speak the language'; 'they mostly present with physical symptoms and don't seem to look for psychological explanations'; 'we don't see many Bangladeshis ourselves, they don't seem to have many problems'; 'they don't like to take problems outside of the family'; 'we don't think they would find it easy to travel outside the area in which they live, so they would not travel to see you'. As a result of these conversations, the therapists offered (a) to consult jointly with referrers at the place where the referrer was normally seeing a family member (GP surgery, social work office, school); and (b) to visit people at home, and to set up a regular day for consultation at the local (very accessible) health centre.

The service relies heavily on interpreters[4] for its functioning. Interpreters have a complex task as bi-cultural workers which includes an advocacy role. The collaboration works well when the therapists and the interpreters function as a staff group, in the sense of working together regularly and creating space and time for discussion and two-way learning and exploration.

The advisory group, in the form of a steering committee, which met for a year, consisted of the staff group, Bangladeshi professionals working in education and social services, and para-professionals working in local community groups. They discussed the kinds of issues that people in the community were concerned about such as poor housing, unemployment and the obstructive behaviour of the Home Office. They also described the many kinds of personal family problems in the community and the impact of racism on people's lives. These discussions confirmed the importance of the therapists attending carefully to the socio-economic problems they encountered in the clinical work, and they adopted a readiness to advocate for their clients with what they often experienced as unhelpful, uncaring, or impervious organisations. The steering committee was also consulted about a name for the emerging service. It was decided that terms related to 'psychology', with its suggestion of Western dualism between mind and body were

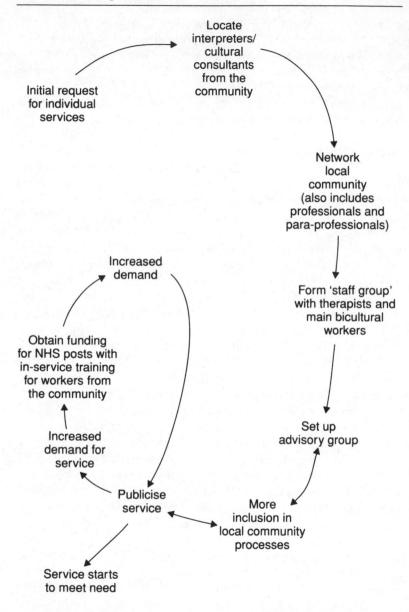

Figure 10.1 A model for the development of a community family counselling service

unsuitable and that 'counselling' was more in line with the communities' notions of advice which people might traditionally seek from the extended family, from elders or from the community. At the next stage, a public meeting for referrers, including voluntary agencies and community groups, was called. This publicised the service enough to get a steady stream of referrals. A brochure for professionals and potential referrers was also produced by the staff group in English and Bengali. The next step in this project is to recruit and formally train Bangladeshi workers to join the main service in mainstream posts. There are two reasons why we consider this step to be crucial in the institution's continuing provision of relevant services. First, it will empower the local community to feel confident in using their local service to help them deal with important family and health problems. Second, in the collaboration within the service, it should provide a mechanism for disseminating knowledge and experience about successful practices in working with clients from this culture.

Subsequent cases

In the first few cases the therapists relied more on their use of themselves and their curiosity than on their knowledge about different cultures – and they were helped by interpreters and the families themselves. However, in the many subsequent cases the therapists have been learning how to use the knowledge they have about Bangladeshi culture without this becoming a straitjacket. They have done this by using the framework for 'good enough' understanding outlined above, by connecting empathically to clients as persons and by carefully checking out family members' views. We have chosen two examples, one from Bangladesh and the other from Pakistan, to illustrate how we access and use their knowledge about clients' culture to guide our curiosity.

The case of Salma Bibi

This case illustrates how an attempt to understand the meaning people give to their lives and symptoms can provide a particular pathway towards finding solutions. Salma Bibi (approximately 38 years-old), was referred by her social worker who was concerned that she might be depressed since she had recently spent increasing time in bed, and was not looking after her nine children who all lived at home in a fifth-floor flat with no lift. They ranged in age from 21 down to 4. Her elderly husband explained angrily that his wife had stopped cooking and cleaning. He implored the therapists to urge her to return to her duties and when asked for his explanation for her behaviour he said she was *pagal* (mad). On asking him to explain further, he did so circularly in terms of her refusal to carry out her duties.

At first meeting, Salma looked extremely dishevelled, with her hair in a great tangle and her sari half hanging off, but she was lucid and calm. She had been in the UK for about three years, and missed her family greatly, finding life in this country very hard.

An initial tentative description of the current problem proffered by the therapist to Salma's husband was that Salma seemed to have so much to do she had gone on strike. At this they both laughed uproariously and his position softened somewhat. He now explained that she had been very worried about their 14-year-old daughter who was being pursued by a local man who wanted to marry her. They did not want the match but were feeling extremely pressured by it – to the extent of recently sending the girl away to distant relatives. Salma's level of self-care had further deteriorated at that point. What she did not say was that she was in the final stages of her tenth pregnancy! She had the baby shortly after, a little boy, and there was a professional network meeting to discuss whether or not this baby was at risk. Their views of the problem are summarised in Figure 10.2. As can be seen, in the wide variety of explanations for Salma's behaviour almost all implied a negative construction of her.

While the later stages of pregnancy would have been an understandable reason for taking to her bed, Salma herself eventually gave a different explanation which emerged in the following way. After the first forty days of her confinement, she started to think about when she might go out for the first time. The therapist asked her who would she get to help her untangle her hair. She said she would not ask anyone to do that because her hair was *jata* and she would have to go through a special ceremony. She explained that her hair had gone into an immediate tangle after she had stepped in the shadow of a *pir* (holyman) and the meaning of this for her was that she had become a special person who would cease normal duties during the period for which this lasted; it would end only with a ceremony at which, amongst other things, her hair would be sorted out. This explanation was clearly news to her husband but its implication was that she would not leave this state until she had returned to Bangladesh to see the *pir*.

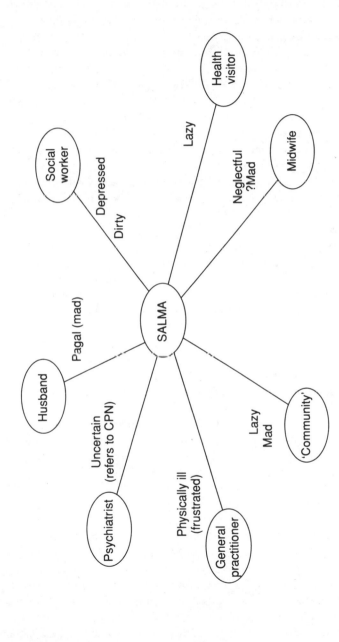

Figure 10.2 Different constructions of Salma's behaviour

She did not seem ready to elucidate it further but now that her own particular meaning had been brought into the conversation it was possible to explore some of the underlying disagreements between herself and her husband, including the original disagreement about whether or not to have a tenth child. She had been against it but had not really felt able to exert her will about it. As it happened she was now very happy with the baby, but the prospect of dealing with him on her own (that is, without the help of the women of her extended family) was daunting. In fact she had never had to bathe a baby before, because that had always been the job of someone else in the family. Her husband had bought a plastic baby bath, but she felt very anxious about using it. At the suggestion of the therapist he filled it with water and then helped his wife to give the baby his first bath. A few weeks later the family returned to Bangladesh for a visit.

Salma's symptoms of confining herself to bed and of her tangled hair and generally dishevelled appearance and the suggestion in her own explanation of a connection with holiness constitutes an expression of a general theme, well known from Bengal and the rest of the Indian Subcontinent. It is the theme which connects symbols denoting madness (*pagalami*) with symbols denoting salvation (*moksa*) (Bhattacharyya, 1986). The ecstatic ascetic exemplifies this unity. The ecstatic ascetic is someone who withdraws from the world of social and especially sexual relationships and who, in return, as a gift from God receives matted locks (Obeyesekere, 1981). The really committed ecstatics denounce all sexual relationships and inflict on themselves great pain as a proof of their union with or marriage to God, but in all cases the symbol of the tangled or matted hair points to the experience of emotional turmoil or painful emotional experiences (ibid.: 33). Salma was thus using a culturally recognised and to her perfectly rational symbol to communicate her upset. Her tangled hair bestowed her with a special status which meant that for the moment at least she was aloof from the ordinary world of cleaning and cooking. It also created a special and powerful identity for a woman who felt particularly disempowered in many aspects of her life, including her daughter and her pregnancy. If this explanation for Salma's predicament was privileged above all the other explanations the solution was also to be found within the same body of ideas. That is to say the family would have to go to Bangladesh.

The therapist's intuition about Salma's predicament and her knowledge about *pirs* and the context of women's lives in Bangladesh, together with the interpreter's additional knowledge about the prevalence and valuing of ideas about matted hair, gave them good grounds for accepting Salma's explanation as a rational one, and subsequently empathising with her as a woman. This acceptance in turn made it possible for Salma's husband to regain confidence in his wife in this new and unfamiliar context. In this way the therapist was able to avoid the potential dangers of either major social work intervention – possibly involving removal of children or psychiatric intervention – possibly involving admission and a labelling of Salma's state as a (Western) psychiatric disorder.

The Khan family

The Khan family was referred to one of the authors following Mr Khan's assault on his 11-year-old son. He had burnt his hand on a hot iron and as a consequence social services had placed him and his three siblings (two brothers and a sister) on the at-risk register. The family's social worker was requesting ongoing work during which it would be decided whether it would be safe for the children to remain in the family.

Mr Khan (52) was an unemployed alcoholic and Mrs Khan (35) worked part time in a chemist. The couple had been in England for sixteen years and despite the long time had not made many friends. They and the children visited Karachi, which was the most recent home of Mr Khan's family, relatively frequently. They were Punjabi Muslims and spoke Urdu as well as very good English, while the children, like so many of the second generation, understood and spoke Urdu but prefered to speak English.

It quickly became clear that everybody in the family considered Mr Khan to be the problem. Mrs Khan described how for so many years she had been left unsupported by her husband to deal with the children, his alcoholism and life in England by herself. She said that she thought that nothing would change until Mr Khan controlled his alcohol problem. This was echoed by every one of the children who all urged their father to control his alcohol intake. Mr Khan himself told a sad story. He was the eldest of ten siblings and often used to get into arguments with his father. He left his parental home as a young man and came to England. Here he worked as a watch salesman and was involved in other small business ventures. He did quite well, was able to buy his own house and provide well for the family until eight years ago when he went bankrupt.

Losing everything materially also meant that he lost his standing and the respect he could previously command both in his own eyes and in the eyes of others. This was when his alcohol problem began in earnest. Burning his son's hand had been an attempt to assert his parental authority which had gone drastically wrong. Now that social services had become involved he was in danger of losing his parental control altogether and with that also the respect and status which despite all, he was enjoying as a man with four children.

It seemed to the therapist that the family was sliding down a twisting spiral: the more the children and Mrs Khan asked Mr Khan to control his alcohol intake the less he felt respected since this broke the rules of hierarchy and order within the traditional Punjabi family. As a consequence the more likely he was to get drunk, which in turn would prompt renewed calls for control and so on. In fact even if he did not drink there were hardly any sources of respect left for him in his life in England. It seemed that this was a cross-cultural predicament with many unresolved aspects.

During the first few sessions the therapist was struck by the repeated use by all members of the family of the words 'respect and control'. The words were uttered in English and yet the way they were used suggested differences from English meaning. Mr Khan was not encouraged to control himself by his family, rather his wife and children asked him to control the alcohol. Similarly although Mr Khan had lost respect, it was not so much a question of him doing something extraordinary to prove himself, but rather a question of others realising that despite adverse circumstances he deserved respect as a man, as a father and as the head of the household. With this idea that the Khans were using English words with Punjabi meaning in mind, the therapist decided to explore the trans-context or the two relevant settings of this family (Turner, 1991:408).

She began this in an early session by exploring how things might be different if the family were living in Karachi. The couple explained that it would be a different world: Mr Khan would probably not be unemployed because his vast network of relatives would help him find a job, he would also receive advice from his many uncles and brothers and Mrs Khan would not feel isolated because the women in the extended family would give her support. After a little while they made clear, however, that this did not mean that they were striving to go back to live in Pakistan. This conversation established to everybody the unique position of the family: it was a family handicapped by the absence of normally available relatives and support systems, yet the values which the couple held and which they would like to pass on to their children still assumed the presence of such support. This meant that they would have to find the resources which normally would be provided by a whole range of people from inside this little unit and mostly from inside the marital relationship.

This opened an avenue for a negotiation between the husband and the wife in the sessions in a manner which would have been unthinkable within the traditional Punjabi framework of family values. Conscious of this the therapist returned to her hunch about the words 'control' and 'respect' and enquired about the Urdu terms. There followed an interchange about *kabu karna* (control) and *izzat* (respect) in which the Khans explained to the therapist the differences between the English and the Punjabi meanings. Gradually in this session and in subsequent ones these concepts were referred to by the couple and by the therapist using the Urdu terms, and in this way the words became symbols of the family's position in two cultural settings.

First, Mr and Mrs Khan agreed that while the husband is the head of the family, his *izzat* (respect) places on him an obligation to take the well-being and wishes of his wife and children into account. Second, during several subsequent sessions they were able to negotiate between themselves so that if he was to *sherab nuu kabuu karna* (control the alcohol) he would need her to talk to him and let him know more about her own feelings and thoughts than they had hitherto been accustomed to. In the absence of a network of male relatives this would denote *izzat* to him. Although Mrs Khan found such direct communication with her husband difficult (in line with Punjabi codes of conduct) she eventually adopted what was for her a new style.

In these sessions the therapist was consciously trying to create an atmosphere in the therapy room which was a mixture of Punjabi and Western themes. The couple had not found a new way of functioning in their new setting. Their London life incorporated many Western ideas which only superficially resembled those with which they grew up. A closer scrutiny revealed important differences particularly in the area of connectedness between relatives (Tamura and Lau, 1992) and in context dependent thinking (Shweder and Bourne, 1982). *Izzat* and *kabu karna* are salient themes in this respect (Krause, 1989) and the use of the Urdu terms in the negotiation between husband and wife became a metaphor for the particular predicament of Mr and Mrs Khan.

As it happens the therapist was knowledgeable both about Urdu and about common Punjabi concepts. This helped both her curiosity and her ability to ask questions at opportune moments. However, as suggested in the framework outlined above, she also needed to ask questions in order to gain an understanding of the particular predicament of Mr and Mrs Khan. When therapists are not familiar with the relevant language and concepts we suggest that they let their curiosity be guided by the family's choice of terms. This requires alertness and sensitivity to language which although sounding familiar, denotes quite different culturally constructed themes of meaning.

SUMMARY

Family therapy is well positioned to address cross-cultural issues and the dual definition of culture both as a blueprint for behaviour, thought and feeling and as a changing body of ideas open to individual interpretation accords well with the aim of most family therapists, namely to empower their clients to take charge of their own lives. In practice this implies that therapists must gather for themselves anthropological and cross-cultural knowledge. Such knowledge cannot be used directly; it can serve as a pool of information from which a general intuition about cultural diversity and themes of meaning can be drawn. To conduct successful therapy, however, therapists must in addition make personal relationships across cultures either inside or outside the therapy room. In a similar way, context-specific connections are needed between mental health institutions and the local communities they are intended to serve.

ACKNOWLEDGEMENTS

The authors wish to thank Hosneara Moobin, Mary Bibi, Hasmat Ara Begum and Meena Malik for being patient teachers, and Dr M. Nasirullah and Dr Bindu Prasad for their encouragement. Also, Harvey Ratner with whom the CFCS was started, and Dr Alan Cooklin for helping to create a context for cross-cultural work. Finally, Joan Garcia for help with the preparation of this chapter.

NOTES

1 See Barth (1969) and Ingold (1986) for the difficulties with this conflation.

2 The use of the phrase 'good enough' is not intended to suggest a mother/child relationship between therapist and family. It is intended to suggest that cross-cultural communication, like any communication, is a reflexive affair and that it is enough of a starting point for therapy that the understanding of the therapist meets a minimum to which clients can react and respond and by which they feel encouraged. In this sense cross-cultural communication requires a 'fit'; it does not require that therapists are able to see things exclusively 'from their clients' point of view'.

3 Harvey Ratner, senior social worker.

4 The interpreters with whom we originally set up the service, Hosneara Moobin, Mary Bibi and Hasmat Ara Begum, and more recently Meena Malik, have taught us an enormous amount about sensitive communication, who can talk to whom about what in the presence of whom, common child-rearing practices, marital and family relations and above all the enjoyment and appreciation of Bengali life.

Chapter 11

Psychotherapy in the context of race and culture: an inter-cultural therapeutic approach

Lennox Thomas

Culture and race are very important in terms of both assessment and treatment when working inter-culturally in a multi-ethnic society. The client may try to escape their implications in some way or the therapist similarly might be in some confusion about her/his own culture and background. The notion of a psychotherapist as (culturally) 'neutral' and/or not needing to be aware of her/his own racism is common. An encounter with such a therapist may not be helpful. Claiming neutrality on the therapist's part puts the client in a difficult position because the therapist has thereby divested herself/himself of those things that might connect with the client's culture and background, be this positively or otherwise. A therapist who claims cultural neutrality also robs the client of the opportunity to speculate or to make observations about the therapist's background, particularly if this has an effect on the therapy in terms of connection or fit.

Some White professionals have great difficulties in hearing the racist experiences of Black people – probably because of their fear of hatred in the transference. This fear usually mobilises defences characterised by comments like 'but this country has always been generous to immigrants' or 'but of course, racism always works both ways'. At this point, the professional is no longer a therapist – basically a caring and containing 'parental' figure – but a squabbling 'child'. It is often in the areas of racism and sexism that professionals working as psychotherapists are at their weakest and not in a position to help their clients who might not only turn to them for solace, but to understand how their inner structures have responded or accommodated these external realities of racism and sexism.

It is most important for a therapist to develop a system of assessment and treatment which not only acknowledges differences – including cultural differences – in the therapeutic or assessment process, but actually uses the differences to sharpen or fine tune the instrument of the assessment. The traditional psychotherapeutic principle of 'hovering attention' in assessment is quite helpful, and would make it possible for the therapist to keep in mind assessment factors pertaining to race, culture, gender and other contextual or power issues. This approach to an inter-cultural assessment relies on a grounding in psycho-analytic theory and a solid understanding of assessment. But the therapist has to keep in mind many issues before meeting the client for the first time. For example, when a client walks into the consulting room to be seen for the first time, it is important to make oneself available to the mental checklist of things that might be needed in order to explore a range of issues in the assessment.

The assessment is very important because it is used as an accelerated method of opening up material for later work with the client in the on-going therapy. If (say) on going therapy is being done on a twelve session contract basis, the process of assessment serves to make material accessible for the limited time available to see the client in therapy. It may be possible to renegotiate a further twelve sessions, but if at assessment there are indications that brief therapy will not be helpful, it may be possible to refer some long-term clients and others to agencies that could see them for longer periods of time.

The experience of working with long-term clients often provides a therapist with the skills to work in an accelerated way with brief therapy. It is very difficult to teach professionals the skills to work the brief therapy method if they have not had the experience of managing or sustaining longer-term therapeutic relationships with very disturbed clients. One has to know the areas to look at and to focus on effectively.

The first part of this chapter discusses questions of culture and race as they apply to the intimate relationship established in the consulting room, illustrating their relevance to psychotherapy by describing parts of case histories of clients seen at Nafsiyat, the Inter-Cultural Therapy Centre in North London, where the author has worked for several years. In the second part, this chapter discusses some specific issues of both a practical and theoretical nature that have impressed the author during his work at Nafsiyat.

RACE AND CULTURE IN THE CONSULTING ROOM

Inter-cultural therapy must be prepared to make a real acknowledgement of the social reality of race and racism. For example, the image of Nafsiyat as an organisation that aims to work with Black and ethnic minorities, addressing questions of persecution, racism and other discriminations, renders it a place where clients see themselves as not being further persecuted by their therapists if they were to talk about their experiences of racial abuse and racism. In fact, clients who have attended Nafsiyat have talked about work with previous therapists who have asked them whether or not they had experienced racism, only to silence them when they began the painful task of recounting these experiences. For example, one counsellor was reported to have suggested to a young Asian man that he had a chip on his shoulder, as a possible explanation for his repeated failure to be promoted at work and being by-passed by other White workers. Whether or not he was a suitable candidate the 'chip on the shoulder' remark is not a useful explorative stance for a therapist to take. This pejorative term is associated usually with the blaming of Black and other peoples, who are unaccepting of the systematic racism in their lives.

It is the responsibility of the therapist – the professional – to bring differences into the consulting room, one of which is race. We cannot allow the client, who might be frightened by the power that we have, always to raise these issues. It should be our duty to ask the clients whether or not they feel comfortable and if they are worried about the issues surrounding our race or skin colour as therapists. It is most important that therapists can give clients permission to talk about racial persecution or discrimination, since they are the people with the power in the consulting room.

There are times when the consulting room has to encompass several different cultural influences. The therapist's idea of being free of any entanglement with the client's culture can sometimes hamper therapy by leading to very difficult transferential relationships later on. The therapist's culture may be predominantly 'British' or, as in the case of the author, it may be derived from the experience of having been raised in a British culture with the vestiges of parental Caribbean culture, and the remnants of an African culture which would have been familiar to the grand-parental generation. There are many different points of understanding and ways of seeing both the outer and inner worlds of such a situation – some culturally specific ways of being in the world which parallel religious or philosophical views.

Because various cultures have different views on the inside and outside, the client's perception of the ways in which situations are dealt with in the family network may vary. For example, a person from a Western background might be much more in tune with the nuclear family (of mother, father and children) than she/he would be with an extended family, while an African or Asian person, raised in her/his culture of origin, might expect to see herself/himself as part of an extended family and so place great emphasis on relationships with a wide range of family members. It might be the case that the grand-parents have much 'say' in the family, and would be relied upon to perform functions, such as the bringing of wisdom or reason to a situation; mediation between the generations; arranging marriages; consulting astrologers or arranging special prayers. The importance that different cultures place on family members, the aunts, uncles and grand-parents might be very different to a British nuclear family's way of thinking. If the therapist fails to take account of all this, the potential for movement or change during the period of assessment or treatment may be missed.

Questions of particular importance to the family could be overlooked because the therapist may not have seen the extended family as having some integral part of the individual or family's treatment. A therapist might not ask the 'right' questions because of an unawareness of these, due to the constraints of her/his own culture. The lack of understanding of other people's cultures can at times be at the root of much conflict or lack of engagement. For example, in Asian and African cultures, it is more acceptable to talk about one's acquisitions, about money or one's aspirations. For this, it would not be unreasonable to expect a pat on the back, perhaps even an enquiry about one's earnings. In Western European societies, this sort of talk could invite accusations of boastfulness and talking, for example, about money or wanting to buy a prestigious car, is unlikely to be rewarded; in a British cultural setting, such talk is likely to invite comments about 'over-reaching' oneself, since modesty and not talking about possessions is more often seen as appropriate and acceptable. So, a meeting between people of very different cultural backgrounds in the therapeutic situation can lead to a great deal of confusion where (for example) one is conditioned to be open and honest about aspirations, while the other has learned to perceive such behaviour as boastful. However, the real situation is much more complicated: while modesty may be seen as a quality to aspire to, it may also be seen as a cultural response to the fear of being envied or tempting fate by being so open and wishing for so much.

Moreover, culture is dynamic and changing and is not a fixed monolithic entity.

Thinking of culture as pure and unadulterated must be avoided, since culture is like life itself, changing and mediated by a variety of factors. Even in families with many close racial and cultural similarities, there are likely to be differences in the ways that members of those families organise themselves into their own family culture. There are certain rules and rituals in families which dictate how much can be discussed with outsiders. This can depend on the type of personalities in the family; for example, social class, ages of children in the family and stages of the family life cycle.

Generational changes in culture undoubtedly exist although there is also continuity of culture across generations. In view of this, there needs to be some understanding of the young people who were born in the UK of Asian, Caribbean and African families. To some extent they form their own cultures, which are different to those of their parents. This cultural emergence is formed by the young people's day-to-day struggle to exist in a society which denies them certain rights, provides them with some opportunities but often does not give them the chance to contribute fully to the society they see as their own. These social and class issues inform their 'culture'. Out of this total experience is born a conceptual understanding of the mental and material existence which gives rise to its own language – its own particular English. This language is part of the sense-making of a generation of people who are British born and part of the wide spectrum of 'Britishness'.

English is the language most often used in inter-cultural therapy. Being a part of the dominant culture and language (or at least perceived as such by the client) the therapist may at times have difficulties in hearing what the client is really saying because of the differential use of English and the issue of power. However, working inter-culturally may require the therapist to conduct therapy in the client's first language. (For example, therapists at Nafsiyat speak at least one other language in addition to English; there are at present thirteen languages spoken at the centre.) If it is not possible to find a therapist who speaks the client's first language, an interpreter may have to be used. When this happens, the therapist can often be presented with complex issues of meaning, since language and communication, being important indicators of emotional and mental states, are essential tools in psychotherapy and counselling.

CASE STUDY 1

Mrs P was a depressed Brazilian woman. Both she and her husband were employed in the travel business in Brazil before getting posted to London for a few years. Mrs P insisted that she would leave her husband if he did not agree to this move. This came about as a result of Mr P's many affairs while in São Paolo. The final straw for Mrs P was discovering that her husband was having an affair with her best friend. She said that she felt like a totally different person since discovering this affair and that she had been 'murdered' by her husband. She mentioned this a couple of times in her session and the therapist was not at all sure what she was saying. Even though Mrs P's feeling state appeared dead and sealed off, it was difficult for the therapist to see this as meaningful and he was very worried about the psychotic content of her thinking. The therapist thought that she did not know the difference between real and unreal, dead or alive. The therapist, seeking to clarify the situation, asked her what she meant by her husband having 'murdered' her. She said: 'Well, I feel as though when he had the affair with my friend, that I was killed.' The therapist puzzled for a moment, then said: 'Oh, I think I understand what you mean. In this country, I think we might say that it was like having our legs cut out from underneath us, or being gutted, or losing one's right arm.'

Comment

It was interesting that when Mrs P used an expression incorporating 'murder', this set up in the professional some thoughts on whether or not her processes were becoming psychotic. What the therapist missed was the use of language which did not particularly have a relationship with reality or unreality, but the client's expression of a grave act perpetrated against her from which she feared she might never recover. She did not describe this as 'being killed' which obscures culpability, but she talked about having 'been murdered' – an expression that implied that a deliberate act had been committed. While the term 'being murdered' might have seemed a strange thing to say, the feeling she experienced of being 'wiped out' was a fact. The concern about Mrs P going into a psychotic mode of communication was understandable. One approach to clarification may have been to have asked Mrs P if this was something that might have been said by other women who had been so hurt and cheated in her own country.

It is interesting in the fine tuning of language how people, using it as a second language, sometimes express feelings more vividly because the skill of censorship has not been sufficiently developed. One is at an advantage in one's first language about precise words which are chosen to express or conceal, but in the absence of this skill, one might be better able to express more clearly those feelings that come from the 'gut' (in figurative English) as opposed to what comes from the intellect. Whether or not feeling as though one's legs had been cut out from underneath one is quite the same as being murdered as a result of infidelity, seems not to matter. The importance for the therapist and client was that a connection was made. The therapist was able to acknowledge the figurative speaking and thinking that was part of the client's repertoire, which would have been difficult to translate.

CASE STUDY 2

Mr D, a young man, wrote requesting therapy for depression, nightmares and an inability to function. He had been a promising student of engineering, while seeking asylum in this country. He wrote to Nafsiyat in neat handwriting in English, stating that he could only have a French-speaking therapist who had some knowledge of his native Zaire. We were fortunate at Nafsiyat to have a French speaking male therapist with a vacancy to see him. This therapist reported that Mr D spoke perfect English and perfect French and they conducted the assessment session in French. Mr D was an asylum-seeker having left Zaire after the slaughter of close political friends. In escaping from the country, he left behind a dear long-term girlfriend, close family and a promising legal career. He was now depressed and on the verge of leaving his engineering course. He was isolated, craving the company of others from his country, and at the same time, fearing involvement in case this might lead to disagreement and further persecution on political grounds in this country.

In the client's second session, he spoke both French and English. The therapist noticed that the emotional high and low tones were expressed in French, and the rest in English. The therapist was puzzled by this, since Mr D had been quite insistent on being in therapy with a French speaker. In the third meeting, the trend continued and Mr D spoke only English. This situation was brought to the clinical discussion group.

Comment

It was considered that the client might have stressed the importance of language in order to get a therapist with a cultural backdrop which could give him a context, perhaps because he felt that his English was not good enough as a means of emotional communication. Other speculations were that he might have found the use of English to have been a useful means of distancing himself from the difficult task of dealing with tragic past events; to speak French perhaps was too spontaneous or immediate for him. The therapist thought that his seeking a French speaker was perhaps his (the client's) way of testing himself on his readiness to deal with what had been left behind. He added that his hunch was that this young man might have developed an uneasiness about him (the therapist) in the transference, because of the possible connections with the French colonisers, since he spoke their language so well.

From the experience of working with refugees who might have been persecuted because of ethnic or religious status in their country, the repetition of that persecution in the form of racism in this country can be quite devastating – as shown by high levels of mental breakdown and suicide in this group. The discussion of this case made it clear that exploration of the client's safety in the sessions with the therapist had not yet begun and probably needed to take place soon. Such a situation is a very real one for those fleeing political violence and persecution, and it is extremely important that the therapist gauges the degree of the client's apprehension or fear quite accurately. In this case, although language was used as a selection criteria for a therapist, the issues raised were not just about language but many others connected with it.

EXPERIENCES AT NAFSIYAT

The organisation of Nafsiyat has developed over many years – changing to suit the needs of a multi-ethnic clientele who often feel very disempowered. Two practical issues are discussed here in some detail – the question of ethnic matching (of therapist and client) and the use of advocates. More general issues that have arisen in providing psychotherapy services for Black and ethnic minorities are then discussed briefly.

Practical issues

The situation at Nafsiyat is that some therapists are Black, some White and all come from a variety of cultures. We work in this way because we believe that it is possible to work with a mixed gender, culture and race team. This presents us all with a challenge. Some of us are on the receiving end of racism, some are from groups with the power to perpetuate racism and others from groups who have previously experienced racism but are now left as inconspicuous minorities, not affected personally by racism. We all have a relationship with racism by the fact that we have a racial identity which has its place in the social pecking order of current racial and cultural supremacy. In a mixed team, discussion and analysis of clinical material is most important since the openness and honesty of its members can help to discover and unlock some of the hidden complexities of race in the counter-transference.

The use of advocates extends the notion of empowering the client so that they are better able to gain access to therapy because the power of the therapist is mediated by another person. It is a way of working developed out of practice as a result of clients finding it difficult to express themselves to the therapist or even to feel comfortable being in the same room. After discussions in the staff group very early in the formation of Nafsiyat, it was decided that not inviting the client to bring a person of their own choice to act as an advocate in therapy sessions might partly relate to the therapist's fear of being exposed, and in part reflect a worry of straying away from the orthodoxy of the psychotherapeutic setting. Clients who are uncomfortable or unable to say what they want to, can bring a friend to help them express themselves more effectively or simply to be there as a support. The friend will be able to mediate the power of the therapist by being in the room and having a role to perform. The client who had hitherto perceived the therapist as frightening, remote or cold has as a support a trusted friend who could help them to understand and explain certain things in the therapy. The friend will be there to support them, act as a prompt, remind the client to say what might have been forgotten or overlooked. The advocate could intervene directly, to disagree with a particular way that the therapist has seen or expressed something in the treatment.

The client is allowed to bring the advocate to all the sessions or some of them, whenever they choose. Interestingly, clients tend not to bring spouses, lovers, children or parents. It is usually a good friend, a trusted health or social work professional on whom the client can rely. From our observation clients choose not to bring family members, probably to regulate the degree of involvement that the family might have with their difficulties. Whether or not an advocate attending with the client can be used as a barometer for measuring engagement or comfort with the therapist has been a subject for speculation. If a client does not bring the advocate, it might indicate that he or she is able to tolerate the sessions and the therapist in the first instance. If the reverse happens and the advocate is brought back to the sessions following an absence or two, it might indicate that the client is not quite at ease, and we would have to think about what might be contributing to this unease. An analysis of the dynamics could reveal that the therapist and his or her power is overtaking the client, that the client is not happy about facing imminent traumatic material in the therapy or indeed that they might need someone to talk to in order to make sense of the content of the session after the therapeutic hour is over. The range and diversity of people coming for psychological help at Nafsiyat and the timing of the sessions can often mean that transferential situations develop quickly and intensely.

Nafsiyat can often be experienced as the last port of call or the only place that might be able to help particular clients. This may be the experience not only of clients but also of the person(s) who have referred them. Accordingly, great store can be set on the therapist as the person who might help where others have failed, or alternatively, as yet another person who will be unable to understand or help the client. It is most important that the therapist has well-developed skills in working transferentially and can therefore assist in the analysis of the interactions that take place between them. In addition to the client's transference and that of the therapist (counter-transference), the concept of the pre-transference has been very useful to us (Curry, 1964).

Race, gender and power

Sometimes clients feel that they need permission to talk about certain things, as they sense the therapist's unease in this area. Fearing that the therapist might not be capable of dealing with the issue, they feel that they have to tread carefully so as not to upset him or her. In such a situation it is clear that clients are facilitating the professional, and this is not their responsibility. The *professional* should facilitate the *client*, making her/him feel at ease in exploring sensitive issues. This situation is parallel to that of Black people making White people feel at ease by telling them how non-racist they might be, or women comforting men by telling them how non-sexist they are. This provides no challenge for either men or White people, and without challenge, the opportunity for entering into the necessary processes of reflection, self-examination and change is usually denied.

The exploration of gender issues in assessment is important, not only for discovering information about the client's history, identity and psychological development, but for the client's negotiation of safety in the consulting room with the therapist. It would not be helpful for a female client to sit through therapy with a male therapist whom she was afraid of, in terms of her personal and physical safety. Not only can this create *impasse* in therapy, it can also be damaging to the client's self-esteem and further disempower her in other situations where she might have used her voice and her personal power to negotiate safety. In these circumstances the therapist will have neglected the client's total position as a woman and as a person seeking empowerment and psychological help. This therapeutic situation creates a conundrum, since in the external world, the client might have been sufficiently skilled to select which train carriage to sit in or bus stop to wait at in order to protect herself from unwanted attention, assault or the fear of both.

During assessment many issues to do with past discrimination may be raised. The therapist may introduce the possibility of gender issues as a topic that the client (male or female) might like to bring to future sessions. For example, the senior nurse who wanted to become an engineer while at school but was discouraged, reflected on how courageous she was as a girl: she felt that she had to mourn the loss of that young girl in order to align herself to the tough choices that she had made in her life. Men have come to assessment and talked about why they think they have never been able to cry or have always had instilled in them the rules of 'being a man'.

One example is that of Kamal, a 22-year-old man born of Kashmiri parents in the Midlands, who came to assessment having written a letter which referred to his not having any sense of direction in his life. Kamal described a happy childhood – he and his two sisters had had a great deal more freedom than other members of his extended Muslim family. He had good relationships with both his professional parents and siblings. He said that now, in adulthood he felt like a different person, quite unlike the person he was in his early childhood. He felt as though he was empty inside, 'not depressed' he hastened to add, but empty, not knowing what to do in his life. He performed quite badly academically and unlike his sisters did not have higher education. He said that he was 'lonely as a teenager'. By the time he was 12 he said that his life had changed and his parents – particularly his father – said that he was 'not allowed to cry'. There was no playing with his sisters and it was made clear to him that 'this is what boys must now do'. He felt as though he had lost a whole part of himself. He was no longer part of his sisters' games, he said that he could 'always hear them laughing and playing' through his bedroom window and that his 'life had just drifted away'. The gentle upbringing that he had shared with his two sisters now prevented him from integrating as a young man. He wondered whether or not psychotherapy could make him into the sort of person who could laugh again and whether or not he could enjoy his sisters' achievements. He felt that his sisters had got everything out of life and that he had nothing. He envied them so much, not only for what they had achieved, but also for what they were as people, confident and happy.

It is important that power issues are analysed in the assessment, taking account of gender, race, disability and social class. Since power organises the way that people behave towards each other in society, it should not escape the full rigour of the psychotherapeutic assessment. With power now on the agenda, there is also a legitimacy for the client to consider how the therapist fits in with and relates to their own reality of power or powerlessness. It is only then that therapy can really be effective, so that what makes up the client's identity is an integral part of the therapy and that opportunities for developing transference are enriched with many possibilities for connection. Being in therapy with a client who is too frightened to speak to the therapist is not only pointless but counter-therapeutic. The personality of the therapist needs to be welcoming, warm and available. If structural or contextual differences between us have made communication difficult, then the very foundations of the relationship must be analysed in order to empower the client who might then be able to access the therapy.

Differences between the client and the therapist can at times lead to a closing off of possibilities to work together. For example: an African-Caribbean male therapist was conducting an assessment interview with an African-Caribbean male client. The latter was quite distressed, feeling that his partner of a couple of years did not understand him and that he had some thoughts of ending the relationship. He said that he remembered his childhood when his parents would put him down or make him feel stupid and that his partner did exactly the same thing. He said that at times, he wished he could break up this pattern, which he had developed, of suffering in silence. The therapist, having become curious about how his partner behaved asked 'can you tell me of times when she is tolerant or more accepting of you?' At that point, the young man's face became frozen, the seconds of silence in the room seemed much longer and the therapist then realised that he had foreclosed on the client, having made an assumption that the partner was a woman. Since the young man had not said specifically that he was in a homosexual relationship, the therapist had assumed that he was heterosexual. The other dilemma for the client was that his choice of when to speak openly about his sexuality was being decided for him, he had no assurance of the therapist's safety or whether or not homophobia – common in society at large – was going to be present in the consulting room with him. The client who was now exposed had to make a decision to go along with the heterosexualised assumption about him, or to speak about something which was very personal, the timing of which was not decided by him.

In assessment, other people have talked about their experience of being class-misfits, having lost connection with their families through the process of education and professionalisation. This has often created a conflict which, externally, informed people of their importance and social power, but internally accused them of being frauds, with the concomitant feelings of shame and unimportance. While many have resolved the situation by intellectually deconstructing the notion of class, the pain of the estrangement from their family often remains.

Stereotypes and transference

Before meeting the client for the first time, a therapist often has a mental picture of the client. This is particularly problematic in a society where people from the minorities have a negative description in the majority culture. If for example, Jewish people or people of African or Asian heritage have a particular description based on stereotypes or negative projections, then it is difficult to separate out the individual from the group. If one's client is from a minority group about which society has a collective descriptive term to which we ascribe a negative social and psychological position, then long before we meet, our pre-transference to the client operates by presenting those pervasive and well-known descriptions. Pre-transference is such that we, as professionals, raised in the context of racism or discrimination, might think that we know the individual client. Having a notion of 'we know the client' might mean that we are developing our familiar responses to those constructs which are part of society and which have now become part of our own thinking. If our pre-transference is not analysed in conjunction with our counter-transference, then we can convince ourselves that we know something about our clients — sometimes before they have even presented themselves for therapy. The unconscious store of pre-judices and projections has to be worked through before we really encounter the real person in therapy. The powerful lure of the stereotype or projection does not find the therapist immune (Thomas, 1992).

Children and adolescents

The concept of identification by proxy is probably difficult to grasp. It is one of the ideas developed as a result of working with a large number of children and adolescents of Asian, African and mixed racial heritage. Some of these children had previously been seen by psychotherapists and other professionals for both assessment and treatment. Many of the children exhibited difficult, disturbing, withdrawn or hard to manage behaviour. Children and young people are referred to Nafsiyat by parents, school psychological services, social workers and counsellors in further education. Parents often reported that their children had attended child guidance for some time, often years, and saw psychotherapists there. Other children had attended special units for children with behavioural problems. Many recall little of the experience or activities with therapists and they often barely described the room where they were seen. What emerged however from some of the children was a pattern in the way they related to the White therapist whom they were seeing.

While for some children communication with the White therapist was unproblematic, for others it emerged that there was little real communication taking place. These children would see the White therapist and communicate with them by putting forward a 'proxy self'. This communication by proxy served the function of protecting the Black child in a society where adults or people with power over

them might be harmful to their psychological and emotional development. By virtue of being a minority in a majority White society, the
child knows that White people have to be 'selected' because some
hurt and hate Black people, while others do not. The child's secret
survival guide, which all Black people have experienced in society
to some extent, is used in order to keep safe. That White people have
to be divided into 'nice ones' and 'ones that you avoid' is a fact in
the internal world of the Black child. In the child's eyes, White
people have to prove themselves to be nice, since the avoidance of
hate is most important in order to preserve self-esteem. Since looking
at White people will not let one know who the nice ones are, life for
the African and Asian child is a matter of taking a series of calculated
risks. They have to rely on their antennae to pick up any sense of
being liked and accepted or otherwise. The concept of racism as the
possible organiser in this behaviour in White people is something
not clearly understood by young people. What is understood at this
age is the notion of fairness and unfairness, and these children know
that what is being done to them is not fair. Sadly, however, some
children are not always sure that racism communicated by dislike or
rejection is not their fault.

To varying degrees, the children of African and Asian heritage
have learnt a way of protecting themselves from rejection, hatred or
attack by screening those White people who have power and
influence in their world. Many young people have described in an
alarming degree of similarity the uneasiness of being a child in the
presence of a White teacher, school dinner lady or bus driver for
example, whose dislike or even hatred of them is such that it is
difficult not to notice. What has surprised them is the fact that other
White adults had not picked up on or noticed the antipathy, and
therefore had not sought to make the situation safe for them.

Miss R, a young student nurse, described her experience of being
raised in a London suburb, one of only three Black children in her
school. She said that putting up with racism in the other children was
not difficult, she learnt how to deal with this. But the racism
experienced from the other children's parents was unbearable. She
remembers one of the other children's mothers in particular, who
regularly called her 'nigger' and told her to go back to her own
country, while casually waiting to collect her own child at the gates
of the infant school. What was shocking to learn was that some other
parents who were present when these incidents took place did not
intervene to help the child, nor was the matter reported to the school

head, anonymously or otherwise. It is not surprising that this young woman now has difficulty relating to some of the White tutors on her course; she finds them untrustworthy and insincere, and although she had a serious grief reaction following her mother's death, and needed some therapeutic help to deal with this, she could not trust her White tutor to talk to about this.

Miss R said that 'after the first few verbal insults, the abusive woman at the school gates no longer needed to say anything further' to her. The sum total of non-verbal communication said exactly what she needed to say from that time onwards. She was so easily controlled by fear and hatred and could tell no one. Her earlier attempts to tell her White foster mother caused her too much upset, and Miss R soon learnt that it was something she had to suffer in silence.

What many of the children who come to Nafsiyat have not been able to understand is that it is not because they were bad or naughty that White people sometimes did not like them. In time, such children learn to protect themselves by projecting the proxy as a part of the self which is usable by anybody, but devoid of the real child and her/his experiences. This false self might be made up of the character-istics that White adults find easy to identify with – perhaps being like the White children in the breakfast cereal adverts or the soap commercials. Being a pretend White child is part of a psychological contortion that a Black child might have to experience in a White society. Putting forward the proxy and protecting the real self is part of the Black child's bid to preserve himself/herself as a whole. It is this split, which enables the child to survive, which can at the same time give rise to disturbance in the child's personality. What is left for debate is whether or not the splitting is pathological or healthy, and whether or not the unfacilitating environment is 'sick' because it has let down the child of Asian or African heritage.

In therapy a relationship by proxy will be in place until the White therapist is considered 'safe', or until the White psychotherapist has developed the sophistication to recognise and analyse the inter-action, the splitting and the manoeuvres that the child has employed for self-protection.

In order properly to access education, television adverts, etc., where White people seem to appear exclusively, the Black child has to pretend a little at times to be White. When these images in educational or advertisement material are mixed, the Black child will develop some legitimacy to be him- or herself. White psychotherapists working with Black children need to understand the dual world that the Black and ethnic minority child occupies. The therapist has to be able to encompass the Black child's total experience, to be aware of their social existence and to know that the revelation of the real self is something that the child will only do when some safety has been established. What is interesting is that the child who has internalised a negative Black self identity (Thomas, 1992), and has learnt to be wary of other Black people, will also have a proxy self in relationships with Black therapists. What is useful about this relationship is that Black psychotherapists, from their own experiences, will be able to identify the operation of the proxy self as a move for self-protection, and will be able to engage with it therapeutically. Those Black therapists who dismiss this child using pejorative terms like 'coconut' or 'bounty' are themselves in the process of struggle to reclaim their own Black identity, since those terms usually serve the function of disavowal or projection.

If the White therapist is found to be a safe person who can see the child in his /her own right, then the task of finding a resolution to the presentation of the proxy can begin.

In Figure 11.1 the relationship between the Black child and the White therapist has just started, and direct communication between

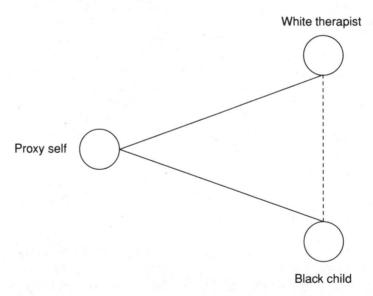

Figure. 11.1 White therapist and Black child: initial position

them is not as strong as the communication between the White therapist and the proxy self which is put forward. From the Black child's viewpoint, the real self has to be protected until he/she has the measure of the White therapist or until the therapist has expressed something of an understanding of the child's dilemma of being in the consulting room with him or her. Protection from misunderstanding or let-down remains until the child's keen observation skills give confirmation that it might be safe in the room with the therapist.

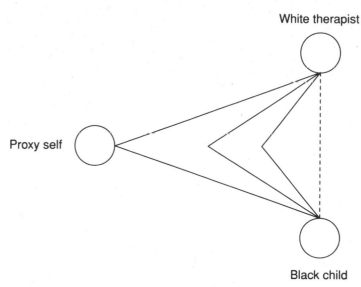

Figure 11.2 White therapist and Black child: intermediate position

In Figure 11.2 communications are becoming more direct and the White therapist is beginning to be experienced as safe, reliant and reliable enough to be used by the Black child. Now the child is able to express feelings and ideas that are closer to the real self to see if they can both bear it. During this process of allowing the White therapist into his or her world, it is always possible that the child may return to the earlier modes of communication. Sometimes it may seem as though progress has been made and there is more openness with the child, at other times it may seem that the fragile progress is reversing and the proxy is being used once again to obscure the child's real feelings.

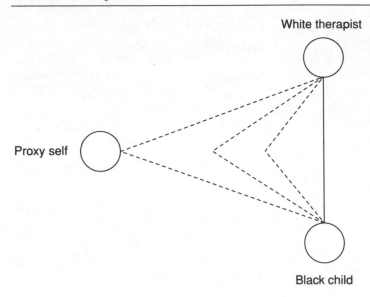

Figure 11.3 White therapist and Black child: ultimate position

Figure 11.3 shows that, although direct communication is now possible – indicated by the bold line between the White therapist and the Black child – the history which made direct communication with the therapist impossible remains. At this point it is possible to use this history to help the child understand it for him or herself. If we were living in a racism-free society, there would be no race obstacle for Black children to overcome on the route towards therapy with White professionals.

Experience at Nafsiyat shows that, for psychotherapy in a multi-ethnic society to be successful, the following conditions must be fulfilled: first, the role of an advocate accompanying a client needs to be addressed carefully; second, there is an obligation on the therapist to facilitate the exploration of sensitive matters around race, culture and gender – and to do so in the context of power issues, both within the therapeutic relationship and in society in general; and finally, in the case of young people, issues of identity have to be analysed, taking account of race so that obstacles to communication are overcome.

Part III

Seeking change

The first part of this book examined the current setting in which mental health care is provided *vis-à-vis* the multi-ethnic nature of society, the meaning of health and illness, etc. The second part considered ways in which issues of importance to community care in a multi-ethnic society are being challenged. Using the insights gained from these two parts, this final part postulates possible ways of working in a constructive and imaginative fashion so that community care for mental health may be suited to the needs of a modern multi-ethnic society.

Chapter 12

The way forward

Suman Fernando

As mental health care shifts from hospital-centred care to care based in the community, new ways of working are being developed. However, this does not mean that the past is necessarily left behind. For one thing, its aftermath, illustrated and described in Chapters 1 and 2, is all around us. The first part of this book indicated the serious problems facing any professional who wishes to play the game of community mental health care in a manner that is fair and equitable to all sections of the community. Clearly the playing field is far from level – especially for people from black and minority ethnic communities. As Chapter 3 pointed out, changes in the law in itself are of limited value – and, in any case, the pressures for change are not necessarily to do with improving the law's sensitivity to cultural difference and racism. In fact, some of the pressures (e.g. for compulsory treatment in the community and for supervision orders), if sustained, may well result in a worsening of the type of inequities currently suffered by black and minority ethnic communities described in Chapter 4. Although people from these communities often turn to voluntary bodies to make up for the deficiencies of the statutory services, Chapter 5 painted a grim picture of the difficulties faced by the black voluntary sector.

Although the basic issues are fairly clear, ways of confronting them are piecemeal and disjointed. It was clear from Chapter 6 that, although the black user movement is emerging, it is not as organised as the user movements involving the majority white communities. And Chapter 7 indicated that, although race equality training should be an essential element in the training of professionals, it is no panacea for racism institutionalised in the structures and systems that constitute mental health services. The conclusion to be drawn from the accounts of innovations within the statutory services described in Chapters 8, 9, 10 and 11 is that, although traditional theories and ways of working may not be all bad, fundamental changes are necessary in professional practice if service provision in the mental health field is to be relevant, appropriate and just in a multi-ethnic society.

This third part of the book examines ways in which change can be pursued in several crucial areas, at theoretical and practical levels. Unfortunately, powerful forces are at work attempting to maintain the status quo in terms of the style and ethos of service provision set over many years by professional groups that have dominated the organisation of services, namely psychiatrists and psychologists. Certainly this domination is being eroded, but the power structure of the next phase is far from clear. The likelihood is that managers of health and social services will play an increasingly prominent role in determining service structure and even day-to-day professional practices. However, there is little evidence to suggest that health service managers are any better placed to deliver fairness and equity, especially if (as is likely) they are primarily accountable to political masters rather than professional bodies. The voice of service users lacks power. If the lessons of the past are not learned adequately and if the injustices and deficiencies recognised in the *present* system are not fully addressed, the likelihood is that the *future* community-based care will be as neglectful of the real needs of people with mental health problems as institution-based care ever was. A real fear in this respect in a multi-ethnic society is that institutional racism coupled with cultural insensitivity, evident for many years in the practices of psychiatry and psychology, will be reproduced, perhaps in different forms but with equal tenacity.

The seriousness of cultural and racial issues in the provision of mental health care is fairly clear, but the way forward in tackling these problems is far from evident. If, as seems likely, the problems stem from the fundamental racism embedded in society, the usefulness of instituting changes limited to health services is sometimes considered problematic. However, I suggest that health services should not be just a reflection of society at large. If anything, health, especially mental health, should be about correcting the ills of society that cause stress. A mental health service in New Zealand working with the Maoris (Waldegrave, 1990) designates their therapy as 'just therapy' – on the basis that justice and mental health go hand-in-hand. This principle, which should underlie all mental health services, has special relevance in a multi-ethnic society.

Unfortunately, the institutions that supervise the practices of the main professional groups involved in mental health care, namely the Royal College of Psychiatrists (RCP), the British Psychological Society (BPS) and the British Association of Social Workers (BASW), do not appear to be addressing issues of race and culture to a significant extent, possibly because they are inherently conservative bodies. However, the Central Council for Education and Training in Social Work (CCETSW), set up directly by the Government, has taken a lead in giving directions on anti-racist practices to social work training.

The way forward is considered in this chapter in several aspects. First, the meaning of what we should understand by 'mental health' requires analysis in order to bring about some unity of purpose among professionals, service users and the community at large. Second, 'diagnosis' needs replacing by a new way of assessing individuals presenting for help, so that they are seen in a family and social context in relation to socio-political systems that they are involved in. Third, therapy – as interventions (by professionals) – must be underpinned by a socially realistic understanding of the realities of life in a modern multicultural society, the meaning of 'culture' as incorporating modern thinking about racism, and the significance of the power wielded by professionals in the name of expertise. Fourth, in order to achieve justice and fairness for all ethnic groups in society, a multicultural approach to mental health service provision must be *anti-racist*, taking on board a contemporary understanding of what 'culture' means and the 'new racism' that dominates British thinking in the 1990s. Finally, needs assessment for mental health problems should take into account those aspects of life that are of significance to the person concerned, rather than 'observations' made by professionals. Underlying all this, indeed for any of this to be effective, there must also be an honest and realistic alliance between service users and professionals.

The picture of an enlightened model of mental health, incorporating a system of assessment that is in touch with the realities of life, leading to socially just interventions worked out in an alliance between service users and professionals, is one ideal that is worth pursuing. Another is that the statutory and voluntary services supplying mental health care are coordinated together and incorporate anti-racist movements within their structures so that they serve all sections of the population equitably. Finally, the third ideal is that service provision is planned and structured on the basis of needs assessment which, both at an individual and at a population level, is informed by social and political realities, including those of racism and cultural differences in society.

A NEW MEANING OF MENTAL HEALTH

The asylum grew up out of a need to establish social order, and society in general was content to leave social rejects to specialists on the basis that their problems had been defined as 'illness'. This state of affairs is changing. The medical domination of thinking about mental health and the domination of doctors in the organisation of services are both seriously questioned. Minority cultural groups (minority that is in a British context but often far from being 'minority' in a world context), people who experience feelings (such as the hearing of 'voices') traditionally attributed to 'illness', some clinical psychologists questioning the concept of 'psychosis', and a host of others, all have something to say about the question of mental health. Users of mental health services are demanding changes in the way help is delivered to people suffering mental health problems – identifying psychiatry itself as a part of the problem. The illness model with its concepts of schizophrenia, manic depression, etc., arose from, and may have been suited to, an institutional, segregationist approach to mental health care. It is unlikely that this same approach suits a model of care centred in the community. It needs to be recognised that 'community care' is not about applying institutional models in the community – or it should not be; it is about different ways of thinking about people with mental health problems living in the community. So, while traditional psychiatry has something to teach us about mental health, we really need to get away from thinking in terms of illness models alone if we are to get to grips with community care.

Kakar (1982), a Western trained psychoanalyst who lives and works in India, states that the term 'mental health' is 'a rubric, a label which covers different perspectives and concerns, such as the absence of incapacitating symptoms, integration of psychological functioning, effective conduct of personal and social life, feelings of ethical and spiritual well-being and so on' (p. 3). In a multicultural society, the thinking derived from Western psychiatry has limited value. Ideologies from other cultures freed from racist judgements must play a significant part in developing a meaningful understanding of mental health for practical purposes. I suggest that we adopt a pragmatic approach, not wasting much time and effort in trying to clarify meanings of words and trying to work systematically from theory to practice. Developing community care is not an academic exercise – it is political action concerning real people, and professionals can help and participate in this venture if they have the proper training or retraining.

The model for mental health needed for service provision is really a very practical one. Essentially it is about issues involved in making life better for people and communities, helping people to cope with stresses or find ways of relieving stresses, deal with emotional problems and generally get on with their lives in as fulfilling a way as possible. Of course such a definition begs a lot of questions – for example, what is a fulfilling life? The dimension of illness prevention should not be ignored, for whatever we think about the genesis of the concept, 'mental illness' exists as a social reality, just as racism exists, or poverty exists. So mental health workers may need to use the illness model for supporting people whose lives have been shattered by being treated as 'ill' for many years – namely those designated as the 'chronically mentally ill'. Vulnerable groups may be identified in relation to pressures in society giving rise to needs that mental health services have to meet. Although the illness model may be needed in individual instances, thinking and planning in terms of 'illness' should be replaced by a consistent method for needs assessment, and the understanding of 'mental health' geared to the action of providing for need.

In implementing mental health care, social and political realities of life and service provision in a multicultural society have to be addressed. It is necessary therefore to recognise the power wielded by the police, the influence of institutionalised racism, and the part played by the psychiatric system (as a constituent of the mental health care system) in enforcing social control. Although psychiatrists have a function in promoting mental health, they are not the main people concerned in this, and perhaps psychiatric expertise is not really geared to health promotion anyway. Promoting mental health through community care is basically a job to be done on the basis of what one might call 'informed common sense', casting the net wide. In this way users of the services have as much say as those who are employed to deliver them; questions of housing, employment and family life become integral parts of what mental health means. Most of all, the effects of discrimination and the processes involved in perpetuating racism, sexism and the other 'isms' that underlie discrimination must be addressed in promoting mental health.

The social realities of contemporary life in a multicultural society must be taken on in an understanding of mental health for practical use in service provision. A clear definition (of mental health) is not necessary, but an understanding of mental health must be based on a historical perspective of psychiatry, especially the influence wielded by the medical model used in defining mental health/illness – a model that has little meaning in non-Western cultural traditions. Multiculturalism should be seen as reflecting the multicultural nature of society as a whole, rather than as a basis for locating any particular person within a fixed cultural group (see pp. 205–208 and also Chapter 1).

In looking for a model of mental health to work with, it is no use turning to experts in 'social psychiatry'. The term social psychiatry has been applied to systems which vary from those based on a strictly medical understanding of illness to the very opposite (sociological) model, which sees illness as an entirely socially constructed label for dealing with social and personal deviancy or rule-breaking (see Chapter 1). Perhaps instead of reaching for some definition of ideal mental health, we should think in terms of helping people to achieve and maintain some form of variable stability. Active interventions to prevent destabilisation can then be thought about, and surely, the concept of illness-prevention may be involved. In other words, I do not think that we can completely get away from continuing to use the illness model at times for individuals, and we should not get too carried away into aiming at some ideal state of mind for everyone. However, when it comes to planning services for communities and individuals, thinking in terms of 'illness' merely confuses the real needs of people living in the real world – and that is what service providers should be concerned about meeting.

Service provision should be about needs of people in the real world. Thus, it should target vulnerable groups (i.e. those whose circumstances merit special consideration), and people whose needs are not being met, institute systems of support, and generally aim to relieve acknowledged stresses. In practice, services must address the realities of people's lives, their limitations and handicaps in dealing with the demands of society, their family life if they have any, homelessness if they are on the street, their wishes and ambitions, the prejudices they face, the ways in which society treats them, their spiritual well-being and so on. Services may well be modelled to respond to distress, crises and problems, rather than symptoms and illness. But providers should not – must not – just wait for people to come forward as users. There has to be 'outreach'. One of the deficiencies in the institutional model of care was that people in need had to fit in to the type of service provided (by specialists), for otherwise no help was forthcoming. There is a danger that all that 'community care' might do is to shift the base from the large institution to the smaller 'resource centre', and perpetuate practices developed in institutions. Service provision based in the community has to deliver services that are appropriate for the life-styles and cultural patterns of *all* people needing care in the community, not just the majority, or those with most influence because of their class, gender or race. And individual differences in needs must be addressed as well as group differences. All this of course has to be set in a context of what is practicable, cost effective and feasible in terms of qualities and abilities of the service providers.

Community care must also face up to what is happening in psychiatry as an institution, challenge the pressures on psychiatry to be even more restrictive than it is, and protect people who may get caught up in discriminatory processes involved in compulsory orders or the inequities in access to services; an equitable service must face up to the collusion between psychiatry and the police, the use of high dose medication, etc. Our mental health model has to address all these issues – in short the realities of life in modern Britain, with its turmoil in inner cities, its homelessness, its racism, its oppression whether in the home or in society at large, etc. – in fact all the ills in our society, if it is to underpin services that are practical and useful. The model must be about real lives of real people in the real world. Mental health promotion must be about encouraging, if not actually ensuring 'integration of psychological functioning, effective conduct of personal and social life, feelings of ethical and spiritual well-being and so on' (Kakar, 1982: 3). But we cannot ignore, must not ignore, the fact that needs vary a great deal, and like it or not we will always have in our community people grappling with serious mental health problems – whether we call it illness or not.

A MULTI-SYSTEMIC APPROACH TO ASSESSMENT

The traditional psychiatrist, conceptualising problems in terms of illness, causes and remedies, carries out assessments in a sort of straight line as shown in Figure 12.1. The disadvantages of this approach are evident in many of the chapters in this book.

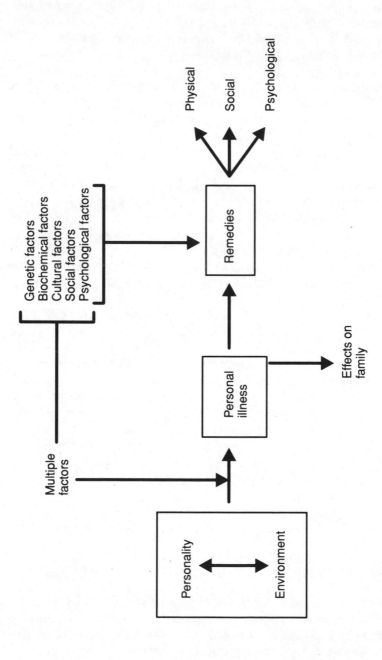

Figure 12.1 Traditional psychiatric assessment

The adoption of a relativist position with respect to concepts about mind and mental health would open up psychiatry to other ways of thinking apart from the traditional illness–cure approach based on a predominantly biological model of human beings. This means, in effect, a cultural and social open-mindedness in understanding mental processes and the aims of 'therapy'. As Jerome Bruner puts it, 'a willingness to construe knowledge and values from multiple perspectives' (1990: 30), acknowledging that what is appropriate in one setting may not be applicable in another. Consequently, the current concepts of mental symptoms must be redefined in terms of (say) 'mental health problems' and the concept of therapy re-evaluated in terms of (say) personal and social interventions – or better still, enabling strategies. This would bring it in line with the sort of thinking needed for community mental health work.

I am not suggesting that we disregard the knowledge within Western psychiatry about the medico-biological dimension of human behaviour, emotions, etc. – that we throw the baby out with the bath water; it is just that there are many baths and many babies – and let's face it, the bath water of psychiatry does need changing. In other words, let us try to put Western values and Western ways of doing things in a global, trans-cultural perspective.

Kleinman has proposed what he calls 'the new transcultural psychiatry' (1977: 3) in which culturally determined explanatory models form the context for an ethnographic assessment that gives a culturally meaningful understanding of symptoms. Apart from seeing an individual's perceptions, emotions and behaviour in terms of their symbolic meaning, problems identified by individuals or families must be seen as reflecting their positions *vis-à-vis* various systems – primarily of course the family system, but beyond that, the judicial, the educational and even the psychiatric system, on the lines suggested by the family therapists Boyd-Franklin and Shenouda (1990). Such an assessment would allow interventions at multiple levels, not excluding the individual level, and is shown in Figure 12.2.

In the model presented in Figure 12.2, the identification of mental health problems linked to a distress-coping model is the basis for starting an assessment. But this central theme is related to a family systems analysis and, more widely, to political and social systems such as education, welfare, policing and psychiatry – the particular emphases depending on the socio-political-cultural context of the individual case. So instead of disorders of thought, belief,

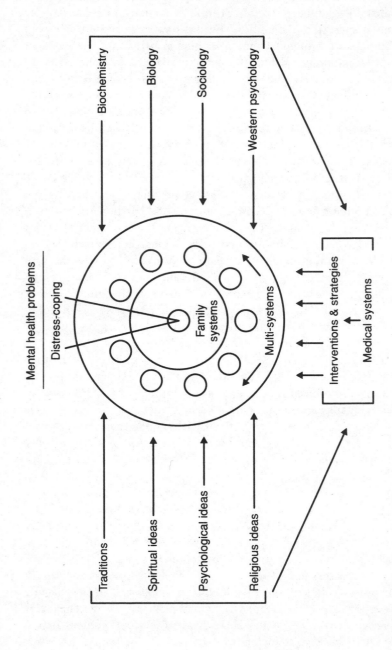

Figure 12.2 Relativist multi-systemic assessment

relationships, behaviour, etc. being analysed as personal illness, we would be identifying problems in thinking, problems in relating, etc., and analyse these in terms of their meanings in a multi-systemic framework. In this analysis, culturally determined explanatory models and information from biology, sociology, etc. (available in Western psychiatry) must be fed into the assessment system.

I believe that this 'relativistic multi-systemic approach' to identifying and analysing mental health problems encompasses a wide range of dimensions but yet addresses the distress of individuals. Such an assessment can form the basis of a range of interventions focused on the individual, the family, or other systems, geared always to the specific needs of the people concerned, seen in the context of the systems they are involved in. This approach is suggested as a way forward to enable psychiatrists to be confident about dropping the illness model while leaving a sound base for psychiatric practice.

How to change?

Strategies for change are as important as the changes themselves. Changes in ways of thinking about human problems often come from ways of working in the field. I suggest making alliances with healers (using the term 'healer' in a wide sense) from Asian and African cultures, and putting resources into developing what are generally called 'complementary' or 'alternative' therapies, but without attempting to take these over – to Westernise them. We can thereby become sensitised to concepts about illness and health held by all sections of our multi-ethnic society, rather than being irrevocably wedded to the current psychiatric dogma about illness, claiming that Western ideas alone are 'scientific'. Objectively speaking, of course, such a claim is not really justified for, as Capra (1982) has pointed out, the ideas and hypotheses (such as those of psychiatry) based on Newtonian physics and Cartesian philosophy are no longer necessarily 'scientific'. Once psychiatry and clinical psychology begin to move into taking account of non-Western cultures, many other changes will occur inevitably. However, in order to make the first moves, the blocks arising from racism need to be overcome. And for that, the disciplines and the professionals working in them must understand the nature of the beast (of racism) and then confront it with anti-racist measures.

THERAPY: THE INTERVENTIONS OF PROFESSIONAL WORKERS

Therapy has acquired a specific meaning in the field of mental health, closely tied up with the concept of illness used to explain mental health problems. The limitations set by this (ethnocentric) meaning of therapy are reflected in the meaning given to the word 'therapy' in *The Concise Oxford Dictionary* (Sykes, 1982) – 'a medical treatment of disease'. The traditional approach of 'giving therapy' in this way is clearly outmoded and also inappropriate in the setting of a multicultural society. The professional activity of professionals (*vis-à-vis* service users) today is best conceptualised as 'interventions' that are helpful, but interventions in which the user plays a crucial and active role. The term intervention then too becomes insufficient, since the process may evolve into a joint venture akin to self-help. Take for example the use of meditation. It may be taught (i.e. intervention) but then becomes self-sustaining (self-help).

The 'care' in mental health care is generally taken to mean the environment in which therapies (interventions) are delivered; a medical definition would be a 'treatment setting'. Thus, care would cover the support systems installed, the networks set up, the safety net provided. But the concept of care too has cultural variations. The traditional Western approach of separating care for physical disabilities from that for mental problems is not universally acceptable. In many cultures, people's social and spiritual needs may be seen as integral to a holistic concept of care that includes mind and body (see Chapter 5). Therefore, mental health services need to take on a holistic approach by including in its remit 'care' for various problems traditionally differentiated as 'social' or physical' or even 'political'. Services based on overall Western approaches to care are not to be dismissed, but it is essential to adapt these for the needs of a modern multi-ethnic society. The work of the Maudsley Outreach Service Team (Chapter 8) shows how the vulnerable and most needy members of society can be engaged if the approach is sensitive to social issues including racism and cultural difference. And the White City Project (Chapter 9) shows the importance of a political dimension to care in the case of people who are discriminated against, disempowered and demoralised. Chapters 9 and 10 show that family therapy and even traditional psychoanalytic psychotherapy may be of use if implemented sensitively with a recognition of current needs.

In a Western setting, a professional approach to therapy usually implies setting strict limits of personal involvement. But in some cultural situations, it may be very important for the professional who is responsible for the interventions to be seen as personally involved. In such a situation, the therapist's attempts to establish professional 'distance' would be perceived by the recipient of therapy as a rejection. For example, many Asian people may not approach professionals who take an extremely detached approach, seeing them as 'off-hand' or uninterested. Further, therapists may need to share their own views (e.g. about social and racial issues) with the people they wish to help, before any progress could be made in gaining the confidence and trust of their clients. The aim of therapy may then resemble, or actually become, joint social action.

Integrating therapies or their equivalents from non-Western cultures as interventions appropriate to the 'new' approach to mental health requires some thought. The traditional Western therapies fall into two broad groups – physical and psychological, the former including medication, electroplexy (ECT), etc., and the latter various forms of psychotherapy, counselling and behavioural therapies. However, interventions derived from other cultures do not fall easily into the same categories. A religious ceremony or fortune-telling may be supportive or even curative (if seen in an illness model) but concerns spiritual matters and belief in power over the future. If a specific 'technology' from one cultural milieu is used in a different one, it may require adaptation – a matter discussed more fully elsewhere (Fernando, 1991).

Thus, in a multicultural setting, professional interventions and care may be perceived very differently by different persons and families. Interventions or social actions proposed by professional workers must be clearly defined to service users, and information about their use (and abuse), legal limits and ethical considerations shared openly with them. Further, professional practices must be structured in a balanced way, to heed the voice of service users, their families and society at large, giving special attention to people and groups in our society that are vulnerable and/or discriminated against. Professionals need to be flexible in their 'limits' of involvement with clients. The seeking of help in some cultures is a personal matter and not a 'clinical' one.

UNDERSTANDING CULTURE

The statement that British society is multicultural is usually taken to mean that there are (culturally) distinct groups of people living in a (culturally) pluralistic society. And the implication inherent in such an assumption is that each group has different needs in terms of mental health care. While accepting that Britain contains within it people who trace their origins to various parts of the world, I take a different view. Clearly, individual families have (family) cultures, and some families may resemble other families in terms of some of their cultural attributes; but the recognition of a common, community culture for each 'cultural' group of people (Asian, African-Caribbean, etc.) does not reflect accurately what is actually the case – except perhaps in extreme instances such as that of socially isolated religious minorities, such as the Hassidic Jews. Nor is such an approach useful for the purpose of planning and providing mental health services. To argue that each cultural group should be considered 'different' is to accept the contention, rejected by homi bhabha (1994), a leading thinker on contemporary culture, that minority cultural groups in Western society have '*pre-given* ethnic or cultural traits set in the fixed tablet of tradition'. homi bhabha goes on:

> The social articulation of difference, from the minority perspective, is a complex, ongoing negotiation that seeks to authorize cultural hybridities that emerge in moments of historical transformation. The 'right' to signify from the periphery of authorized power and privilege does not depend on the persistence of tradition; it is resourced by the power of tradition to be reinscribed through the conditions of contingency and contradictoriness that attend upon the lives of those who are 'in the minority'.
>
> (1994: 2, emphasis in original)

In contrast to the usual perception of relatively fixed 'cultures', I would argue for considering 'culture' as something that is subject to a fluidity of movement, and for cultural difference as the product of various forces impinging on people. 'Culture' of a group is something that 'emerges' from society at large, including historical heritage, but by no means dominated by traditions. This approach to culture is not just more accurate in terms of what is actually the case in British (and indeed most European and North American) societies, but it is also more realistic in terms of models of 'cultural difference' on which the planning and delivery of mental health care should be based.

In simple terms, groups seen as 'cultural groups' in Britain are not socially isolated from each other and mental health needs of an individual cannot be deduced by reference to his/her culture any more than to his/her place of residence. A person's (or family's) cultural group may say something about the mental health needs of the majority of people seen as belonging to that particular 'cultural group' (just as the residential address may do in terms of housing, deprivation, etc., or as gender may do in the case of some types of need) but no more. On the contrary, it would be very misleading to make assumptions about mental health needs of individuals (or families) by reference to their broader 'cultures', because this often leads to stereotyping. The stereotypes of the all-caring Asian family may well have arisen because (by Western standards) Asian people were judged to have 'close' families, but it is a common experience of Asians that their needs are ignored on the basis that social support should be left to 'the family' (Webb-Johnson, 1991).

The notion of culture as 'a movement back and forth, not making a claim to any specific or essential way of being' (Renee Green quoted in homi bhabha, 1994: 3) has consequences for psychological evaluation of people and families from minority ethnic communities. First, concepts, such as 'culture-clash' and 'cultural dissonance', that come easily to professionals as explanations for the mental health problems of people (or families) from such communities, lose their impact; these concepts are seen as no more applicable to people from minority cultures than to those from majority cultures. Second, as 'culture' is seen as 'emergent' rather than fixed by tradition, the questions to be asked (in providing mental health care) are about the forces impinging on the groups of people identified as 'cultural groups'. These may relate to housing, education, racial attacks, police harassment, family interactions, etc. It is not a specifically 'cultural' approach that is needed – with emphasis on identifying 'cultural factors', cultural stresses, etc. – but one based on 'need', based in turn on the experiences of these groups in contemporary society. Of course the needs have to be interpreted in terms of the person or family concerned.

Finally, a mental health worker, faced with someone from a culture unfamiliar to the worker, is now freed from the task of evaluating exactly what the particular culture (of the client) is like, and from attempting to obtain specialist knowledge for this purpose. The professional can therefore concentrate on analysing the needs of the individual (or family), the source of any knowledge that is needed for interpreting need being the person or family itself. In other words, the identification of need and its analysis can be freely conducted by working out with the client(s) the latter's perceptions of need to be integrated into a language of mental health. The difference between this approach and the traditional cultural approach of obtaining knowledge of 'culture' before assessing need (seen as something 'special'), is that here, 'culture' does not form the basis of the approach in the first place, although 'culture' would play a large part in the final analysis.

ANTI-RACIST MEASURES

The fact that racism is integrated into British society means that judgements made about 'culture' are naturally affected by attitudes held about race. And racist notions of culture are pervasive in professional training and professional work in general. Therefore the incorporation of anti-racist measures in all aspects of work is essential – in training professionals, in developing their modes of assessment, and in their interventions. This is no simple matter however. Anti-racist training carried out in an insensitive manner may merely provoke resistance and, worse still, complacency, but to avoid the subject because of the possible drawbacks is no solution. The argument sometimes raised – that anti-racism merely perpetuates racism – does not stand examination. Non-resistance is not an answer to evil forces.

While on the one hand overt racism, with racial attacks and the upsurge of racist political parties, has risen in prominence in the 1990s, 'subtle racism' – always more dangerous than overt racism in non-totalitarian societies – has adapted its form. Racism is now being articulated in terms of 'culture', social standing, etc. rather than in (now) old-fashioned biological terms. The 'new racism', identified by Barker (1981), explored by Husband (1994) and elaborated by Gilroy (1987, 1993) was discussed in Chapter 1. But the meaning of culture too is changing (as described above), and so the dynamic interaction between 'culture' and 'race' is bound to change. Anti-racist training must keep up with the times.

The main points made in Chapter 7 are worth repeating. Anti-racist training of professionals must be backed up by management within the context of general policies, supported by organisational structures and geared to developing (racial) equity in practice. In order to be effective, such training must be meaningful to the professionals being trained in terms of their professional work. Training by itself is of little use without a more general anti-racist drive within institutions, including the professional bodies that provide direction to the professionals involved in mental health service provision – especially clinical psychologists, psychiatrists and social workers. Further, as the involvement of the voluntary sector increases, as it well might, and service users have a greater influence on the directions taken by services, these groups of people too must incorporate anti-racist measures deliberately and purposefully, for otherwise, the *natural* racist tendencies are likely to dominate these 'sectors' too.

Charles Husband (1994) has emphasised the need for anti-racism, whether in terms of training or more generally, to be informed by the 'Black perspective'. As society changes, so does the experience of its black and ethnic minorities – and their perspective on social issues, mental health, professional practices, psychiatry, etc. Increasingly, black people (using the word 'black' in a political sense) are composed of British-born citizens, clear in their own minds about their rights as citizens but aware and cognisant of their background. Their self-perception as black people stems from a mixture of racial and cultural identities – loosely termed 'ethnic' identity – linked inevitably to the status (or lack of it) of black people in society at large. But the nature of the racism they face is related to the *here and now*. The kind of anti-racist measures that are instituted, and the content of anti-racism training in mental health work must take account of the past, the history of racism, colonial oppression, slavery, etc., but, in the final analysis, anti-racism must be related to the here and now – the current experiences of today's black people – *their* perspectives.

In summary, as society changes, the social position, self-perception and reaction to racism of black people in British society is changing. The ways in which racism is manifested are changing too and so the meaning and implications of racism itself, including its relationship with 'culture', is changing. Therefore, anti-racism that is incorporated into training must change with the times in order to be effective at least in stemming the tide of racism, if not in counteracting it fully.

NEEDS ASSESSMENT

It is not the aim of this section to review the techniques of 'needs assessment', but to comment on the effects of what may well happen in practice. Needs assessment, as a concept, has been proposed as a way of enabling mental health services to become sensitive to the needs of the communities they serve. But the question of whether it turns out to be an advance depends entirely on the meanings attached to the concept in practice. Indeed the battle for capturing 'needs assessment' in order to perpetuate the medical domination of the mental health scene has begun. The RCP has already published a book, *Measuring Mental Health Needs* (Thornicroft *et al.*, 1992), which attempts to establish 'needs' as a predominantly medical matter based on measures of traditional 'illness'. The danger of government policy following suit is high, considering the power exercised by professional groups and the political advantages of using 'psychiatry' to obscure social problems and maintain control over minorities in society. This must be resisted.

Needs cannot be measured on the basis of illness rates, on which so-called 'epidemiological information' is based (see Chapter 2). It is seriously misleading to make the diagnosis of an illness (say 'schizophrenia') as the starting point for needs assessment. If professionals work to a systems analysis model (as outlined above), needs may be related to the deficiencies identified in the systems concerned, or the way the person or family deals with each system. An extrapolation of such assessments to groups of people could lead to estimates of overall population needs once details of its composition (in terms of ethnicity, social class, etc.) are known.

Then there are the social needs that stem from poverty, homelessness, discrimination, etc. which require a social analysis. Unmet need here is not just – or even mainly – a responsibility of health services, and so mental health need from this viewpoint must encompass a wide range of social and political issues. Inadequate resourcing and the lack of the political will to accept social realities may well interact with the reluctance of professionals to take on what they identify as 'political issues', to produce types of needs assessment that are unrelated to real lives of real people.

Examining quality of service provision in an honest and realistic fashion must be closely linked to needs assessment, and the assessment of quality requires an understanding of social issues, including the implications of dealing with a culturally diverse population and the deep-seated impact of racism. When need is being assessed, cultural appropriateness of the service that should be provided to meet an identified need (a day centre, for example), or the presence of an effective anti-racist approach in the way it is provided, may be crucial. But most of all, the quality of a service must be judged by its ability to meet the needs of the whole community it serves and to do so equitably and fairly. To provide equitable services for all the community requires detailed analysis of the needs of the different communities and the individuals within the community. And for such a process to take place, genuine dialogue with the community, service users and professionals is required.

Further, in identifying different needs of groups in the community, the type of 'attention' (to need) given or implied in the process of service provision must be acceptable to the service users. For example, if an illness model underlies the assessment of need of black people, the likelihood is that medication to suppress 'dangerousness' would be given greater prominence than (say) counselling to combat the effects of racism or financial help to deal with poverty. It may not be appropriate to provide hostels run as institutions for people with so-called 'long-term mental health problems' – designated in the institutional era as 'revolving-door patients', (see Chapter 8). Instead flexible outreach services may be the approach needed.

In summary, the needs being assessed must be seen in context and through the experiences (and preferably the eyes of) the people who are deemed to have the need. Needs assessment is not about 'epidemiological information' or measuring levels of disability. Most of all, it is not a follow-on from diagnosis. However, considering the purchaser–provider split and the system of contracting services (introduced into both Health and Social Services), a practical approach may be (a) to develop systems of measuring need as widely as possible in community surveys, with the involvement of service users, and (b) to commission services that are geared to these needs, using at that point (and not before then) whatever models of illness and health may be appropriate for the individuals that become clients of the systems. Clearly all the services must have basic standards including anti-racist practice and attention to cultural diversity congruent with the nature of the community concerned.

STRATEGIES FOR SERVICE PROVISION

The way forward for service development is unclear. If the statutory authorities confront the power of vested interests and the medical dominance over mental health thinking, they may find ways of grasping the nettle of their own institutionalised racism at the same time. This would enable service development to go along the road to becoming a culturally sensitive service, by discarding honestly and fully the useless parts of the present psychiatric service; surely ethnic minorities should and would eagerly cooperate by participating in building up a modern service suitable for a multi-ethnic society. Otherwise, there is no option but for black and ethnic minorities to persevere in hammering away at the (present) monolithic institutions as they find them, while at the same time seeking ways and means of evolving methods of mental health care for their own groups. In the latter case, it is inevitable that different minority groups would need to concentrate on their own communities (while maintaining links across communities), in spite of the divisiveness this creates in terms of society at large. In other words, ethnically separate services may be necessary in many areas, at least in the short term, although integrated multi-ethnic services should be the ideal to be aimed at in the long term.

The history of recent ventures in providing services that were designed to meet problems of special significance to black and minority ethnic groups provide salutary lessons about developing mental health care in a multicultural *racist* society. Many projects started by black people for black people have foundered on the question of finance. The experience of the black voluntary sector (Chapter 5) is significant here. The impression is that, when government funding is available, the conditions attached to its use are often too restrictive, and private (charitable) agencies are often reluctant to finance projects for more than two or three years, thereby placing too heavy a burden on people of good will. Some statutorily funded projects that are clearly successful and led by prominent black workers have been quietly taken over and/or restricted in their activities by subtle means. The few imaginative and constructive projects specifically designed to address issues of importance to black and minority ethnic communities, although not necessarily set up as 'separate' services (three of which are described in this book), have not been taken up as examples of how things should be done *generally* in the statutory sector, but remain (if they survive at all), as isolated oases – the exceptions to the general rule. It seems that if mental health services that confront racism and take account of culture are to be effective in the longer term, a strong base independent of statutory (state) control is desirable.

CONCLUSIONS

The outlook for fundamental changes in professional practices is not hopeful – at least in the near future. However, to consider the most powerful discipline in the field at present, psychiatry, it is self-evident that its narrow reductionist approach to human problems is too old-fashioned and, in any case, out of line with modern scientific thinking about mind and matter. Therefore, psychiatry is *bound* to change very fundamentally, sooner or later, and we can all help it along into constructive paths. However, if it changes in ways that would enable psychiatry to play a helpful role in a multi-ethnic society for *all* its people (and not just continue with what amounts to an imperial tradition *vis-à-vis* black people), there may be certain consequences for society at large. For example, if psychiatrists do not use the illness model as a means of controlling people, social deviance and protest would in effect be 'demedicalised', something that may be seen as a drawback with respect to overall social policy. However, I suggest that the gain to psychiatry from establishing itself as a system that is uninvolved in the racism of social control and sensitive to individuals of all cultures will be that it can then take part in promoting social justice – a much more satisfying role for most psychiatrists than the present one of collusion with social control.

Clinical psychology as a profession has become increasingly powerful in the mental health scene as a (seemingly) preferable alternative to psychiatry. Clearly, its ethnocentricity and its historic racism does not bode well for black and ethnic minorities. However, on the face of it at least, insights of (Western) clinical psychology, by offering alternative approaches to the illness-ridden thinking of psychiatry, do allow scope for culturally sensitive work, once racism itself is confronted.

The political influence of social work as a discipline is apparently on the wane – at least in the mental health field. This is most unfortunate because this is the only discipline that has seriously attempted to address fundamental issues of race and culture in its training schemes for mental health workers. This does not mean that social workers in the field are less racist in their *practices* than are other professionals, for much of the racism that black people suffer from within the mental health services stems from institutional practices which are only slightly influenced by the isolated and/or particular behaviour of individuals. But at least many social workers do have a lead over other professionals because they have been trained to (and often do) recognise the racism of the mental health system.

Managers are the newest players in the game of mental health to exercise power, having been given the impetus to do so by the purchaser–provider systems which place them in key positions in both health and social services. Managers can now influence planning and delivery of services very directly and often voice an eagerness to challenge traditional practices in the mental health field. The extent to which they may be able to do so effectively is not clear. But, if managers take decisive action, informed by all sections of the community – including service users – and do not succumb to so-called 'scientific' arguments for continuing traditional practices, real change for the better may well be on the cards. However, the indications are that many managers, confused by the complexity of issues about mental health, multiculturalism, racism, etc., choose the soft option of restricting their actions to making tokenistic appointments of (say) 'development workers' with little power, holding consultative meetings with 'stakeholders' without allowing non-professionals into positions of power and giving greater emphasis to cost than to quality of service. Indeed many purchasers of health and social services appear to have lost their way in mental health needs assessments of populations and so may well be taken over by the rapidly organising (medical) psychiatric lobby that is emerging with 'scientific' illness-orientated measures of needs.

The organisation of mental health services at present leaves much to be desired considering the multi-ethnic composition of society. The ideal is that eventually all services will be accessible to and appropriate for all ethnic groups – multi-ethnic services for a multi-ethnic society. However, in the present climate, where issues of race and culture are inadequately addressed in service provision, it is inevitable that services geared to the needs of particular ethnic groups must co-exist side-by-side with more general, 'generic', services. The balance in any particular district depends on the circumstances prevailing there. However, whether 'generic' or 'ethno-specific', each service must aim to be based on a working together of professionals and service users. And anti-racist measures, based on a clear understanding of contemporary racism and a meaningful understanding of 'culture', must be an integral part of the service.

Although there are few signs of fundamental change of the type implied in this book to be necessary, there are indications that attitudes to mental health and the services needed for people with mental health problems are slowly changing. It is hoped that this book shows how things can be different and that its readers are provided with an opportunity to savour the ways in which, by careful and sensitive training and practice, mental health care can be rendered appropriate for the needs of those who require it, can be just and fair to all sections of the community, and can make contact with real problems of real people.

FURTHER READING

Beliappa, Jayanthi (1991) *Illness or Distress? Alternative Models of Mental Health.* Confederation of Indian Organisations, London.

bhabha, homi k. (1994) *The Location of Culture.* Routledge, London. Especially Introduction and Chapter 9.

Boyle, Mary (1990) *Schizophrenia. A Scientific Delusion?* Routledge, London. Especially Chapters 2 and 8.

Christie, Y. and Blunden, R. (1991) *Is Race on Your Agenda? Improving Mental Health Services for Black and Minority Ethnic Groups.* Kings Fund, London.

D'Ardenne, Patricia and Mahtani, Aruna (1989) *Transcultural Counselling in Action.* Sage, London.

Fanon, Frantz (1986) *Black Skin, White Masks.* Translated by Charles Lam Markmann. Pluto Press, London (originally published as *Peau Noire, Masques Blanc.* Editions de Seuil, Paris 1952).

Fernando, Suman (1991) *Mental Health, Race and Culture.* Macmillan/MIND, London. Especially Chapters 4, 7 and 8.

Gilroy, Paul (1993) *Small Acts. Thoughts on the Politics of Black Cultures.* Serpents Tail, London. Especially Chapter 1.

Healey, David (1990) *The Suspended Revolution. Psychiatry and Psychotherapy Re-examined.* Faber & Faber, London. Especially Chapter 1.

Howitt, Dennis (1991) *Concerning Psychology. Psychology Applied to Social Issues.* Open University Press, Milton Keynes. Especially Chapter 6.

James, Winston and Harris, Clive (1993) *Inside Babylon. The Caribbean Diaspora in Britain.* Verso, London.

Jenner, F. A., Monteiro, A. C. D., Zagalo-Cardoso, J. A. and Cunha-Oliveira, J. A. (1993) *Schizophrenia. A Disease or Some Ways of Being Human?* Sheffield Academic Press, Sheffield.

Kakar, Sudhir (1982) *Shamans. Mystics and Doctors. A Psychological Inquiry into India and its Healing Traditions.* Unwin, London.

Kareem, J. and Littlewood, R. (eds) (1992) *Intercultural Therapy. Themes, Interpretations and Practice.* Blackwell, London. Chapters 2 and 3.

Lindow, Vivien (1994) *Purchasing Mental Health Services: Self-Help Alternatives.* MIND, London.

Rogers, Ann, Pilgrim, David and Lacey, Ron (1993) *Experiencing Psychiatry. Users' Views of Services.* Macmillan/MIND, London.

Romme, Marius and Escher, Sandra (1993) *Accepting Voices.* MIND, London.

Rose, Steven, Lewontin, R. C. and Kamin, Leon (1984) *Not In Our Genes.*

Biology, Ideology and Human Nature. Penguin, Harmondsworth. Especially Chapters 5 and 8.

Webb-Johnson, Amanda (1991) *A Cry for Change. An Asian Perspective on Developing Quality Mental Health Care.* Confederation of Indian Organisations, London. Especially sections 6, 7 and 9.

Wellman, David T. (1977) *Portraits of White Racism.* Cambridge University Press, Cambridge.

References

Adams, C. (1987) *Across Seven Seas and Thirteen Rivers: Life Stories of Pioneer Sylheti Settlers in Britain*. THAP Books, London.

Allport, G. (1954) *The Nature of Prejudice*. Addison-Wesley, Reading, MA.

Andersen, H. and Goolishan, H. (1988) 'Human systems as linguistic systems. Preliminary and evolving ideas about the implications for clinical theory'. *Family Process* 27 (3): 371–393.

Angelou, M. (1986) 'Still I rise' in *And Still I Rise*. Virago Press, London (pp. 41–42).

Aponte, H. (1977) 'Anatomy of a therapist' in P. Papp (ed.) *Family Therapy Full Length Case Studies*. Gardner Press, New York.

Aponte, H. (1985) 'The negotiations of values in therapy'. *Family Process* 24 (3): 323–338.

Aponte, H. (1986) 'If I don't get simple I cry'. *Family Process* 25 (4): 531–548.

Aponte, H. (1990) 'Too many bosses. An eco-structural intervention with a family and its community'. *Journal of Strategic and Systemic Therapies* 9: 49–63.

Auerswald, E. (1968) 'Interdisciplinary versus ecological approach'. *Family Process* 7: 209–215.

Aziz, K. M. A. (1979) *Kinship in Bangladesh*. International Centre for Diarrhoeal Disease Research, Monograph Series No. 1, Dacca.

Banton, M. and Harwood, J. (1975) *The Race Concept*. David & Charles, London.

Banton, R., Clifford, P., Frosh, S., Lousada, J. and Rosenthal, J. (1985) *The Politics of Mental Health*. Macmillan, London.

Barker, M. (1981) *The New Racism*. Junction Books, London.

Barnes, D. M. (1987) 'Biological issues in schizophrenia'. *Science* 235: 430–433.

Barnes, M. and Berke, J. (1971) *Two Accounts of a Journey Through Madness*. MacGibbon & Kee, London.

Barth, F. (1969) *Ethnic Groups and Boundaries*. George Allen & Unwin, London.

BASW (1977) *Mental Health Crisis Services – A New Philosophy*. British Association of Social Workers, Birmingham.

Bateson, G., Jackson, D., Haley, J. and Weakland, J. (1956) 'Toward a theory of schizophrenia'. *Behavioural Science* 1: 251–264.

Bayer, R. (1981) *Homosexuality and American Psychiatry: The Politics of Diagnosis.* Basic Books, New York.

Beard, J. M., Malamud, T.J. and Rossman, E. (1974) 'Psychiatric rehabilitation and long-term re-hospitalisation: The findings of two studies'. *Schizophrenia Bulletin* 11: 622–635.

Bebbington, P. E. (1978) 'The epidemiology of depressive disorder'. *Culture, Medicine and Psychiatry* 2: 297–341.

Bebbington, P. E., Hurry, J. and Tennant, C. (1981) 'Psychiatric disorders in selected immigrant groups in Camberwell'. *Social Psychiatry* 16: 43–51.

Beliappa, J. (1991) *Illness or Distress? Alternative Models of Mental Health.* Confederation of Indian Organisations, London.

Benedict, P. K. and Jacks, I. (1954) 'Mental illness in primitive societies', *Psychiatry* 17: 377–384.

Benedict, R. (1935) *Patterns of Culture.* Routledge & Kegan Paul, London.

Bentall, R. P. (1990) 'The syndromes and symptoms of psychosis or why you can't play "Twenty Questions" with the concept of schizophrenia and hope to win', in R. P. Bentall (ed.) *Reconstructing Schizophrenia.* Routledge, London (pp. 23–60).

Bentall, R. P., Jackson, H. F. and Pilgrim, D. (1988) 'Abandoning the concept of "schizophrenia": some implications of validity arguments for psychological research into psychotic phenomena'. *British Journal of Clinical Psychology* 27: 303–324.

bhabha, homi k. (1994) *The Location of Culture.* Routledge, London.

Bhattacharyya, D. P. (1986) *Pagalami: Ethnopsychiatric Knowledge in Bengal.* Maxwell School of Citizenship and Public Affairs, Syracuse.

Billig, M. (1979) *Psychology, Racism and Fascism.* A F & R Publications, Birmingham.

Blom-Cooper, L., Brown, M., Dolan, R. and Murphy, E. (1992). *Report of the Committee of Inquiry into complaints about Ashworth Hospital.* HMSO, London.

Boyd-Franklin, N. (1989) *Black Families in Therapy.* Guilford Press, New York.

Boyd-Franklin, N. and Shenouda, N. T. (1990) 'A multisystems approach to the treatment of a black, inner-city family with a schizophrenic mother'. *American Journal of Orthopsychiatry* 60 (2): 186–195.

Boyle, M. (1990) *Schizophrenia. A Scientific Delusion?* Routledge, London.

Breggin, P. R. (1991) *Toxic Psychiatry.* St Martin's Press, New York.

Breggin, P. R. and Breggin, G. R. (1993) 'A biomedical programme for urban violence control in the US: The dangers of psychiatric social control'. *Changes* 11(1): 59–71.

Browne, D. (1991) *Black people, mental health and the courts: An exploratory study into the psychiatric remand process as it affects black defendants at magistrates court.* National Association for the Care and Rehabilitation of Offenders, London.

Browne, D. (1995) (in press) *An Element of Compulsion.* Commission for Racial Equality, London.

Bruner, J. (1990) *Acts of Meaning*. Harvard University Press, Cambridge, MA.

Bryan, B., Dadzie, S. and Scafe, S. (1986) *The Heart of the Race: Black Women's Lives in Britain*. Virago, London.

Burrell, G. and Morgan, G. (1979) *Sociological Paradigms and Organisational Analysis*. Heinemann, London.

Campbell, D., Draper, R. and Huffington, C. (1989) *Second Thoughts on the Theory and Practice of the Milan Approach to Family Therapy*. Karnac Books, London.

Capra, F. (1982) *The Turning Point. Science, Society and the Rising Culture*. Wildwood House, London.

Carothers, J. C. (1951) 'Frontal lobe function and the African'. *Journal of Mental Science* 97: 12–48.

Carothers, J. C. (1953) *The African Mind in Health and Disease. A Study in Ethnopsychiatry*. WHO Monograph Series No. 17, World Health Organisation, Geneva.

Carrithers, M. (1992) *Why Humans Have Culture. Explaining Anthropology and Social Diversity*. Oxford University Press, Oxford.

Cartwright, S. A. (1851) 'Report on the diseases and physical peculiarities of the Negro race', *New Orleans Medical and Surgical Journal*, May, 1851, 691–715. Reprinted in A. C. Caplan, H. T. Engelhardt and J. J. McCartney (eds), Paper 3.3, *Concepts of Health and Disease*, Addison-Wesley, Reading, MA (pp. 305–325).

CCETSW (1993) CCETSW Paper 19.19. 1987 revised 1993. *Requirements and guidance for the training of social workers to be considered for approval in England and Wales under the Mental Health Act 1983*. Central Council for Education and Training in Social Work, London.

Cecchin, G. (1988) 'Hypothesising-circularity-neutrality revisited: an invitation to curiosity'. *Family Process* 26(4): 3–14.

Chambon, A. (1989) 'Refugee families' experiences: three family themes'. *Journal of Strategic and Systemic Therapy* 8: 3–13.

Chen, E. Y. H., Harrison, G. and Standen, P. J. (1991) 'Management of first episode psychotic illness in Afro-Caribbean patients'. *British Journal of Psychiatry* 158: 517–522.

Cobb, A. (1993) *Safe and Effective? MIND's Views on Psychiatric Drugs, ECT and Psychosurgery*. MIND Publications, London.

Cooper, D. (1970) *Psychiatry and Anti-Psychiatry*. Paladin, London.

Cope, R. (1989) 'The compulsory detention of Afro-Caribbeans under the Mental Health Act'. *New Community* 15(3): 343–356.

Cope, R. and Ndegwa, D. (1990) 'Ethnic differences in admission to a regional secure unit'. *Journal of Forensic Psychiatry* 3: 365–378.

Curry, A. (1964) 'Myth, transference and the black psychotherapist'. *Psychoanalytic Review* 51: 547–554

D'Ardenne, P. and Mahtani, A. (1989) *Transcultural Counselling in Action*. Sage, London.

Darton, D., Gorman, J. and Sayce, L. (1994) *Eve Fights Back. The Successes of MIND's Stress on Women Campaign*. MIND Publications, London.

Dell, S., Grounds, A., James, K. and Robertson, G. (1991) *Mentally Disordered Remand Prisoners*. Report to the Home Office.

Demerath, N. J. (1942) 'Schizophrenia among primitives'. *American Journal of Psychiatry* 98: 703–707.

Devereux, G. (1939) 'Mohave culture and personality' *Character and Personality* 8: 91–109.

DHSS (1970) *Worcester Development Project: Feasibility Study for a Model Reorganisation of Mental Health Services.* HMSO, London.

DHSS (1975) *Better Services for the Mentally Ill.* HMSO, London.

DHSS (1976) *A Review of the Mental Health Act 1959.* HMSO, London.

DHSS (1993) *Caring for People.* HMSO, London.

DoH (1993a) *The Patient's Charter.* HMSO, London.

DoH (1993b) *Legal Powers on the Care of Mentally Ill People in the Community:* Report of the Internal Review. DoH, London.

DoH (1994) *Being Heard.* The Report of a Review Committee on NHS Complaints Procedures. HMSO, London.

DoH and Home Office (1992). *Review of Health and Social Services for Mentally Disordered Offenders and Others Requiring Similar Services: Services for People from Black and Ethnic Minority Groups; Issues of Race and Culture. A Discussion Paper.* DoH/Home Office, London.

DoH and Welsh Office (1993) *Code of Practice: Mental Health Act 1983.* HMSO, London.

Dobzhansky, T. (1971) 'Race equality', in R. H. Osborne (ed.) *The Biological and Social Meaning of Race.* Freeman, San Francisco (pp. 13–24).

Eagles, J. M. (1991) 'The relationship between schizophrenia and immigration. Are there alternatives to psychosocial hypotheses?' *British Journal of Psychiatry* 159: 783–789.

Falicov, C. (1982) 'Mexican families', in M. McGoldrick, J. Pearce and J. Giordano (eds) *Ethnicity and Family Therapy.* Guilford Press, New York.

Fanon, F. (1952) *Peau Noire, Masques Blancs.* Editions de Seuil, Paris. (Trans. C. L. Markmann (1967) *Black Skin, White Masks.* Grove Press, New York.) (pbk edn, Pluto Press, London 1986.)

Fenton, S. and Sadiq, A. (1993) *The Sorrow in My Heart. Sixteen Asian Women Speak About Depression.* Commission for Racial Equality, London.

Fernando, S. (1988) *Race and Culture in Psychiatry.* Croom Helm, London. (pbk edn, Routledge, London 1990.)

Fernando, S. (1991) *Mental Health, Race and Culture.* Macmillan/MIND, London.

Foucault, M. (1967) *Madness and Civilisation.* (Trans. R. Howard.) Tavistock, London.

Foucault, M. (1988) *Politics Philosophy Culture. Interviews and Other Writings 1977–1984* (ed. L. D. Kritzman). Routledge, London.

Francis, E. (1991) 'Mental health, anti-racism and social work training', in CCETSW (ed.) *One Small Step Towards Racial Justice.* Central Council for Education and Training in Social Work, London (pp. 81–95).

Frederick, J. (1991) *Positive Thinking for Mental Health.* Black Mental Health Group (ISIS), London.

Freire, P. (1972) *Pedagogy of the Oppressed.* Penguin, Harmondsworth.

Freud, S. (1913) *Totem and Taboo. Some Points of Agreement between the*

Mental Lives of Savages and Neurotics. Hugo Heller, Vienna. (Trans. and published in English by Routledge & Kegan Paul, London 1950.)

Fryer, P. (1984) *Staying Power. The History of Black People in Britain.* Pluto Press, London.

Galton, F. (1869) *Hereditary Genius: An Inquiry into its Laws and Consequences.* Macmillan, London.

Gilroy, P. (1987) *There Ain't No Black in the Union Jack. The Cultural Politics of Race and Nation.* Hutchinson, London.

Gilroy, P. (1993) 'One nation under a groove'. in *Small Acts. Thoughts on the Politics of Black Cultures.* Serpent's Tail, London (pp. 19–48).

Gold, J. (1985) 'Cartesian dualism and the current crisis in medicine – a plan for a philosophical approach'. Discussion Paper. *Journal of the Royal Society of Medicine* 78: 663–666.

Goldner, V. (1988) 'Generation and gender: Normalities and covert hierarchies'. *Family Process* 27: 17–31.

Gordon R. (1993) *Community Care Assessments. Practical Legal Framework.* Longman, London.

Gorman, J. (1994) 'View from the top'. *OPENMIND* 67 (March/April): 18–19.

Gostin, L. (1986) *Mental Health Services – Law and Practice.* Shaw & Sons, London.

Hall, G. S. (1904) *Adolescence, its Psychology and its Relations to Physiology, Anthropology, Sociology, Sex, Crime, Religion and Education*, Vol. II. D. Appleton, New York.

Hall, S. (1978) 'Racism and reaction', in CRE (ed.) *Five Views of Multiracial Britain.* Commission for Racial Equality, London (pp. 23–35).

Hall, S., Critcher, C., Jefferson, T., Clarke, J. and Roberts, B. (1978) *Policing the Crisis. Mugging, the State and Law and Order.* Macmillan, London.

Harrison, G. (1990) 'Searching for the causes of schizophrenia: The role of migrant studies'. *Schizophrenia Bulletin* 16: 663–671.

Haughton, P. and Sowa, T. (1993) *Black Perspectives in the Voluntary Sector.* Thames/LWT Telethon Report, London.

Hill, M. (1994) 'Who do you think we are?' *Diaspora* March.

Hinds, A. (1992) *Report on organisations serving the Afro-Caribbean community.* West Indian Standing Conference, London.

Hodge, J. L. and Struckmann, D. K. (1975) 'Some components of the Western dualist tradition', in J. L. Hodge, D. K. Struckmann and L. D. Trost (eds) *Cultural Bases of Racism and Group Oppression* (Pt 4). Two Riders Press, Berkeley (pp. 122–195).

Holland, D. (1992) 'How cultural systems become desire: a case study of an American romance', in R. D'Andrade and C. Strauss (eds) *Human Motivation and Cultural Models.* Cambridge University Press, Cambridge (pp. 61–89).

Holland, S. (1988) 'Defining and experimenting with prevention', in S. Ramon and M.D. Giannichedda (eds), *Psychiatry in Transition: The British and Italian Experiences.* Pluto, London.

Holland, S. (1990a) 'Psychotherapy, oppression and social action: Gender, race, and class in Black women's depression', in R. J. Perelberg and A. C.

Miller (eds) *Gender and Power in Families*. Routledge, London (pp. 256–269).

Holland, S. (1990b) 'From social abuse to social action via psychotherapy'. Paper presented at a conference: Psychoanalytic therapy and Ethnic Minorities held at Ealing Hospital, London.

Holland, S. (1991) 'From private symptom to public action'. *Psychology and Feminism* 1(1): 58–62.

Holland, S. (1992) 'From social abuse to social action', in J. Ussher, and P. Nicholson (eds) *Gender Issues in Clinical Psychology*. Routledge, London (pp. 68–77).

Holloway, F. (1994) 'Need in community psychiatry: a consensus is required'. *Psychiatric Bulletin* 18: 321–323.

Home Office (1991) *Police and Criminal Evidence Act 1984 (Section 66): Code of Practice*. HMSO, London.

Home Office and Central Office of Information (1977) *Racial Discrimination. A Guide to the Race Relations Act 1976*. HMSO, London.

hooks, b. (1993) *Sisters of the Yam: Black Women and Self-Recovery*. Turnaround, London.

Howitt, D. (1991) *Concerning Psychology. Psychology Applied to Social Issues*. Open University Press, Milton Keynes.

Husband, C. (1982) '"Race", the continuity of a concept', in C. Husband (ed.) *Race in Britain. Continuity and Change*. Hutchinson, London (pp. 11–23).

Husband, C. (1994) *'Race' and the Nation: The British Experience*. Paradigm Books, Curtin University of Technology, Bentley, Western Australia.

Ilahi, N. (1980) *Psychotherapy services to ethnic communities*. Department of Psychotherapy, Ealing General Hospital, London.

Ingold, T. (1986) *Evolution and Social Life*. Cambridge University Press, Cambridge.

IRR (1993) *Community Care: The Black Experience*. Institute of Race Relations, London.

Jenner, F. A., Monteiro, A. C. D., Zagalo-Cardoso, J. A. and Cunha-Oliveira, J. A. (1993) *Schizophrenia. A Disease or Some Ways of Being Human?* Sheffield Academic Press, Sheffield.

Jones, E. (1993) *Family Systems Therapy. Developments in the Milan-systemic Therapies*. John Wiley & Sons, Chichester.

Jones, J. M. (1972) *Prejudice and Racism*. Addison-Wesley, Reading, MA.

Jones, J. S. (1981) 'How different are human races?' *Nature* 293: 188–190.

Jones, M. (1968) *Social Psychiatry in Practice*. Penguin, Harmondsworth.

Jones, S. (1993) *The Language of the Genes. Biology, History and the Evolutionary Future*. HarperCollins, London.

Joseph, T. (1984) *UK School Report*. Painting on acrylic canvas, exhibited at Sheffield City Art Galleries, Sheffield.

Jung, C. G. (1930) 'Your Negroid and Indian behaviour'. *Forum* 83(4): 193–199.

Kakar, S. (1978) *The Inner World: A Psycho-analytic Study of Childhood and Society in India* (2nd edn). Oxford University Press, Oxford.

Kakar, S. (1982) *Shamans, Mystics and Doctors*. Unwin, London.

Kendell, R. E. and Kemp, I. W. (1989) 'Maternal influenza in the aetiology of schizophrenia'. *Archives of General Psychiatry (Chicago)* 46: 878–882.

King, D. J. and Cooper, S. J. (1989) 'Viruses, immunity and mental disorder'. *British Journal of Psychiatry* 154: 1–7.

Kleinman, A. (1977) 'Depression, somatization and the "new cross-cultural psychiatry".' *Social Science and Medicine* 11: 3–10.

Kleinman, A. (1987) 'Anthropology and psychiatry: The role of culture in cross-cultural research on illness'. *British Journal of Psychiatry* 151: 447–454.

Kleinman, A. (1988) *Rethinking Psychiatry. From Cultural Category to Personal Experience.* The Free Press, New York.

Kraepelin, E. (1921) *Manic-Depressive Insanity and Paranoia.* (Trans. and edited by R. M. Barclay and G. M. Robertson.) Livingstone, Edinburgh.

Krause, I-B. (1989) 'The sinking heart: A Punjabi communication of distress'. *Social Science and Medicine* 29: 563–575.

Krause, I-B. (1993) 'Family therapy and anthropology: A case for emotions'. *Journal of Family Therapy* 15: 35–56.

Krause, I-B. (1994) 'Numbers and meaning: A dialogue in cross-cultural psychiatry'. *Journal of the Royal Society of Medicine* 87: 278–285.

Kuipers, L., Leff, J. and Lam, D. (1992) *Family Work for Schizophrenia. A Practical Guide.* Gaskel/Royal College of Psychiatrists, London.

Laing, R. D. (1967) *The Politics of Experience.* Pantheon Books, New York.

Lambo, A. (1969) 'Traditional African Cultures and Western medicine' in F. N. L. Poynter (ed.) *Medicine and Culture.* Wellcome Institute of the History of Medicine, London (pp. 201–210).

Latimer, M. (1992) *Funding Black Groups. A Report into the Charitable Funding of Ethnic Minority Organisations.* Directory of Social Change, London.

Lau, A. (1984) 'Transcultural issues in family therapy'. *Journal of Family Therapy* 6: 91–112.

Lau, A. (1990) 'Psychological problems in adolescents from ethnic minorities'. *British Journal of Hospital Medicine,* 44: 201–205.

Leff, J. (1973) 'Culture and the differentiation of emotional states'. *British Journal of Psychiatry* 123: 299–306.

Lieberman, J. A. and Koreen, A. R. (1993) 'Neurochemistry and neuroendocrinology of schizophrenia: A selective review'. *Schizophrenia Bulletin* 19: 371–429.

Littlewood, R.(1992a) 'How universal is something we can call therapy?', in J. Kareem and R. Littlewood (eds) *Intercultural Therapy Themes, Interpretations and Practice.* Blackwell Scientific, Oxford (pp. 38–56).

Littlewood, R. (1992b) Psychiatric Diagnosis and Racial Bias: Empirical and Interpretive Approaches. *Social Science and Medicine* 34: 141–149.

Littlewood, R. and Lipsedge, M. (1989) *Aliens and Alienists. Ethnic Minorities and Psychiatry.* Unwin Hyman, London.

Lorenz, K. (1966) *On Aggression.* Methuen, London.

Lorenz, K. (1974) *Civilised Man's Eight Deadly Sins.* Methuen, London.

McDougall, W. (1920) *The Group Mind.* Cambridge University Press, Cambridge.

McDougall, W. (1921) *Is America Safe for Democracy?* Scribner, New York.

McGoldrick, M. (1982) 'Ethnicity and family therapy: An overview', in M. McGoldrick, J. Pearce and J. Giordano (eds) *Ethnicity and Family Therapy*. Guilford Press, New York (pp. 3–130).

McGoldrick, M., Pearce, J., and Giordano, J. (1982) *Ethnicity and Family Therapy*. Guilford Press, New York.

McGovern, D. and Cope, R. (1987) 'The compulsory detention of males of different ethnic groups with special reference to offender patients'. *British Journal of Psychiatry* 150: 505–512.

McNamee, S. and Gergen, K. (1992) *Therapy as Social Construction*. Sage, London.

Maloney, C. (1986) *Behaviour and Poverty in Bangladesh*. University Press, Dhaka.

Masson, J. (1988) *Against Therapy*. Atheneum, New York (pbk edn, Fontana, London 1990).

Maudsley, H. (1867) *The Physiology and Pathology of Mind*. D. Appleton, New York.

Mednick, S. A., Machon, R. A., Huttanen, M. O. and Bonett, D. (1989) 'Adult schizophrenia following prenatal exposure to an influenza epidemic'. *Archives of General Psychiatry (Chicago)* 45: 189–192.

Mental Health Act Commission (1987) *Second Biennial Report 1985–1987*. HMSO, London.

Mental Health Act Commission (1989) *Third Biennial Report 1987–1989*. HMSO, London.

Mental Health Act Commission (1991) *Fourth Biennial Report 1989–1991*. HMSO, London.

Mental Health Act Commission (1993) *Fifth Biennial Report 1991–1993*. HMSO, London.

Mental Health Media (1992) 'From anger to action: Advocacy, empowerment and mental health'. Video made by Mental Health Media, London.

Messent, P. (1992) 'Working with Bangladeshi families in the east end of London'. *Journal of Family Therapy* 14(3): 287–304.

MIND (1993a) *MIND's Policy on User Involvement*. National Association for Mental Health, London.

MIND (1993b) *MIND's Policy on Black and Minority Ethnic People and Mental Health*. National Association for Mental Health, London.

MIND (1993c) *MIND's Policy on Women and Mental Health*. National Association for Mental Health, London.

Minuchin, S. and Montalvo, B. (1967) *Families of the Slums*. Basic Books, New York.

Molnar, S. (1983) *Human Variation. Races, Types and Ethnic Groups* (2nd edn). Prentice-Hall, Englewood Cliffs, NJ.

Montalvo, B. and Gutierrez, M. (1988) 'The emphasis on cultural identity: A developmental-ecological constraint', in C. Falicov (ed.) *Family Transitions: Continuity and Change over the Life Cycle*. Guilford Press, New York (pp. 181–209).

Moodley, P. and Perkins, R. (1991) 'Routes to psychiatric in-patient care in an inner London borough. *Social Psychiatry and Psychiatric Epidemiology* 26: 47–51.

Morris, D. (1967) *The Naked Ape*. Cape, London.

Morris, D. (1969) *The Human Zoo*. Cape, London.

Multiple Media (1984) 'We're not mad, we're angry'. Video made by a collective of psychiatric system survivors. Available from National Association for Mental Health Publications, London.

Murphy, G. (1938) *An Historical Introduction to Modern Psychology*. Routledge & Kegan Paul, London.

Obeyesekere, G. (1981) *Medusa's Hair. An Essay on Personal Symbols and Religious Experience*. University of Chicago Press, Chicago.

O'Brian, C. P. (1990) 'Family therapy with black families'. *Journal of Family Therapy* 12(1): 3–16.

O'Callaghan, E., Sham, P., Takei, N., Glover, G. and Murray, R. M. (1991) 'Schizophrenia after prenatal exposure to 1957 A2 influenza epidemic'. *Lancet* 337: 1248–1250.

Offer, D. and Sabshin, M. (1966) *Normality: Theoretical and Clinical Concepts of Mental Health*. Basic Books, New York.

Perelberg, R. (1990) 'Equality, asymmetry and diversity: On conceptualisations of gender', in R. Perelberg and A. Miller (eds) *Gender and Power in Families*. Routledge, London (pp. 34–60).

Perelberg, R. (1992) 'Familiar and unfamiliar types of family structure: Towards a conceptual framework', in J. Kareem and R. Littlewood (eds) *Intercultural Therapy, Themes, Interpretations and Practice*. Blackwell Scientific, Oxford (pp. 112–132).

Perelberg, R. and Miller, A. (eds) (1990) *Gender and Power in Families*. Routledge, London.

Pina, J. C. (1986) *Sons of Adam, Daughters of Eve; The Peasant World View in Alto Minho*. Clarendon Press, Oxford.

Pipe, R., Bhat, A., Mathews, B. and Hampstead, J. (1991) 'Section 136 and African/Afro Caribbean minorities'. *International Journal of Social Psychiatry* 37(1): 14–23.

Prince, R. (1968) 'The changing picture of depressive syndromes in Africa'. *Canadian Journal of African Studies* 1: 177–192.

Prins, H. Blacker-Holst, T., Francis, E. and Keitch, I. (1993) *Report of the Committee of Inquiry into the Death in Broadmoor Hospital of Orville Blackwood and A Review of the Deaths of Two Other Afro-Caribbean Patients. Big, Black and Dangerous?* Special Hospitals Service Authority, London.

Pritchard, J. C. (1835) *A Treatise on Insanity and Other Disorders Affecting the Mind*. Sherwood, Gilbert & Piper, London.

Radford, M. (1993) 'A personal view of psychiatry following a visit to Madison, USA'. Unpublished paper.

RCP (1987) *Community Treatment Orders*. Royal College of Psychiatrists, London.

RCP (1993) *Community Supervision Orders*. Royal College of Psychiatrists, London.

Ritchie, J. H., Dick, D. and Lingham, R. (1994) *The Report of the Inquiry into the Care and Treatment of Christopher Clunis*. HMSO, London.

Rogers, A., Pilgrim, D. and Lacey, R. (1993) *Experiencing Psychiatry: Users' Views of Services*. Macmillan/MIND, London.

Rushton, J. P. (1990) 'Race differences, r/K theory, and a reply to Flynn'. *The Psychologist: Bulletin of the British Psychological Society* 5: 195–8.

Rustin, M. (1991) *The Good Society and the Inner World*. Verso, London.

Sabshin, M. (1967) 'Psychiatric perspectives on normality'. *Archives of General Psychiatry (Chicago)* 17: 258–264.

Sadhoo, N. (1990) 'Endless stress'. *Social Work Today* August, pp.16–18.

Said, E. W. (1978) *Orientalism*. Routledge & Kegan Paul, London.

Sartre, J- P. (1948) *Antisemite and Jew*. Schocken Books, New York.

Scheff, T. J. (1966) *Being Mentally Ill: A Sociological Theory*. Aldine, Chicago.

Scott, R. D. (1960) 'A family-orientated psychiatric service to the London Borough of Barnet'. *Health Trends* 12: 65–68.

Scull, A. (1977) *Decarceration. Community Treatment and the Deviant. A Radical View*. Prentice Hall, Englewood Cliffs, NJ. (2nd edn Polity Press, Cambridge, 1984.)

Shoenberg, E. (1972) *A Hospital Looks at Itself*. Bruno Casirer, London.

Shweder, R. and Bourne, E. (1982) 'Does the concept of the person vary cross-culturally', in A. Marsella and G. White (eds) *Cultural Conceptions of Mental Health and Therapy*. D. Reidel, Dordrecht (pp. 97–137).

Siegler, M. and Osmond, H. (1974) *Models of Madness, Models of Medicine*. Macmillan, New York.

Simon, B. (1978) *Mind and Madness in Ancient Greece. The Classical Roots of Modern Psychiatry*. Cornell University Press, London.

Sinha, D. (1993) 'Indigenisation of psychology in India and its relevance', in V. Kim and J. W. Berry (eds) *Indigenous Psychologies*. Sage, London (pp. 30–43).

Speck, R. and Attneave, C. (1974) *Family Networks*. Vintage Books, New York.

Stevens, A. and Raftery, J. (1992) 'The purchasers' information requirements on mental health needs and contracting for mental health services', in G. Thornicroft, C. R. Brewin and J. Wing (eds) *Measuring Mental Health Needs*. Gaskell, London (pp. 42–61).

Sykes, J. B. (1982) *The Concise Oxford Dictionary*. Clarendon Press, Oxford.

Szasz, T. S. (1962) *The Myth of Mental Illness*. Secker & Warburg, London.

Szasz, T. S. (1970) *The Manufacture of Madness*. Dell Publishing, New York.

Tamura, T. and Lau, A. (1992) 'Connectedness versus separateness: Applicability of family therapy to Japanese families'. *Family Process* 31(4): 319–340.

Thomas, A. and Sillen, S. (1972) *Racism and Psychiatry*. Brunner/Mazel, New York.

Thomas, L. (1992) 'Racism and psychotherapy: Working with racism in the consulting room – an analytic view', in J. Kareem and R. Littlewood (eds) *Intercultural Therapy. Themes, Interpretations and Practice*. Blackwell Scientific, Oxford (pp. 133–145).

Thornicroft, G., Brewin, C. R. and Wing, J. (1992) *Measuring Mental Health Needs*. Gaskell/Royal College of Psychiatrists, London.

Torrey, E. F. (1973) 'Is schizophrenia universal? An open question'. *Schizophrenia Bulletin* 7: 53–57.

Trivedi, P. (1992) 'Untitled' in *Survivors' Poetry: From dark to light.* Survivors' Press, London (p. 82).

Tuke, D. H. (1858) 'Does civilization favour the generation of mental disease?' *Journal of Mental Science* 4: 94–110.

Turner, J. (1991) 'Migrants and their therapists: A trans-context approach'. *Family Process* 30: 407–419.

von Bertalanffy, L. (1962) 'General systems theory: A critical review'. *Yearbook of the Society of General Systems Theory* 7: 1–21.

Waldegrave, C. (1990) 'Just therapy'. *Dulwich Centre Newsletter* 1: 5–46.

Walters, M., Carter, B., Papp, P. and Silverstein, O. (1988) *The Invisible Web: Gender Patterns in Family Relationships.* Guilford Press, New York.

Watts, F. N. and Bennett, D. H. (1983) *Theory and Practice of Psychiatric Rehabilitation.* John Wiley & Sons, Chichester.

Watts-Jones, D. (1992) 'Cultural and integrative therapy issues in the treatment of a Jamaican woman with panic disorder'. *Family Process* 31: 105–118.

Watzlawick, P., Beavin, J. and Jackson, D. (1967) *Pragmatics of Human Communication.* W. W. Norton, New York.

Webb-Johnson, A. (1991) *A Cry for Change. An Asian Perspective on Developing Quality Mental Health Care.* Confederation of Indian Organisations, London.

Webb-Johnson, A. (1993) *Building on Strengths. Enquiry into Health Activity in the Asian Voluntary Sector.* Confederation of Indian Organisations, London.

Wellman, D. (1977) *Portraits of White Racism.* Cambridge University Press, Cambridge.

Wenham, M. (1993) *Funded to Fail – Nuff Pain No Gain.* London Voluntary Service Council, London.

Wessely, S., Castle, D., Der, G. and Murray, R. (1991) 'Schizophrenia and Afro-Caribbeans. A case-control study'. *British Journal of Psychiatry* 159: 795–801.

Westwood, S., Couloute, J., Desai, S., Mathew, P. and Piper, A. (1989) *Sadness in my heart: Racism and mental health. A research report.* Leicester Black Mental Health Group, University of Leicester, Leicester.

White, M. and Epstein, D. (1990) *Narrative Means to Therapeutic Ends.* Dulwich Centre Publications, Adelaide.

Whittington, C. and Holland, R. (1985) 'A framework for theory in social work'. *Issues In Social Work Education* 5(1): 25–50.

Wilson, M. (1993) *Mental Health and Britain's Black Communities.* Kings Fund, London.

Wing, J. (1989) 'Schizophrenic psychoses: Causal factors and risks', in P. Williams, G. Wilkinson and K. Rawnsley (eds) *The Scope of Epidemiological Psychiatry.* Routledge, London (pp. 225–239).

Wing, J. and Haley, A. M. (1972) *Evaluating a Community Psychiatric Service.* Oxford University Press, London.

Wood, D. (1993) *The Power of Words. Uses and Abuses of Talking Treatments.* National Association for Mental Health, London.

Subject index

Name index

362.2   Mental health in a
Men   multi-ethnic

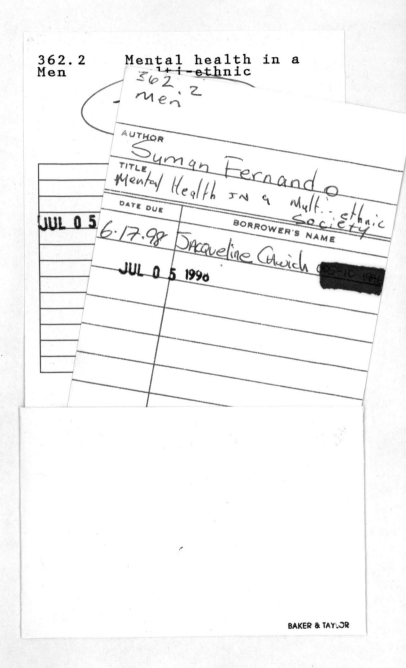